AMERICA'S BYWAYS™ OF THE
WEST COAST

come **CLOSER** *to* the heart and soul of *your* **AMERICA**

America's Byways Series | MOBIL TRAVEL GUIDE

We gratefully acknowledge our inspection team for their efficient and perceptive evaluations of the establishments listed in this book and the establishments for their cooperation in showing their facilities and providing information about them.

Thanks also go to the National Scenic Byways Program and the coordinators of the individual Byways for all their help and support in the coordination of this project.

VICE PRESIDENT, PUBLICATIONS: **Kevin Bristow**
MANAGING EDITOR: **Pam Mourouzis**
MANAGER OF PUBLISHING PRODUCTION SERVICES: **Ellen Tobler**
CONCEPT AND COVER DESIGN: **ABS Graphics, Inc. Design Group**
EDITOR: **Tere Drenth**
PRINTING ACKNOWLEDGEMENT: **North American Corporation of Illinois**

Copyright © 2004 EMTG, LLC. All rights reserved. Except for copies made by individuals for personal use, this publication may not be reproduced in whole or in part by any means whatsoever without prior written permission from Mobil Travel Guide, 1460 Renaissance Drive, Suite 401, Park Ridge, IL 60068; 847/795-6700; info@mobiltravelguide.com.

Mobil, Exxon, and Mobil Travel Guide are trademarks of Exxon Mobil Corporation or one of its subsidiaries. All rights reserved. Reproduction by any means, including, but not limited to, photography, electrostatic copying devices, or electronic data processing is prohibited. Use of information contained herein for solicitation of advertising or listing in any other publication is expressly prohibited without prior written permission from Exxon Mobil Corporation. Violations of reserved rights are subject to prosecution.

The information contained herein is derived from a variety of third-party sources. Although every effort has been made to verify the information obtained from such sources, the publisher assumes no responsibility for inconsistencies or inaccuracies in the data or liability for any damage of any type arising from errors or omissions.

Neither the editors nor the publisher assumes responsibility for the services provided by any business listed in this guide or for any loss, damage, or disruption in your travel for any reason.

ISBN: 0-9727-0227-X

Manufactured in the United States of America.

10 9 8 7 6 5 4 3 2 1

America's Byways Series | MOBIL TRAVEL GUIDE

Table of Contents

America's Byways of the West Coast

MAPS

Alaska
- Alaska's Marine Highway A5
- Glenn Highway A6
- The Seward Highway A7

California
- Arroyo Seco Historic Parkway—Route 110 .... A8
- Big Sur Coast Highway—Route 1 .... A9
- Death Valley Scenic Byway A10
- San Luis Obispo North Coast Byway—Route 1 .... A11
- Tioga Road/Big Oak Flat Road A12
- Volcanic Legacy Scenic Byway A13

Oregon
- Cascade Lakes Scenic Byway A14
- Hells Canyon Scenic Byway A15
- Historic Columbia River Highway A16
- McKenzie Pass-Santiam Pass Scenic Byway A17
- Outback Scenic Byway A18
- Pacific Coast Scenic Byway A19
- Roque-Umpqua Scenic Byway A20
- West Cascades Scenic Byway A21

Washington
- Chinook Scenic Byway A22
- Mountains to Sound Greenway—I-90 .... A23
- Strait of Juan de Fuca Highway—SR 112 .... A24

A WORD TO OUR READERS A25

OVERVIEW OF THE NATIONAL SCENIC BYWAYS PROGRAM A27

INTRODUCTION A29

continued on next page

America's Byways Series | MOBIL TRAVEL GUIDE
Table of Contents

AMERICA'S BYWAYS OF THE WEST COAST

Alaska
Alaska's Marine Highway 1
Glenn Highway 9
The Seward Highway 17

California
Arroyo Seco Historic Parkway—Route 110 25
Big Sur Coast Highway—Route 1 33
Death Valley Scenic Byway 43
San Luis Obispo North Coast Byway—Route 1 49
Tioga Road/Big Oak Flat Road 57
Volcanic Legacy Scenic Byway 65

Oregon
Cascade Lakes Scenic Byway 73
Hells Canyon Scenic Byway 79
Historic Columbia River Highway 85
McKenzie Pass-Santiam Pass Scenic Byway 91
Outback Scenic Byway 97
Pacific Coast Scenic Byway 103
Roque-Umpqua Scenic Byway 115
Volcanic Legacy Scenic Byway 123
West Cascades Scenic Byway 129

Washington
Chinook Scenic Byway 135
Mountains to Sound Greenway—I-90 141
Strait of Juan de Fuca Highway—SR 112 153

Alaska's Marine Highway AK

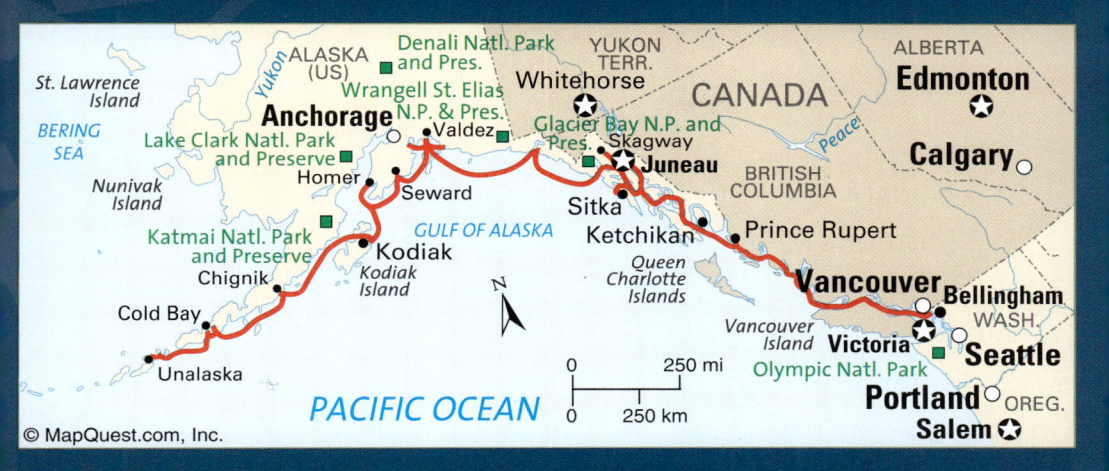

WEST COAST **A5**

AK Glenn Highway

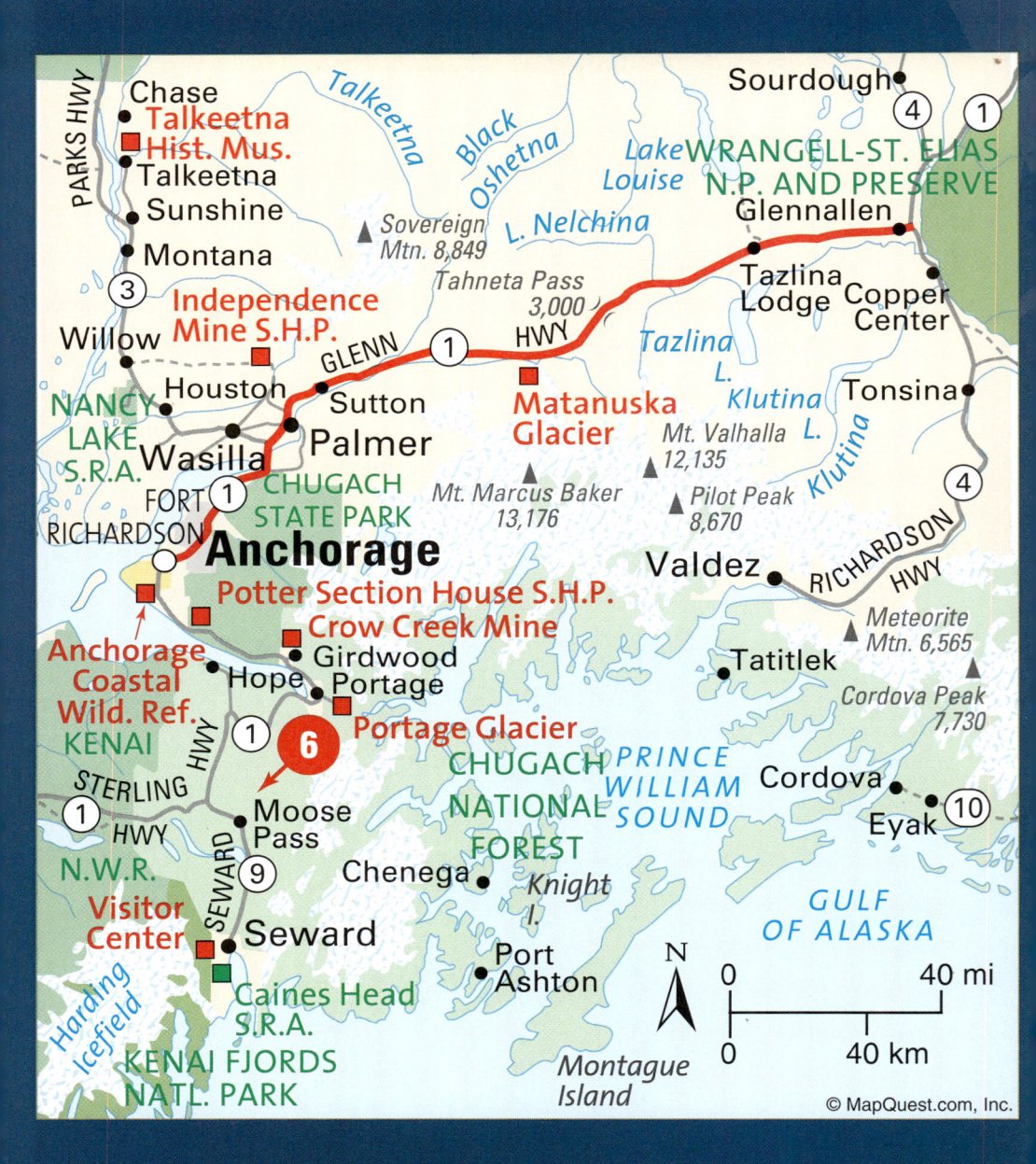

The Seward Highway AK

CA — Arroyo Seco Historic Parkway—Route 110

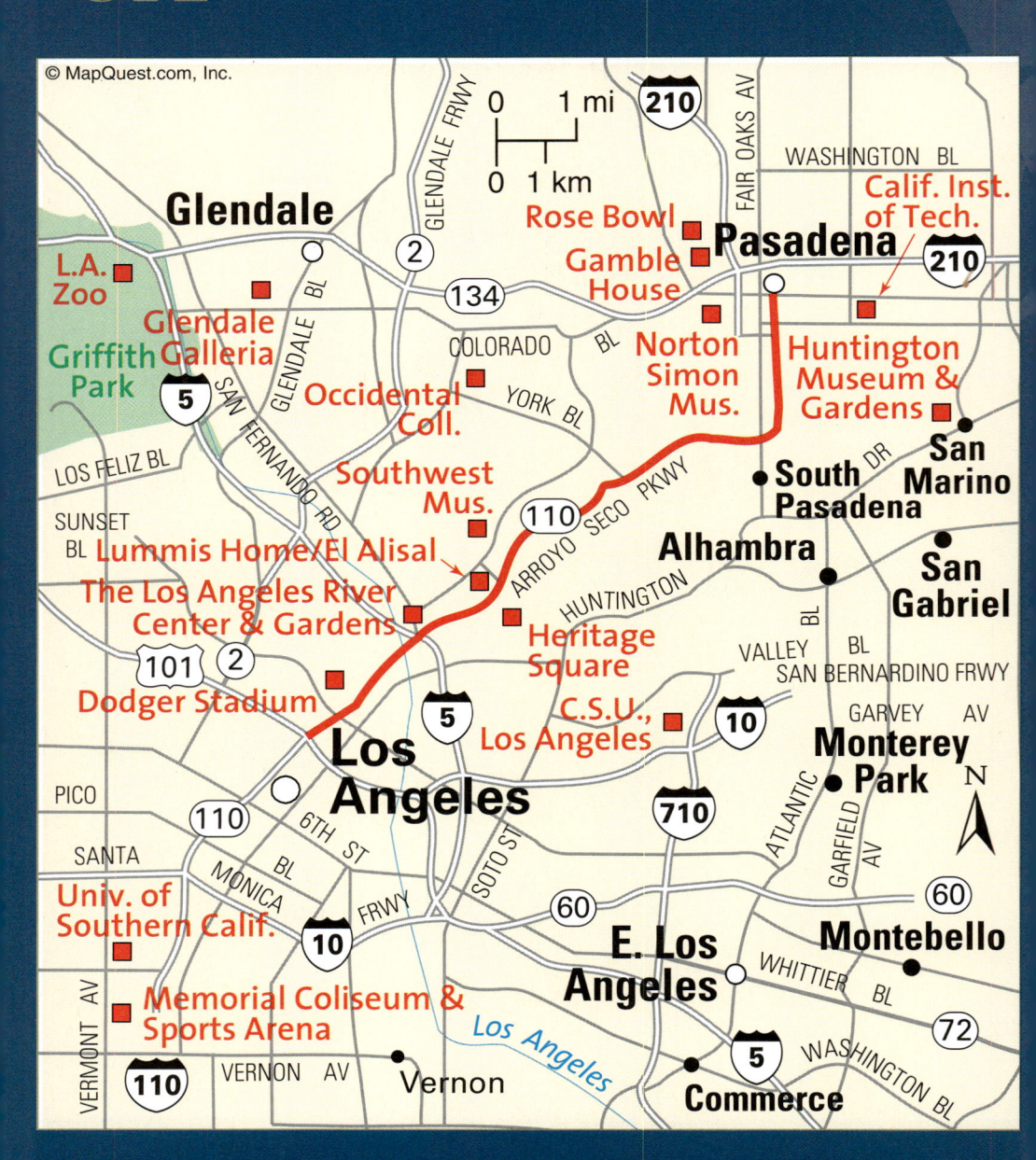

Big Sur Coast Highway—Route 1

CA Death Valley Scenic Byway

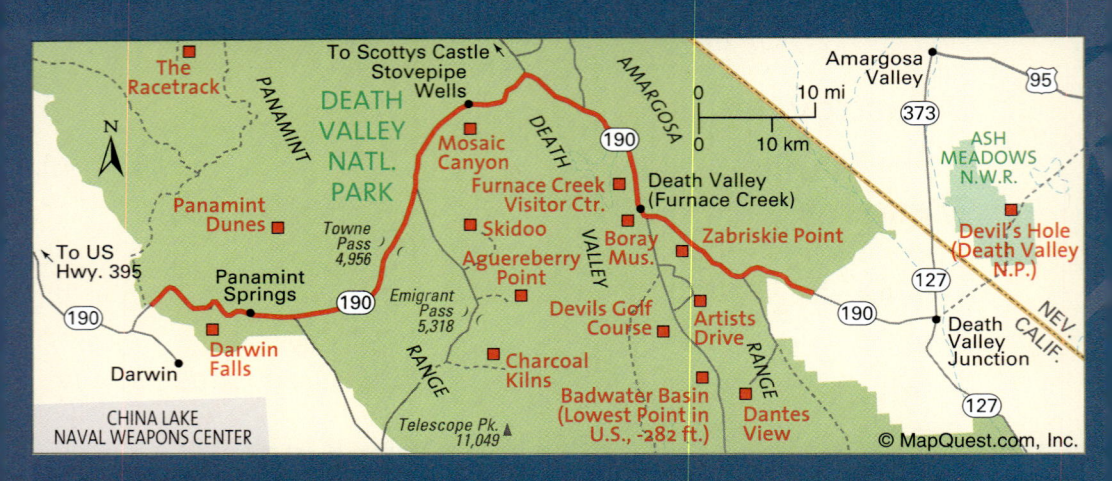

San Luis Obispo North Coast Byway—Route 1

CA — Tioga Road/Big Oak Flat Road

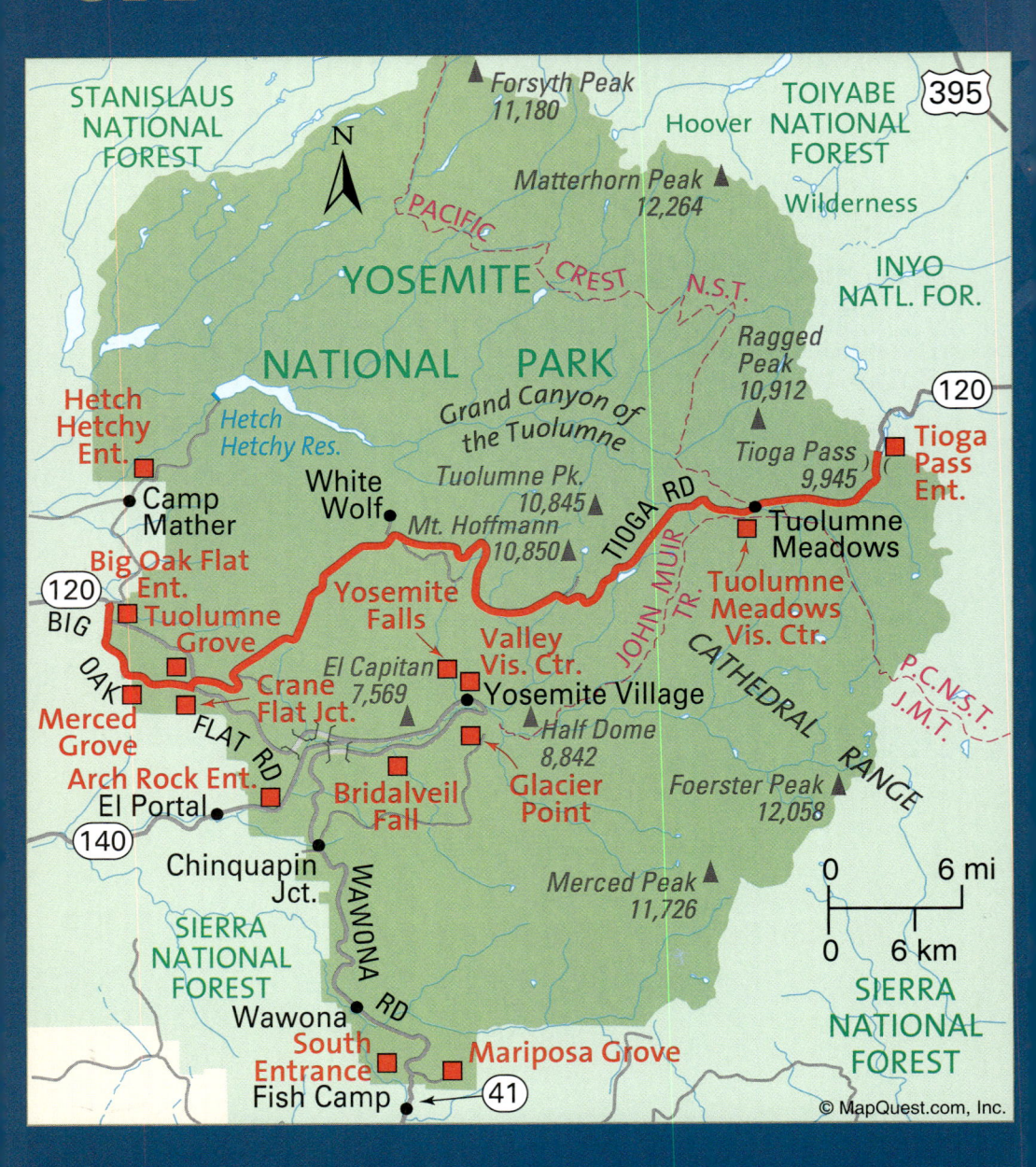

Yosemite National Park

Stanislaus National Forest

Toiyabe National Forest
- Hoover Wilderness
- 395

Inyo Natl. For.

- Forsyth Peak 11,180
- Matterhorn Peak 12,264
- Pacific Crest N.S.T.
- Ragged Peak 10,912
- Tioga Pass 9,945
- 120
- **Tioga Pass Ent.**

- **Hetch Hetchy Ent.**
- Hetch Hetchy Res.
- Camp Mather
- White Wolf
- Grand Canyon of the Tuolumne
- Tuolumne Pk. 10,845
- Mt. Hoffmann 10,850
- TIOGA RD
- Tuolumne Meadows
- Tuolumne Meadows Vis. Ctr.
- John Muir Tr.

- 120
- **Big Oak Flat Ent.**
- Tuolumne Grove
- BIG OAK FLAT RD
- Yosemite Falls
- Crane Flat Jct.
- El Capitan 7,569
- Valley Vis. Ctr.
- Yosemite Village
- Half Dome 8,842
- Glacier Point
- Foerster Peak 12,058
- CATHEDRAL RANGE
- P.C.N.S.T./J.M.T.

- **Merced Grove**
- **Arch Rock Ent.**
- El Portal
- 140
- Bridalveil Fall
- Merced Peak 11,726

- Chinquapin Jct.
- **Sierra National Forest**
- WAWONA RD
- Wawona
- **South Entrance**
- Fish Camp
- **Mariposa Grove**
- 41

- **Sierra National Forest**

0 — 6 mi
0 — 6 km

© MapQuest.com, Inc.

A12 AMERICA'S BYWAYS™

Volcanic Legacy Scenic Byway
also covers OR

OR — Cascade Lakes Scenic Byway

Hells Canyon Scenic Byway — OR

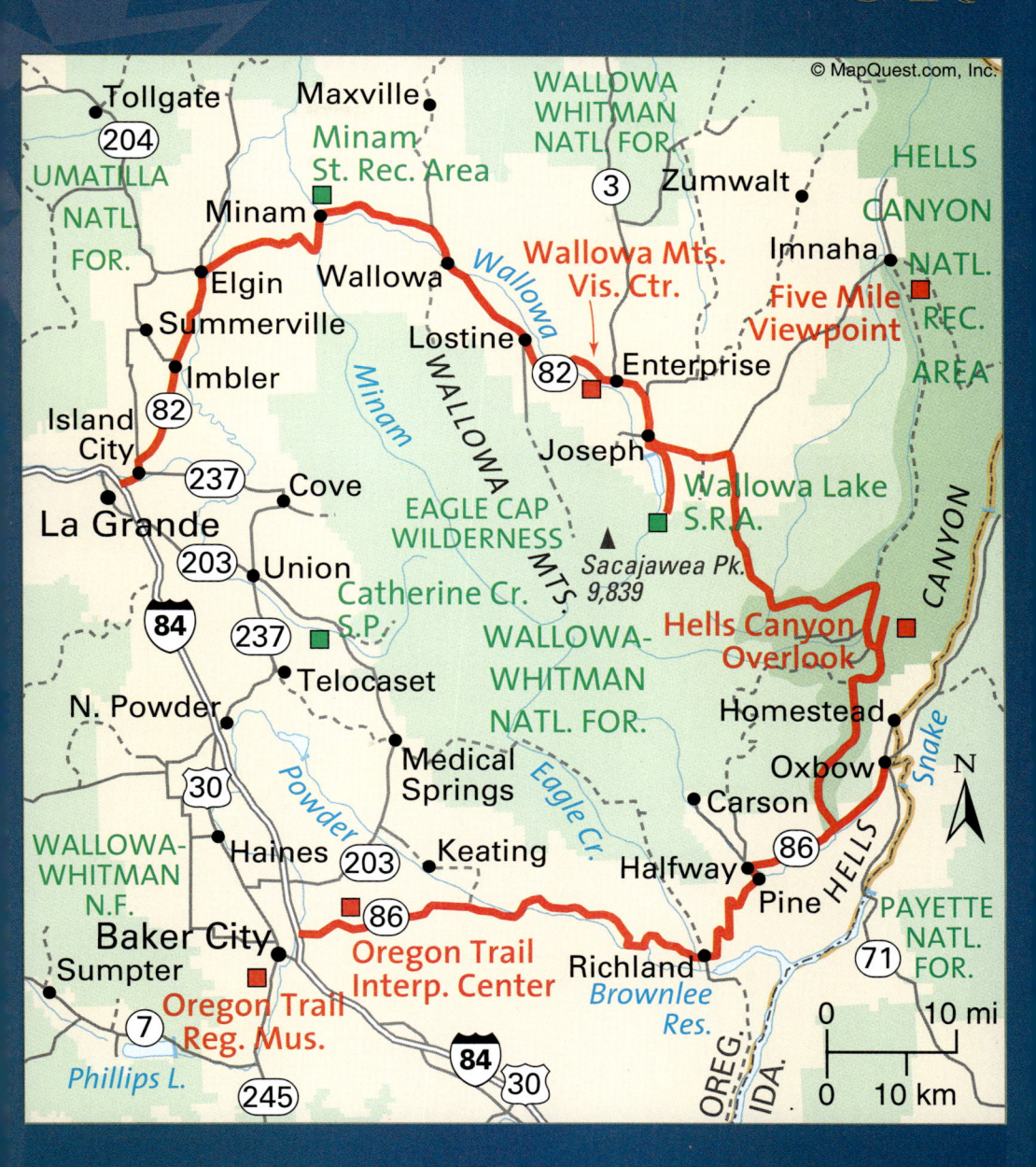

ns/headings
OR · Historic Columbia River Highway

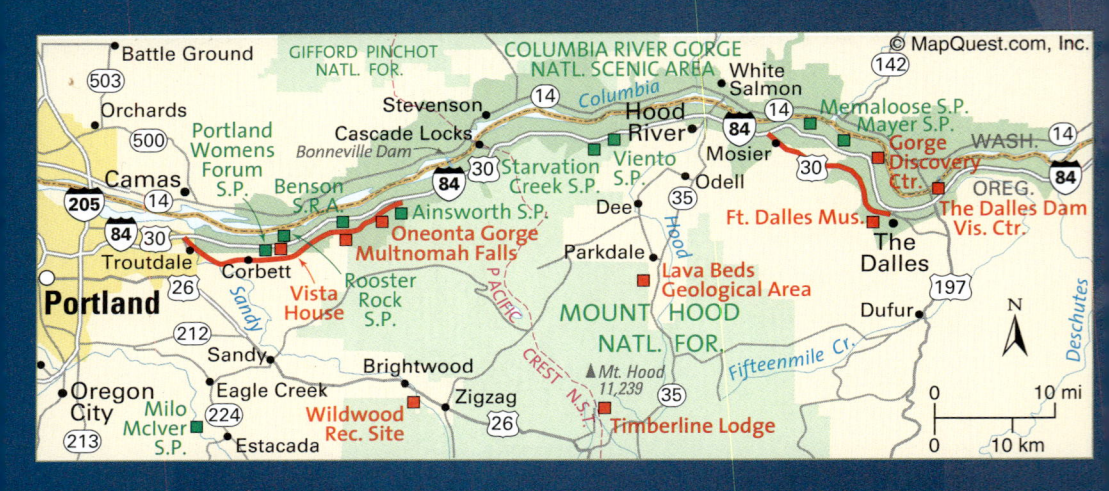

A16 AMERICA'S BYWAYS™

McKenzie Pass-Santiam Pass Scenic Byway — OR

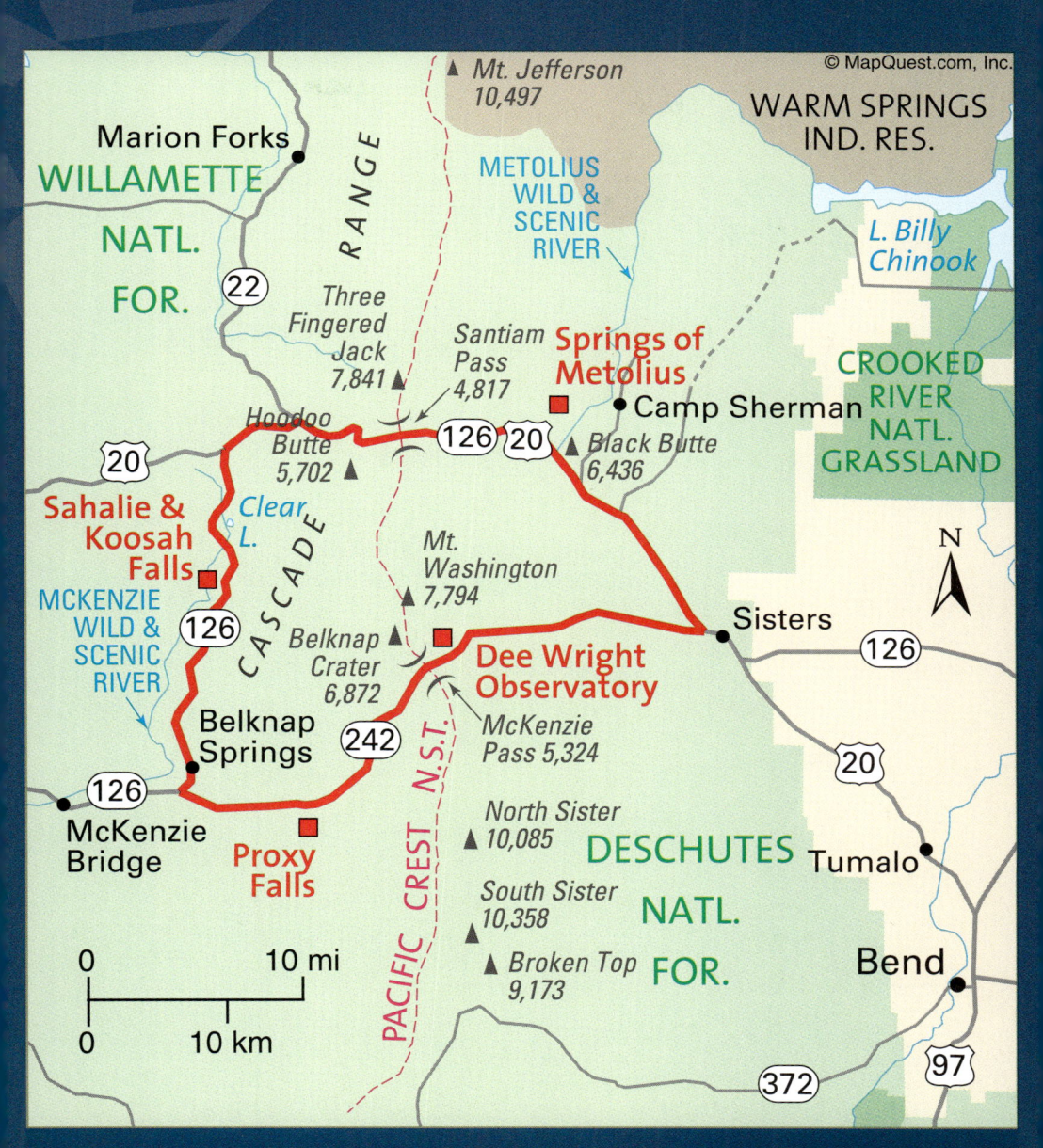

OR Outback Scenic Byway

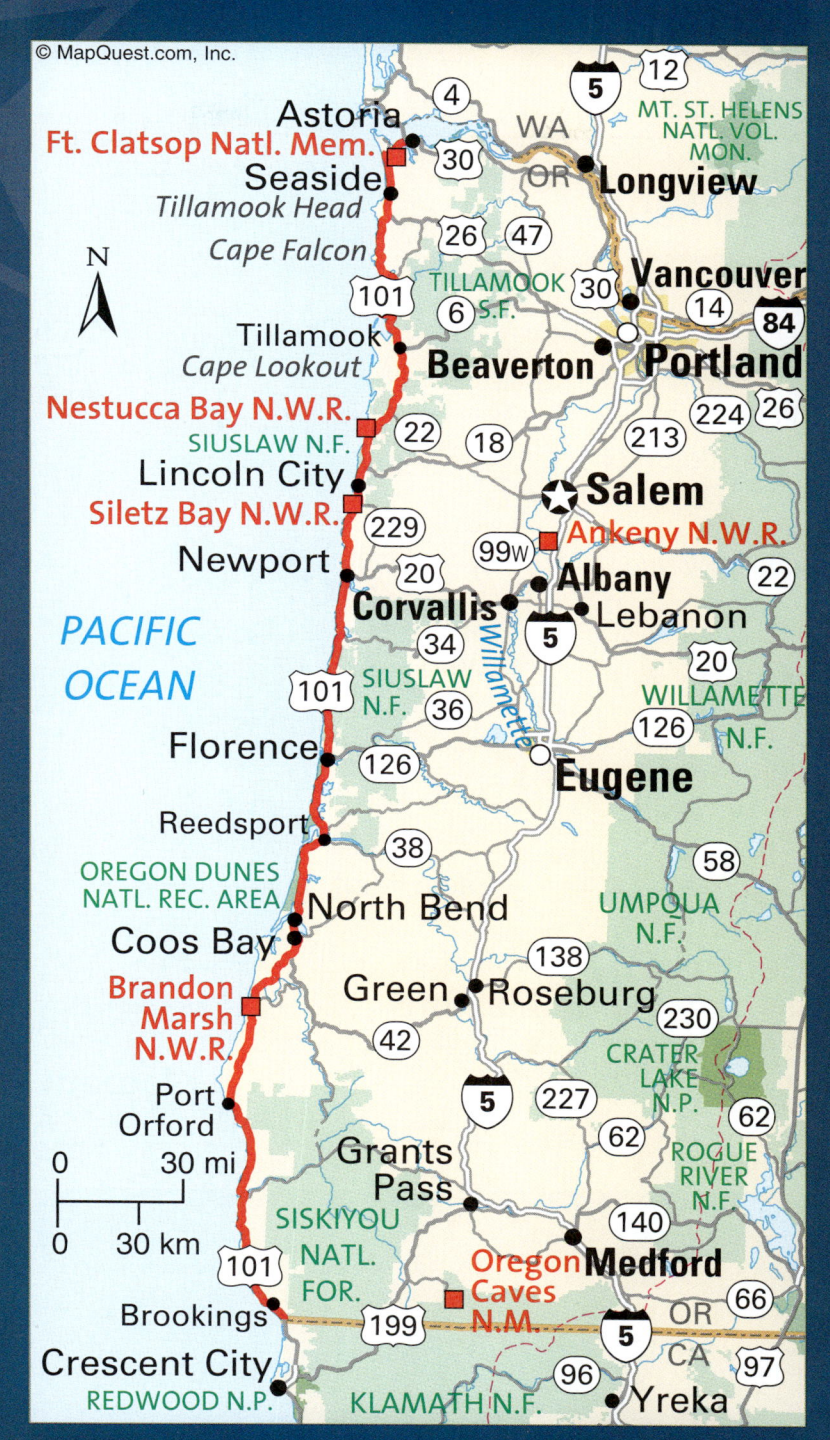

Pacific Coast Scenic Byway — OR

OR — Rogue-Umpqua Scenic Byway

West Cascades Scenic Byway — OR

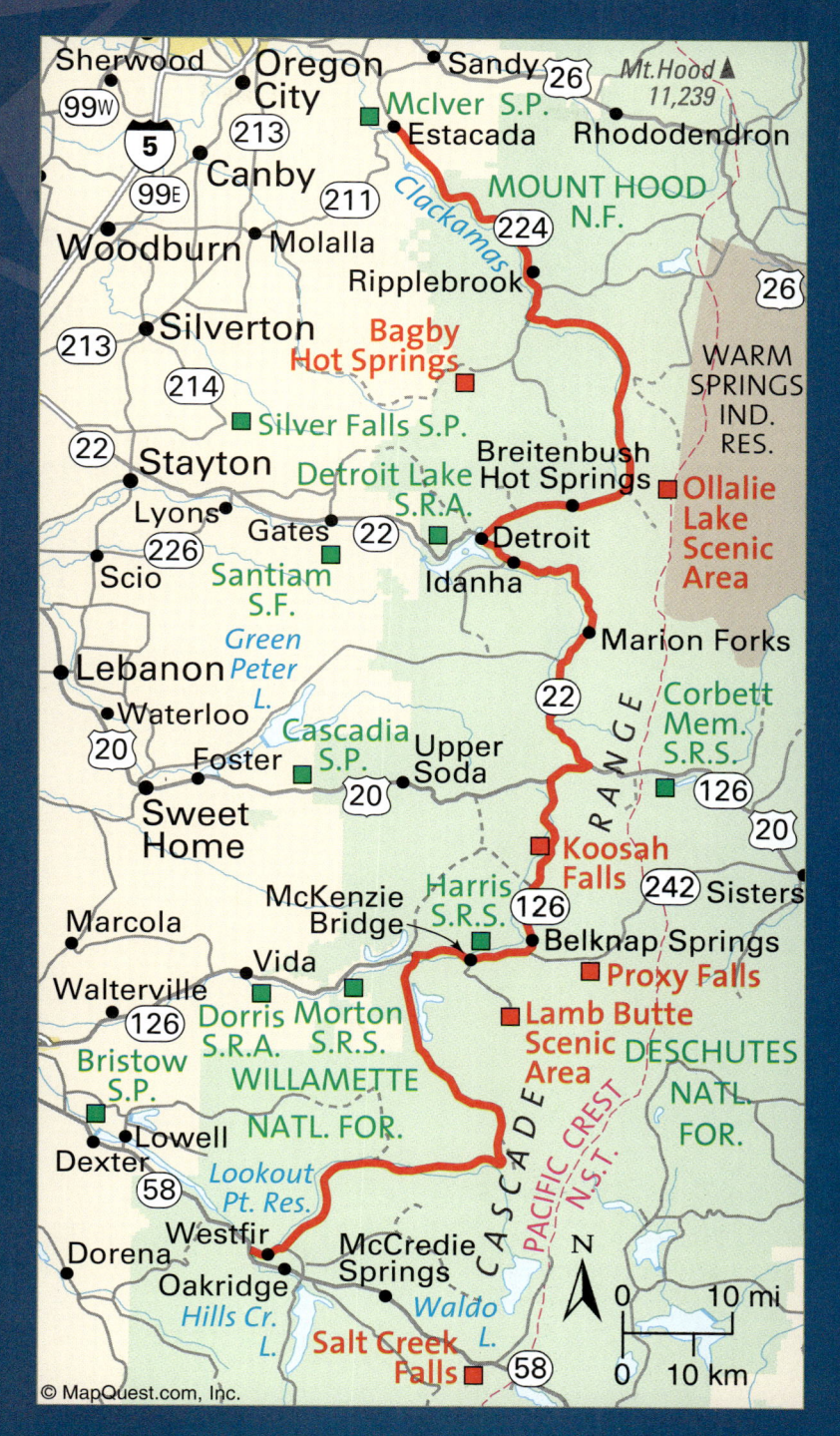

WA Chinook Scenic Byway

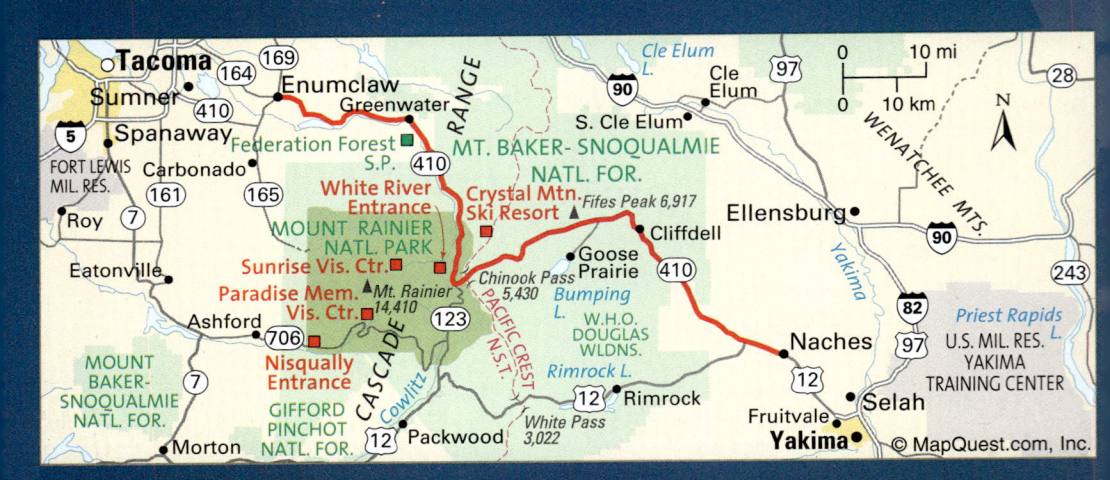

Mountains to Sound Greenway—I-90

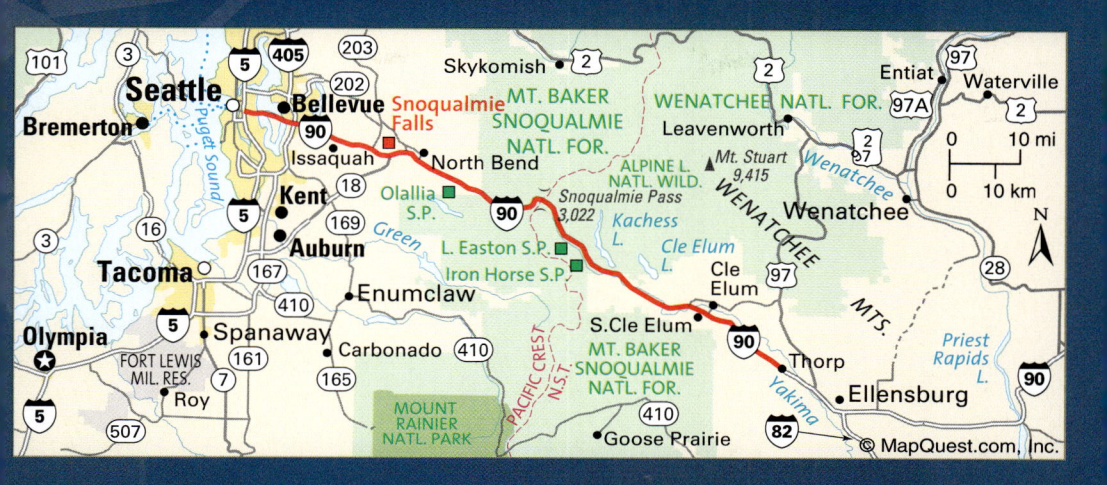

WA Strait of Juan de Fuca Highway—SR 112

America's Byways Series | MOBIL TRAVEL GUIDE

A Word to Our Readers

Travelers are on the roads in great numbers these days. They're exploring the country on day trips, weekend getaways, business trips, and extended family vacations, visiting major cities and small towns along the way. Because time is precious and the travel industry is ever-changing, having accurate, reliable travel information at your fingertips is critical. Mobil Travel Guide has been providing invaluable insight to travelers for more than 45 years, and we are committed to continuing this service well into the future.

The Mobil Corporation (known as Exxon Mobil Corporation since a 1999 merger) began producing the Mobil Travel Guide books in 1958, following the introduction of the US highway system in 1956. The first edition covered only five southwestern states. Since then, our books have become the premier travel guides in North America, covering the 48 contiguous states and Canada. Now, Mobil Travel Guide presents a brand-new series in partnership with the National Scenic Byways Program. We also recently introduced road atlases and specialty publications; a robust new Web site; as well as the first fully integrated, road-centric travel support program called MobilCompanion, the driving force in travel.

Since its founding, Mobil Travel Guide has served as an advocate for travelers seeking knowledge about hotels, restaurants, and places to visit. Based on an objective process, we make recommendations to our customers that we believe will enhance the quality and value of their travel experiences. Our trusted Mobil One- to Five-Star rating system is the oldest and most respected lodging and restaurant inspection and rating program in North America. Most hoteliers, restaurateurs, and industry observers favorably regard the rigor of our inspection program and understand the prestige and benefits that come with receiving a Mobil star rating.

The Mobil Travel Guide process of rating each establishment includes:

- Unannounced facility inspections
- Incognito service evaluations for Mobil Four- and Five-Star properties
- A review of unsolicited comments from the general public
- Senior management oversight

For each property, more than 450 attributes, including cleanliness, physical facilities, employee attitude, and courtesy, are measured and evaluated to produce a mathematically derived score, which is then blended with the other elements to form an overall score. These quantifiable scores allow comparative analysis among properties and form the basis that Mobil Travel Guide uses to assign its Mobil One- to Five-Star ratings.

This process focuses largely on guest expectations, guest experience, and consistency of service, not just physical facilities and amenities. It is fundamentally a relative rating system that rewards those properties that continually strive for and achieve excellence each year. Indeed, the very best properties are consistently raising the bar for those that wish to compete with them. These properties proactively respond to consumers' needs even in today's uncertain times.

Only facilities that meet Mobil Travel Guide's standards earn the privilege of being listed in our books. Deteriorating, poorly managed establishments are deleted. A Mobil Travel Guide listing constitutes a positive quality

A WORD TO OUR READERS

recommendation; every listing is an accolade, a recognition of achievement. Our Mobil One- to Five-Star rating system highlights its level of service. Extensive in-house research is constantly underway to determine new additions to our lists.

- The **Mobil Five-Star Award** indicates that a property is one of the very best in the country and consistently provides gracious and courteous service, superlative quality in its facility, and a unique ambience. The lodgings and restaurants at the Mobil Five-Star level consistently and proactively respond to consumers' needs and continue their commitment to excellence, doing so with grace and perseverance.
- Also highly regarded is the **Mobil Four-Star Award,** which honors properties for outstanding achievement in overall facility and for providing very strong service levels in all areas. These award-winners provide a distinctive experience for the ever-demanding and sophisticated consumer.
- The **Mobil Three-Star Award** recognizes an excellent property that provides full services and amenities. This category ranges from exceptional hotels with limited services to elegant restaurants with a less-formal atmosphere.
- A **Mobil Two-Star property** is a clean and comfortable establishment that has expanded amenities or a distinctive environment. A Mobil Two-Star property is an excellent place to stay or dine.
- A **Mobil One-Star property** is limited in its amenities and services but focuses on providing a value experience while meeting travelers' expectations. The property can be expected to be clean, comfortable, and convenient.

Allow us to emphasize that we do not charge establishments for inclusion in our guides. We have no relationship with any of the businesses and attractions we list and act only as a consumer advocate. In essence, we do the investigative legwork so that you won't have to.

Keep in mind, too, that the hospitality business is ever-changing. Restaurants and lodgings—particularly small chains and standalone establishments—change management or even go out of business with surprising quickness. Although we make every effort to double-check information during our annual updates, we nevertheless recommend that you call ahead to make sure the place you've selected is still open and offers all the amenities you're looking for. We've provided phone numbers; when available, we also list Web site addresses.

We hope that your travels are enjoyable and relaxing and that our books help you get the most out of every trip you take. If any aspect of your accommodation, dining, or sightseeing experience motivates you to comment, please drop us a line. We depend a great deal on our readers' remarks, so you can be assured that we will read your comments and assimilate them into our research. General comments about our books are also welcome. You can write to us at Mobil Travel Guide, 1460 Renaissance Drive, Suite 401, Park Ridge, IL 60068, or send an e-mail to info@mobiltravelguide.com.

Take your Mobil Travel Guide books along on every trip you take. We're confident that you'll be pleased with their convenience, ease of use, and breadth of dependable coverage.

Happy travels!

America's Byways Series | MOBIL TRAVEL GUIDE

Overview of the National Scenic Byways Program

WHAT ARE AMERICA'S BYWAYS™?

Under the National Scenic Byways Program, the US Secretary of Transportation recognizes certain roads as National Scenic Byways or All-American Roads based on their archaeological, cultural, historic, natural, recreational, and scenic qualities. There are 96 such designated Byways in 39 states. The Federal Highway Administration promotes the collection as America's Byways™.

America's Byways™ are a distinctive collection of American roads, their stories and treasured places. They are roads to the heart and soul of America. Byways are exclusive because of their outstanding qualities, not because Byways are confined to a select group of people.

Managing the intrinsic qualities that shape the Byway's story and interpreting the story are equally important in improving the quality of the visitors' experience. The National Scenic Byways Program is founded upon the strength of the leaders for individual Byways. It is a voluntary, grassroots program. It recognizes and supports outstanding roads. It provides resources to help manage the intrinsic qualities within the broader Byway corridor to be treasured and shared. Perhaps one of the underlying principles for the program has been articulated best by the Byway leader who said, "The program is about recognition, not regulation."

WHAT DEFINES A NATIONAL SCENIC BYWAY AND AN ALL-AMERICAN ROAD?

To be designated as a National Scenic Byway, a road must possess at least one of the six intrinsic qualities described below. To receive an All-American Road designation, a road must possess multiple intrinsic qualities that are nationally significant and contain one-of-a-kind features that do not exist elsewhere. The road or highway must also be considered a destination unto itself. That is, the road must provide an exceptional traveling experience so recognized by travelers that they would make a drive along the highway a primary reason for their trip.

Anyone may nominate a road for possible designation by the US Secretary of Transportation, but the nomination must be submitted through a state's official scenic byway agency and include a corridor management plan designed to preserve and enhance the unique qualities of the Byway.

The Byways themselves typically are supported through a network of individuals who volunteer their time and effort. It is a bottom-up, grassroots-oriented program. Local citizens and communities create the vision for their Byway, identify the resources comprising the intrinsic qualities, and form the theme or story that stirs the interest and imagination of visitors about the Byway and its resources. Local citizens and communities decide how best to balance goals, strategies, and actions for promoting the Byway and preserving its intrinsic qualities. The vision, goals, strategies, and actions for the Byway are laid out in the required corridor management plan.

Nomination is not about filling out an application. It's all about telling the Byway's story. That's the premise that is driving the FHWA's work on requesting nominations for possible national designation. Nominees might want to think of their Byway's nomination as a combination of the community's guide and a visitor's guide for the Byway.

OVERVIEW OF THE NATIONAL SCENIC BYWAYS PROGRAM

WHAT ARE INTRINSIC QUALITIES?

An intrinsic quality is a scenic, historic, recreational, cultural, archaeological, or natural feature that is considered representative, unique, irreplaceable, or distinctly characteristic of an area. The National Scenic Byways Program provides resources to the Byway community and enhances local quality of life through efforts to preserve, protect, interpret, and promote the intrinsic qualities of designated Byways.

- **Archaeological quality** involves those characteristics of the Byway corridor that are physical evidence of historic or prehistoric life that is visible and capable of being inventoried and interpreted.

- **Cultural quality** is evidence and expressions of the customs or traditions of a distinct group of people. Cultural features include, but are not limited to, crafts, music, dance, rituals, festivals, speech, food, special events, and vernacular architecture that are currently practiced.

- **Historic quality** encompasses legacies of the past that are distinctly associated with physical elements of the landscape, whether natural or man-made, that are of such historic significance that they educate the viewer and stir an appreciation of the past.

- **Natural quality** applies to those features in the visual environment that are in a relatively undisturbed state. These features predate the arrival of human populations and may include geological formations, fossils, landforms, water bodies, vegetation, and wildlife.

- **Recreational quality** involves outdoor recreational activities directly associated with, and dependent upon, the natural and cultural elements of the corridor's landscape.

- **Scenic quality** is the heightened visual experience derived from the view of natural and man-made elements of the visual environment.

For more information about the National Scenic Byways Program, call 800/4BYWAYS or visit the Web site www.byways.org.

America's Byways Series | MOBIL TRAVEL GUIDE

Introduction

America's Byways™ are a distinctive collection of American roads, their stories, and treasured places. They are the roads to the heart and soul of America. This book showcases a select group of nationally designated Byways and organizes them by state, and within each state, alphabetically by Byway. Information in this book is collected from two sources:

- The National Scenic Byways Program (NSBP) provides content about the Byways themselves—quick facts, the Byway story, and highlights. NSBP's information contributors include federal, regional, and state organizations, as well as private groups and individuals. These parties have been recognized as experts in Byways and are an authoritative source for the Byways information that appears in this book.

- Information in this book about lodgings, restaurants, and most sights and attractions along the Byways comes from Mobil Travel Guide, which has served as a trusted aid to auto travelers in search of value in lodging, dining, and destinations since its inception in 1958. The Mobil One- to Five-Star rating system is the oldest and most respected lodging and restaurant inspection and rating program in North America. This trusted, well-established tool directs you to satisfying places to eat and stay, as well as to interesting events and attractions in thousands of locations.

The following sections explain the wealth of information you'll find about the Byways that appear in this book: information about the Byway, things to see and do along the way, and places to stay and eat.

Quick Facts

This section gives you an overview of each Byway, including the following quick facts:

LENGTH: The number of miles from one end of the Byway to the other.

TIME TO ALLOW: How much time to allow to drive the entire length. For some Byways, the suggested time is several days because of the length or the number of attractions on or near the Byway; for others, the time is listed in hours.

BEST TIME TO DRIVE: The season(s) in which the Byway is most appealing. For some Byways, you also discover the peak season, which you may want to avoid if you're looking for a peaceful, uncrowded drive.

BYWAY TRAVEL INFORMATION: Telephone numbers and Web sites for the Byway organization and any local travel and tourism centers.

SPECIAL CONSIDERATIONS: Words of advice that range from the type of clothing you'll want to bring to winter-weather advisories.

RESTRICTIONS: Closings or other cautionary tips.

BICYCLE/PEDESTRIAN FACILITIES: Explains whether the Byway is safe and pleasant for bicycling and/or walking.

INTRODUCTION

THE BYWAY STORY

As explained in the preceding section titled "Overview of the National Scenic Byways Program," a road must possess intrinsic qualities and one-of-a-kind features to receive a National Scenic Byway or All-American Road designation. An All-American Road must also be considered a destination unto itself. This section describes the unique qualities of each Byway, with a separate section for each of its intrinsic qualities. Here you'll find information about the history and culture of the roadway, the wildlife and other natural features found along the Byway, and the recreational opportunities that are available to visitors to the area.

HIGHLIGHTS

Some local Byway organizations suggest tours or itineraries that cover all or part of the Byway. Where these itineraries are available, they're included in this book under the heading "Highlights."

THINGS TO SEE AND DO

Mobil Travel Guide offers information about nearly 20,000 museums, art galleries, amusement parks, historic sites, national and state parks, ski areas, and many other types of attractions. A white star on a black background ★ signals that the attraction is a must-see—one of the best in the area. Because municipal parks, public tennis courts, swimming pools, and small educational institutions are common to most towns, they generally are not mentioned.

When a Byway goes through or comes quite close to a particular town, city, or national park, attractions in those towns or parks are included. Otherwise, attractions are limited to those along the Byway.

Attractions for the entire Byway are listed alphabetically by name. Following an attraction's description, you'll find the months, days, and, in some cases, hours of operation; the address/directions, telephone number, and Web site (if there is one); and the admission price category. The following are the ranges we use for admission fees:

- **FREE**
- **DONATION**
- **$** = Up to $5
- **$$** = $5.01-$10
- **$$$** = $10.01-$15
- **$$$$** = $15.01 and up

PLACES TO STAY

For each Byway, recommended lodgings are listed in alphabetical order, based on the cities in which they're located. In general, only lodgings that are close to or located right on the Byway are listed.

Each lodging listing gives the name, address/location (when no street address is available), neighborhood and/or directions from downtown (in major cities), phone number(s), Web site (if available), total number of guest rooms, and seasons open (if not year-round). Also included are details on business, luxury, recreational, and dining facilities on the property or nearby. A key to the symbols at the end of each listing can be found in the "Terms, Abbreviations, and Symbols in Listings" section of this Introduction.

Because most lodgings offer the following features and services, information about them does not appear in the listings unless exceptions exist:

- Year-round operation with a single rate structure
- Major credit cards accepted (note that Exxon or Mobil Corporation credit cards cannot be used to pay for room or other charges)
- Air-conditioning and heat, often with individual room controls
- Bathroom with tub and/or shower in each room
- Cots and cribs available

- Daily maid service
- Elevators
- In-room telephones

For every property, we also provide pricing information. Because lodging rates change frequently, we list a pricing category rather than specific prices. The pricing categories break down as follows:

- ¢ = Up to $90
- $ = $91-$150
- $$ = $151-$250
- $$$ = $251-$350
- $$$$ = $351 and up

All prices quoted are in effect at the time of publication; however, prices cannot be guaranteed. Note that in some locations, short-term price variations may exist because of special events or holidays. Certain resorts have complicated rate structures that vary with the time of year; always confirm rates when making your plans.

All listed establishments have been inspected by experienced field representatives and/or evaluated by a senior staff member. Our ratings are based on detailed inspection reports of the individual properties, on written evaluations of staff members who stay and dine anonymously, and on an extensive review of reader comments. Rating categories reflect both the features a property offers and its quality in relation to similar establishments.

Here are the definitions for the star ratings for lodgings:

- ★★★★★: A Mobil Five-Star lodging provides consistently superlative service in an exceptionally distinctive luxury environment, with expanded services. Attention to detail is evident throughout the hotel, resort, or inn, from bed linens to staff uniforms.
- ★★★★: A Mobil Four-Star lodging provides a luxury experience with expanded amenities in a distinctive environment. Services may include, but are not limited to, automatic turndown service, 24-hour room service, and valet parking.
- ★★★: A Mobil Three-Star lodging is well appointed, with a full-service restaurant and expanded amenities, such as a fitness center, golf course, tennis courts, 24-hour room service, and optional turndown service.
- ★★: A Mobil Two-Star lodging is considered a clean, comfortable, and reliable establishment that has expanded amenities, such as a full-service restaurant on the premises.
- ★: A Mobil One-Star lodging is a limited-service hotel, motel, or inn that is considered a clean, comfortable, and reliable establishment.

PLACES TO EAT

For each Byway, dining establishments are listed in alphabetical order, based on the cities in which they're located. These restaurants and other eateries are either right on or close to the Byway chapter in which they're listed. All establishments listed have a full kitchen and offer table service and a complete menu. Parking on or near the premises, in a lot or garage, is assumed.

Each listing also gives the cuisine type, address (or directions if no street address is available), neighborhood and/or directions from downtown (in major cities), phone number, Web site (if available), meals served, days of operation (if not open daily year-round), reservation policy, and pricing category. We also indicate whether a children's menu is offered. The pricing categories are defined as follows per diner and assume that you order an appetizer, entrée, and one drink:

- $ = Up to $15
- $$ = $16-$35
- $$$ = $36-$85
- $$$$ = $86 and up

All listed establishments have been inspected by experienced field representatives and/or evaluated by a senior staff member. Our ratings are based on detailed inspection reports of the individual properties, on written evaluations of staff members who stay and dine anonymously, and on an extensive review of reader comments. Rating categories reflect both the

INTRODUCTION

features a property offers and its quality in relation to similar establishments.

The Mobil star ratings for restaurants are defined as follows:

- ★★★★★: A Mobil Five-Star restaurant offers one of few flawless dining experiences in the country. These establishments consistently provide their guests with exceptional food, superlative service, elegant décor, and exquisite presentations of each detail surrounding a meal.
- ★★★★: A Mobil Four-Star restaurant provides professional service, distinctive presentations, and wonderful food.
- ★★★: A Mobil Three-Star restaurant has good food, warm and skillful service, and enjoyable décor.
- ★★: A Mobil Two-Star restaurant serves fresh food in a clean setting with efficient service. Value is considered in this category, as is family friendliness.
- ★: A Mobil One-Star restaurant provides a distinctive experience through culinary specialty, local flair, or individual atmosphere.

TERMS, ABBREVIATIONS, AND SYMBOLS IN LISTINGS

The following terms, abbreviations, and symbols are used throughout the Mobil Travel Guide lodging and restaurant listings to indicate which amenities and services are available at each establishment. We've done our best to provide accurate and up-to-date information, but things do change, so if a particular feature is essential to you, please contact the establishment directly to make sure that it is available.

Continental breakfast: Usually coffee and a roll or doughnut.

In-room modem link: Every guest room has a connection for a modem that's separate from the main phone line.

Laundry service: Either coin-operated laundry facilities or overnight valet service is available.

Luxury level: A special section of a lodging, spanning at least an entire floor, that offers

Locals recommend

Byway experts from around the country recommend special restaurants and/or lodgings along their particular Byways that can make your trip even more pleasant. You'll see these special recommendations throughout this book. Look for this symbol next to the hotel or restaurant name:

increased luxury accommodations. Management must provide no less than three of these four services: separate check-in and check-out, concierge, private lounge, and private elevator service (with key access). Complimentary breakfast and snacks are commonly offered.

MAP: Modified American plan (lodging plus two meals).

Movies: Prerecorded videos are available for rental or check-out.

Prix fixe: A full, multicourse meal for a stated price; usually available at finer restaurants.

Valet parking: An attendant is available to park and retrieve your car.

VCR: VCRs are present in all guest rooms.

VCR available: VCRs are available for hookup in guest rooms.

- Pet allowed
- Fishing
- Horseback riding
- Snow skiing nearby
- Golf, nine-hole minimum, on premises
- Tennis court(s) on premises
- Swimming
- In-house fitness room
- Jogging
- Major commercial airport within 10 miles
- Nonsmoking guest rooms
- SC Senior citizen rates
- Business center

A32

SPECIAL INFORMATION FOR TRAVELERS WITH DISABILITIES

The Mobil Travel Guide [D] symbol indicates establishments that are at least partially accessible to people with mobility problems. Our criteria for accessibility are unique to our publications. Please do not confuse them with the universal symbol for wheelchair accessibility.

When the [D] symbol follows a listing, the establishment is equipped with facilities to accommodate people using wheelchairs or crutches or otherwise needing easy access to doorways and rest rooms. Travelers with severe mobility problems or with hearing or visual impairments may or may not find the facilities they need. Always phone ahead to make sure that an establishment can meet your needs.

All lodgings bearing our [D] symbol have the following facilities:

- ISA-designated parking near access ramps
- Level or ramped entryways to buildings
- Swinging building entryway doors a minimum of 39 inches wide
- Public rest rooms on the main level with space to operate a wheelchair and handrails at commode areas
- Elevator(s) equipped with grab bars and lowered control buttons
- Restaurant(s) with accessible doorway(s), rest rooms with space to operate a wheelchair, and handrails at commode areas
- Guest room entryways that are at least 39 inches wide

- Low-pile carpet in rooms
- Telephones at bedside and in the bathroom
- Beds placed at wheelchair height
- Bathrooms with a minimum doorway width of 3 feet
- Bath with an open sink (no cabinet) and room to operate a wheelchair
- Handrails at commode areas and in the tub
- Wheelchair-accessible peepholes in room entry door
- Wheelchair-accessible closet rods and shelves

All restaurants bearing our [D] symbol offer the following facilities:

- ISA-designated parking beside access ramps
- Level or ramped front entryways to the building
- Tables that accommodate wheelchairs
- Main-floor rest rooms with an entryway that's at least 3 feet wide
- Rest rooms with space to operate a wheelchair and handrails at commode areas

Alaska's Marine Highway
✼ ALASKA

Quick Facts

LENGTH: 8,834 miles.

TIME TO ALLOW: Allow one month to take in all the sights.

BEST TIME TO DRIVE: The highway is beautiful year-round. Summer is the high season, so make reservations early. During the winter months, the frequency of trips to some communities is reduced.

BYWAY TRAVEL INFORMATION: Alaska's Marine Highway: 800/642-0066; Byway local Web sites: www.dot.state.ak.us/amhs/index.html, www.dot.state.ak.us.

SPECIAL CONSIDERATIONS: All vehicles, including large trucks, RVs, and trailers, can be accommodated on the highway's ships, provided space is available. Electrical current on board is 110-volt, 60-cycle, AC power.

RESTRICTIONS: Fees vary from under $50 to hundreds of dollars depending on how far you go and whether you are bringing your car. Call Alaska's Marine Highway System for a schedule.

BICYCLE/PEDESTRIAN FACILITIES: All ferries accommodate bicycles and walk-on travelers. You must leave you bike on the car deck; access to the deck is prohibited while underway except for specific trips. You also have access to your vehicle while the vessel is in port. Bicycles, kayaks, and very small boats (inflatables under 100 pounds) are charged at the Alternate Means of Conveyance rate, which is limited to one per customer. If the boat exceeds 100 pounds, it will be charged at the Vehicles to 10 Feet rate. Larger boats must be on a trailer and will be charged the appropriate amount by length.

I f you want to see Alaska, take the ferry. Alaska's Marine Highway is made up of a state-owned fleet of nine ferries that travel scenic coastal routes totaling more than 8,000 miles. From the southern terminus in Bellingham, Washington, the ferries ply waters lined with the lush, green rain forests of British Columbia and Alaska's Inside Passage. Voyagers pass glaciers and fjords in Prince William Sound and the windswept Aleutian Islands, rich in cultural, archeological, and seismic history.

In southeastern Alaska, northbound travelers can end their sail in Haines or Skagway to connect to the Yukon or other Alaska scenic highways, such as the Haines Highway and the Taylor/Top of the World Highway. The mainline vessels are the Taku, Matanuska, Malaspina, Kennicott, and Columbia. These workhorses of the Inside Passage travel from Bellingham, Washington; Prince Rupert, British Columbia; and southeastern Alaska coastal communities.

The *Bartlett* travels routes in south-central Alaska and Prince William Sound. The *Tustumena* travels the Gulf of Alaska and the Aleutian Islands. During the summer, the state's newest ferry, the *M/V Kennicott*, provides several Gulf of Alaska crossings to the south-central communities of Valdez and Seward.

THE BYWAY STORY

Alaska's Marine Highway tells archaeological, cultural, historical, natural, recreational, and scenic stories that make it a unique and treasured Byway.

Alaska

✣ *Alaska's Marine Highway*

Archaeological

Although you may not see much archaeology from the ferry, stops along the way offer a look at some of Alaska's most intriguing archaeological sites. Much of the archaeological evidence left behind is the work of native Alaskans, and some sites along the Byway are of Russian and American origin.

Petroglyphs can be found on the Byway near Kodiak, near Petersburg in the Tongass National Forest, and in Sitka. In Wrangell, visitors will be delighted to find Petroglyph State Historic Park, where beautiful circles and designs are carved into large stones. A short hike from the ferry landing takes explorers to a collection of more than 40 petroglyphs from an unknown time and culture, although the native Tlingit people could be descendents of the artists. Archaeologists have made guesses about the significance of the designs on the boulders, but they could be anything from artwork to a record of the past.

In Ketchikan, archaeology and today's cultures come together at the Totem Bight State Historic Park. When native people left their villages to find work in the new towns in Alaska, they also left collections of totem poles behind. During the 1930s, the Civilian Conservation Corps (CCC) came to salvage what was left of these totem poles and re-create what had been lost. An even more recent archaeological excavation began at Sitka in 1995 to uncover Baranof Castle, built in 1837. Work at this site has uncovered many artifacts from the time Russians first began to inhabit Sitka. The occupations and way of life for native Alaskans and new Alaskans become evident through each discovery.

Cultural

Three distinct cultures have come to call Alaska their home over the last few centuries, and these cultures are present at every port along Alaska's Marine Highway. The native cultures have been joined over the years by Russian and American cultures to create a rich history and a thriving present.

The lives of residents, along with the industries that allow them to survive in the Land of the Midnight Sun, are around every corner as you enjoy the decks of the ferry or the streets of one of Alaska's towns. Alaska's Marine Highway takes you through fishing villages and historic towns. Watching a fishing boat on the ocean, you may catch a glimpse of one of the huge halibut that fishing boats bring in.

Nearly every stop on the Byway reveals more history of the native Alaskans who have lived here for centuries. The native people celebrate festivals and wear authentic clothing. Feasts and festivals that involve dancing, singing, arts, and crafts traditionally occur during the winter, when all the work of the summer has been done. Many of the festivals are held in honor of animal spirits. Some of the native cultures believe that the hunt will be continually good when the spirits of animals are honored. The festivals and traditions you witness on the Byway may be the most memorable part of your trip.

Historical

The history of coastal Alaska dates back to unrecorded times, when the first native Alaskans were just getting used to the beautiful, yet extreme, territory they lived in. Over many centuries, Alaska has come to be appreciated by different cultures that wanted to stake a claim in the area. From Russian Orthodox missionaries to American gold miners, the history of Alaska and its coastline is unique and full of stories. As you travel along Alaska's Marine Highway, each port unravels more of the past.

Kodiak Island was the site of the first permanent Russian colony in 1784. The same Russian trappers who were willing to brave the elements in Siberia were also willing to settle the land across the Bering Strait if it meant finding more furs. As settlement progressed, a Russian Orthodox mission was established to keep peace between native peoples and the Russians until the parcel of land was sold to the United

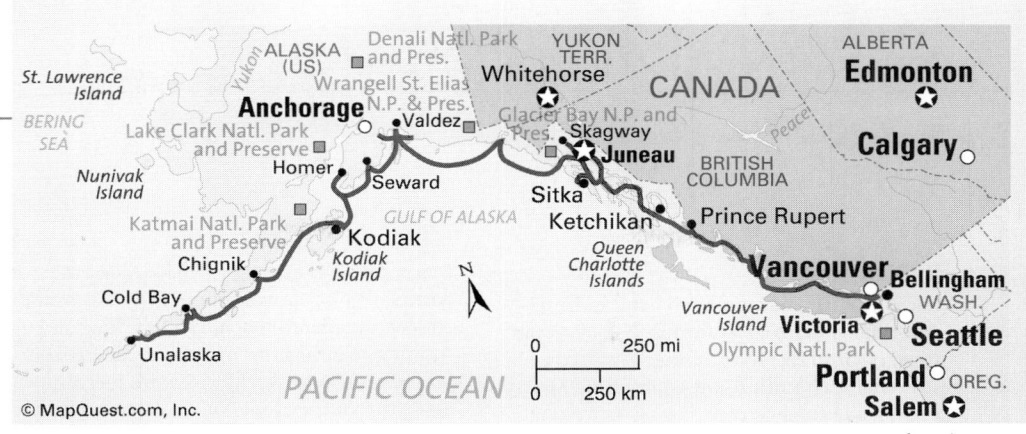

States. Today, towns like Sitka, Unalaska, Seldovia, and many others display pieces of Russian history and influence in Alaska.

Development in Alaska really began in 1867 when "Seward's Icebox" became a US territory. News of gold in the arctic spread like wildfire, and prospectors gathered in mining communities to try their luck. Ketchikan became the gateway to the Klondike Gold Rush, and Skagway became the destination. Skagway still maintains its reputation as a gold rush town with the Klondike Gold Rush National Historic Park. All through the Inside Passage and on to south-central Alaska, miners established communities in places that promised wealth. Some were successful, and many were not, but stories of Alaska were told far and wide in the lower 48 states.

The first tourists to Alaska traveled along the coast for a look at the lands that they had heard so much about. They usually took a steamship on a route developed along Alaska's Inside Passage to see the mystical northern territory, and its glaciers and dense forests. Traveling along the coastline remains one of the world's favorite ways to see Alaska—Alaska's Marine Highway preserved the sightseeing tactics of the first Alaskan tourists.

Natural

Some of the most unique wonders of the world are clustered in the northern corner—a very large corner—known as Alaska. Filled with majestic sea creatures, geological movements, and land overrun with glaciers and forests, Alaska's scenic coastline abounds with natural wonders. In the daylight, you may see a whale as it splashes its tail against the water. At night, the Northern Lights may fill the sky.

As you travel along the shores of Alaska, you observe the unspoiled natural features of the north. Alaska's Marine Highway travels through the Tongass National Forest and along the Chugach National Forest, allowing you to get a good look at both the land and the sea. These beautiful water passageways display rock outcroppings, forest-covered mountainsides, and even glaciers. Although Norway is known best for having fjords, Alaska has its own collection. The state has 100,000 glaciers, most located on the coast. Also notice the smoldering islands along the Alaska Peninsula. These islands are part of the Pacific "Ring of Fire," where underwater volcanoes create island volcanoes that can be seen from the ferry.

Few Byways offer a view of such fascinating sea creatures. Whales, seals, fish, and seabirds are all an integral part of an experience on Alaska's Marine Highway. Stop in Seward to visit the Alaska Sealife Center, where interactive displays tell all about Alaska's wildlife. The route actually passes through nine wildlife preserves and national parks, where you're sure to catch a glimpse of something interesting. Both baleen whales and killer whales can be spotted at Glacier Bay National Park and Preserve. At Kodiak Island, nearly 2 million seabirds live along the shores, while brown bears roam the spruce forests. As you continue, you may be surprised at the kinds of sights that surface on your voyage.

Alaska

Alaska's Marine Highway

Recreational

Recreation and adventure go hand in hand, and what is more adventurous than an ocean voyage? From the decks of the ships to the streets of each town to the trails of the forests, you'll find plenty of places to explore along Alaska's Marine Highway. Nearly 98 percent of the land along the Byway is publicly owned, which makes wilderness experiences and recreational opportunities virtually endless. While you ride the ferry, you can dine, lounge, and even camp on the decks.

One of the benefits of traveling Alaska's Marine Highway is being able to take your favorite recreational activities with you—mountain biking, kayaking, hiking, or whatever other activities beckon along the coast. At each community, you'll find opportunities to get out and explore, with miles of trails, plenty of parks, and places to stay available at every stop. If you're traveling the Byway for a look at local history and culture, spend time in the communities along the way. Stopping in the Tongass National Forest or the Chugach National Forest allows you to see some of Alaska's beautiful forests and perhaps some of its wildlife. If you're an angler, you may want to try salmon fishing in some of Alaska's rivers.

Scenic

Be sure to bring enough film for your camera. Visiting the coastline of Alaska is like visiting the shores of a fantasy land. Traveling the coast by Alaska's Marine Highway transforms the adventure to a sea voyage, where the wonders of the north are waiting to be discovered. From volcanoes to glaciers, a collection of natural wonders are visible from the decks. You'll see evergreen islands and majestic fjords. Glacier-carved mountains rise up from the shoreline, overshadowing a peaceful fishing village. And at night, the Northern Lights may glide across the black sky.

As you travel among the villages and towns of the three main sections of the marine Byway, the scenery changes, and nature displays different spectacles from her bag of tricks. Along the Alaskan Peninsula, volcanic activity exists on smoldering islands that are still growing and forming. Winding through the Inside Passage, you pass many of the 1,500 islands there. All along the journey, look for Alaskan sea life that can be seen only from the decks of a boat—or on one of television's nature channels.

Each stop on the route takes you to towns and villages with displays of history and culture. Parts of the scenery on the Byway are found in the Russian Orthodox churches and the remnants of booming gold rush towns. Snowcapped mountains in the background and the crisp Alaskan atmosphere only heighten the appeal of each place along the way. And within each city, you are likely to find rivers, trails, or bays, where eagles soar and seals still gather.

HIGHLIGHTS

Alaska's Marine Highway takes you through a variety of towns (listed here alphabetically) along the southern Alaskan coastline.

- **Haines:** Located at the northern extent of the Inside Passage route, this community is situated along the Chilkat River. This is a popular port community, linked to the traditional highway system that connects to the Alaska Highway via the Haines state scenic byway. The community is also popular for its bald eagle population in the autumn. In October, the world's largest number of bald eagles gather in Haines to take advantage of the late salmon run. This amazing gathering of eagles is the basis of the Chilkat Bald Eagle Preserve and annual Alaska Bald Eagle Festival held in their honor.

- **Homer:** Located on the Kenai Peninsula, Homer is the home port for a large fleet of halibut charter operators fishing the rich and scenic waters of Kachemak Bay. The Spit is where all the action in Homer takes place. Both commercial fishing boats and leisure fishermen gather at The Spit for boating and fishing. Also located in Homer is the Alaska

Maritime National Wildlife Refuge. The refuge is home to seabirds, which find a habitat in the rocks and reefs of Alaskan islands.

- **Juneau:** Juneau is the capital of Alaska and a historic community with a range of tourism-oriented services and cultural events. The community was settled as a gold mining district and is now the service hub for southeastern Alaska. It is also the gateway to Glacier Bay National Park.

- **Ketchikan:** Ketchikan is known as the Gateway to Alaska and is the state's salmon capital. The community is known for its historic Creek Street district and timber industry.

- **Kodiak:** Kodiak, the nation's largest commercial fishing port, was once the capital of Russian America. The community is located on Kodiak Island, a national wildlife preserve, allowing outstanding wildlife viewing opportunities.

- **Petersburg:** This town is known as Little Norway due to its Scandinavian roots and has several festivals to celebrate the heritage of its residents. Visitors to the community often believe they are visiting a Norwegian community due to its architecture and commonly spoken language.

- **Seward:** If you hear names like "Resurrection Bay" and "Marathon Mountain," you are probably at the romantic town of Seward on the Seward Highway. The town was named to honor William H. Seward, who helped the United States purchase Alaska from Russia. Near Seward, you'll find Kenai Fjords National Park and the Chugach National Forest headquarters. While in Seward, don't miss a visit to the Alaska Sealife Center. Celebrating Independence Day in Seward means running or watching the Mount Marathon Race and participating in events all around the city.

- **Sitka:** Numerous volcanic mountains rise out of the ocean and provide a stunning ocean backdrop for this fishing community. Sitka was the Russian capital of North America in the 19th century, as well as the first state capital of Alaska. It still offers visitors a great taste of that period in Alaskan history. The community is also a center for Tlingit native culture.

- **Skagway:** Skagway is a community with a rich history that includes the Klondike Gold Rush. The history of that period is displayed by a National Park Service site and by the city's historic architecture. The White Pass and Yukon Route historic railway traverses the 3,000-foot mountain pass to the Yukon, Canada.

- **Unalaska/Dutch Harbor:** Unalaska/Dutch Harbor is the westernmost point of the Marine Highway. Located in the Aleutian Islands, it was the first Russian-American community. The town was invaded by the Japanese during World War II.

- **Valdez:** Valdez is the terminus of the Trans-Alaskan Pipeline and the Richardson State Scenic Byway. The area is home to the World Extreme Skiing Competitions as well as many other outstanding winter activities. Don't miss the scenic walking trail.

- **Whittier:** Whittier is an important hub connecting the Marine Highway to the Alaska Railroad and to the rest of Alaska, including Anchorage, Fairbanks, and Denali National Park. The community is also linked by highway to the rest of Alaska.

Alaska

✤ *Alaska's Marine Highway*

THINGS TO SEE AND DO

Driving along Alaska's Marine Highway will certainly keep your senses engaged, but if you yearn to get out of the car and stretch your legs, or if you'd like to make a mini-vacation out of your trip, check out these attractions along the route.

ALASKA SEALIFE CENTER. *301 Railway Ave, Seward (99664). Phone 907/224-6300; toll-free 800/224-2525. www.alaskasealife.org.* The Alaska SeaLife Center offers an unrivaled up-close and personal experience with Gulf of Alaska marine wildlife. Witness 1,500-pound Steller sea lions gliding past underwater viewing windows, puffins diving in a carefully crafted naturalistic habitat, and harbor seals hauled out on rocky beaches. Alaskan king crab, sea stars, and Pacific octopus also await you, as well as a variety of intertidal creatures and deep-sea fishes. Open daily; closed Thanksgiving, Dec 25. **$$$**

BALD EAGLE PRESERVE AND ANNUAL FESTIVAL. *113 Haines Hwy, Haines (99827). Phone 907/766-3094. baldeaglefest.org/info.html.* In October, the world's largest number of bald eagles gather in Haines to take advantage of the late salmon run. This amazing gathering of eagles is the basis of this annual festival that is held in the eagles' honor.

CHUGACH NATIONAL FOREST. *3301 C St, Anchorage (99503). Phone 907/743-9500. www.fs.fed.us/r10/chugach/.* The Chugach National Forest is the second largest forest in the National Forest System. Roughly the same size as the states of Massachusetts and Rhode Island combined, the Chugach (pronounced CHEW-gatch) is the most northern of national forests, only 500 miles south of the Arctic Circle. One-third of the Chugach is composed of rocks and moving ice. The remainder is a diverse and majestic tapestry of land, water, plants, and animals. The mountains, lakes, and rivers of the Kenai Peninsula, the islands and glaciers of Prince William Sound, and the copious wetlands and birds of the Copper River Delta make this national forest a mecca for adventurers.

GLACIER BAY NATIONAL PARK AND PRESERVE. *Gustavus (99826). Phone 907/784-3295. www.nps.gov/glba/.* The Glacier Bay Visitor Center is located on the second level of the Glacier Bay Lodge, and the first portion of the Forest Loop Train is accessible to wheelchairs. **FREE**

KATMAI NATIONAL PARK AND PRESERVE. *King Salmon (99613). Phone 907/246-3305. www.nps.gov/katm/.* At least 14 volcanoes in the park are active, although none is erupting at this time. The park, located on the Alaska Peninsula, across from Kodiak Island, also offers wilderness not often seen in the lower 48, with brown bears and fish as its most well-known inhabitants. Open year-round.

★ **KENAI FJORDS NATIONAL PARK.** *Seward (99664). Phone 907/224-3175. www.nps.gov/kefj/.* Kenai Fjords National Park includes one of the four major ice caps in the United States, the 300-square-mile Harding Icefield, and coastal fjords. Located on the southeastern Kenai Peninsula, the national park is a pristine and rugged land supporting many unaltered natural environments and ecosystems. Here a rich, varied rain forest is home to tens of thousands of breeding birds, and adjoining marine waters support a multitude of sea lions, sea otters, and seals. The most popular visitor activity at Kenai Fjords is viewing the park from a tour boat. The boats are privately owned, and the many operators offer tours of varying lengths and features. Authorized commercial guides provide camping, fishing, and kayaking services. Air charters fly over the coast for flight seeing and access to the fjords. Boat tours and charters are available from Seward. In summer, boat tours ply the coast, observing calving glaciers, sea birds, and marine mammals. **$**

KLONDIKE GOLD RUSH NATIONAL HISTORIC PARK. *Skagway (99840). Phone 907/983-9224. www.nps.gov/klgo/.* This park explores the rich and fascinating history of the Klondike Gold Rush of 1897-1898. Fifteen restored buildings in the Skagway Historic District, the 33-mile

Chilkoot Trail (fee), and part of the White Pass Trail are included in the park. Open year-round. **FREE**

✪ **KODIAK ISLAND NATIONAL WILDLIFE REFUGE.** *1390 Buskin River Rd, Kodiak (99615). Phone 907/487-2600. www.r7.fws.gov/ nwr/Kodiak/kodnwr.html.* The Kodiak Island Refuge includes about two-thirds of Kodiak Island, as well as 50,000 acres of Afognak Island, which is north of Kodiak. Wildlife abounds in the area, because the coastline is always nearby, yet the interior of the islands offer dense vegetation that feeds the native brown bears, red foxes, river otters, short-tailed weasels, little brown bats, tundra voles, and up to 2 million sea birds. Hunting, fishing, cabins (fee). Open year-round.

PETROGLYPH BEACH STATE HISTORIC PARK. *Wrangell (99929). Phone 907/874-2381. www.wrangell.com/visitors/attractions/history/ petroglyph.* Petroglyphs—or rock carvings—were artistic works by Native Americans, and Petroglyph Beach offers some of the best examples that still survive today.

TONGASS NATIONAL FOREST. *204 Siginaka Way, Sitka (99835). Phone 907/747-6671. www.fs.fed.us/r10/tongass.* Tongass National Forest, the largest national forest in the US, is the definition of "wilderness;" in fact, one-third of the Tongass (5.7 million acres) is managed as wilderness, so that Alaska retains its undeveloped character. Hardy visitors can expect to see eagles, bears, deer, and a variety of other animals, birds, and fish in this vast national forest. Hunting, fishing, cabins (fee).

WHITE PASS AND YUKON ROUTE OF THE SCENIC RAILWAY OF THE WORLD. *Skagway (99840). Phone toll-free 800/343-7373. www.whitepassrailroad.com.* This historic railway traverses the 2,865-foot White Pass on a 3-hour, 40-mile fully narrated trip. Longer trips also originate in Skagway and travel to Lake Bennett, British Columbia; Whitehorse, Yukon Territory; and the Chilkoot Trail. **$$$$**

WRANGELL-ST. ELIAS NATIONAL PARK AND PRESERVE. *106.8 Richardson Hwy, Cooper Center (99573). Phone 907/822-5234. www. nps.gov/wrst/.* The park-preserve, totaling more than 13 million acres, is often called the "mountain kingdom of North America," because the Chugach, Wrangell, and St. Elias mountain ranges converge here. The park-preserve boasts North America's largest collection of glaciers and peaks above 16,000 feet. Open year-round. **FREE**

PLACES TO STAY

If you choose to include an overnight stay in your trip along this Byway, Mobil Travel Guide recommends staying the night at one of the following lodgings.

★★★ **ALASKA WATERFRONT HOMER INN & SPA.** *895 Ocean Dr, Homer (99603). Phone 907/235-2501; toll-free 800/294-7823. www.alaskawaterfront.com.* 5 rooms, 2 story. Custom seaside suites on beautiful Kechemak Bay featuring a secluded sand beach, hot tub, king-size beds, spectacular ocean and glacier views, and an array of specialty spa treatments. **$$**

★★★ **ARCTIC SUN LODGING.** *61995 Mission Rd, Homer (99603). Phone 907/235-2283; toll-free 888/479-6259. www.alaskaarcticsun.com.* 6 rooms, 2 story. Featuring rooms with views of Kachemak Bay and the Kenai Mountains. **$**

★★★ **LAND'S END RESORT.** *4786 Homer Spit Rd, Homer (99603). Phone toll-free 800/478-0400. www.lands-end-resort.com.* 80 rooms, 2 story. Featuring bay windows with views of Kechemak Bay. An on-site beachfront spa is available to guests at no extra charge, offering in-room massage and physical therapy. **$$**

7

Alaska

❋ *Alaska's Marine Highway*

★★ **VICTORIAN HEIGHTS BED & BREAKFAST.** *61495 Race Ct, Homer (99603). Phone 907/235-6357. akms.com/victorian.* 4 rooms, 2 story. Located in the hills overlooking Kachemak Bay, the Kenai Mountain Range, and several glaciers. All rooms have private baths, comfortable furnishings, and simple—but elegant—décor. $

★★ **ALASKA WOLF HOUSE BED & BREAKFAST.** *1900 Wickersham Ave, Juneau (99802). Phone 907/586-2422; toll-free 888/586-9053.* 5 rooms, 2 story. Built on the mountainside in a 4,000-square-foot western red cedar log home with open beams, natural skylights, and large windows. A gourmet breakfast is provided every morning. $

★★ **THE HIGHLANDS BED & BREAKFAST.** *421 Judy Ln, Juneau (99801). Phone toll-free 877/463-5404. www.juneauhighlands.com.* 4 rooms, 2 story. Located in historical downtown Juneau with modern amenities and private entrances and baths. $

★★ **BROOKSIDE INN BED & BREAKFAST.** *1465 Richardson Hwy, Valdez (99686). Phone 907/835-9130. www.brooksideinnbb.com.* 6 rooms, 2 story. Built in 1898, the inn is located three minutes from downtown Valdez and Prince William Sound. $

★★ **L & L'S BED & BREAKFAST.** *533 W Hanagita St, Valdez (99686). Phone 907/835-4447. www.lnlalaska.com.* 5 rooms, 3 story. Located minutes from downtown Valdez, the Alaska Marine Ferry Terminal, nature trails, and the visitor center, with drop-off and pickup from the airport and ferry provided. $

PLACES TO EAT

A long day of driving is sure to make you hungry. At the end of your journey, take a table at one of the following restaurants.

★★ **THE CHART ROOM RESTAURANT.** *4786 Homer Spit Rd, Homer (99603). Phone 907/235-2500. www.lands-end-resort.com.* American menu. Breakfast, lunch, dinner. One of Alaska's oldest continually operating restaurants, featuring upscale local cuisine. $$

★ **DUGGAN'S GALLEY.** *120 W Bunnell St, Homer (99603). Phone 907/235-7747.* Irish menu. Closed Mon. Lunch, dinner. Popular local café that features fresh local ingredients and live music on Fri and Sat. $

★★ **THE ROOKERY RESTAURANT.** *Otter Cove in Eldred Passage across the Bay from the Homer Spit, Homer (99603). Phone 907/235-7770. www.ottercoveresort.com/rookery.htm.* American menu. Lunch, dinner. Located at Otter Cove in Eldred Passage with extensive views of the abundant natural wildlife. Tour and charter boats available. $$

★★★ **THE FIDDLEHEAD RESTAURANT.** *429 W Willoughby Ave, Juneau (99801). Phone 907/586-1042.* American menu. Lunch, dinner. Creative contemporary cuisine utilizing the best local ingredients. $$

★★ **HANGAR ON THE WHARF.** *Suite 5, Fisherman's Wharf, Juneau (99801). Phone 907/586-5018. www.hangaronthewharf.com.* American menu. Lunch, dinner. Juneau's only waterfront restaurant, featuring southeast Alaska's largest selection of microbrews in a converted aircraft hangar. $

★★ **THANE ORE HOUSE.** *4400 Thane Rd, Juneau (99801). Phone 907/586-3442.* American menu. Lunch, dinner. Rustic setting with regional Alaskan specialties and unique seating. Song and dance floor show in adjacent theater. $

★★ **ALASKA'S BISTRO.** *100 Fidalgo, Valdez (99686). Phone 907/835-5688.* Mediterranean menu. Lunch, dinner. Upscale harborside dining with an extensive wine bar. $$

★★★ **THE ROSE CACHE.** *321 Egan St, Valdez (99686). Phone 907/835-8383.* American menu. Closed Mon. Dinner. Relaxed and elegant dining with local ingredients. Reservations required. $$

Glenn Highway
✳ ALASKA

Quick Facts

LENGTH: 135 miles.

TIME TO ALLOW: 8 hours.

BEST TIME TO DRIVE: Summer is beautiful with wildflowers and forests in full bloom. Winter sometimes includes days during which travel is not recommended.

BYWAY TRAVEL INFORMATION: Matanuska-Susitna Convention and Visitor Bureau: 907/746-5000; Byway local Web site: www.alaskavisit.com.

SPECIAL CONSIDERATIONS: Tour buses travel the Glenn Highway corridor extensively during the summer tourist season. The Glenn Highway is subject to avalanches; when traveling during winter, check road and weather information prior to the trip and carry appropriate winter gear. Pull-offs are plowed and available for viewing in the winter.

RESTRICTIONS: The Glenn Highway can be safely traversed by two-wheel-drive vehicles. Most of the state park facilities beyond Sutton are closed during the winter.

BICYCLE/PEDESTRIAN FACILITIES: The Glenn Highway accommodates pedestrians and bicyclists with separated trails between East Anchorage and Chugiak. No pedestrians are allowed on the controlled access facility between Chugiak and the Parks Highway, but tour bikers are. Between the Parks Highway and Sutton, both pedestrians and bicyclists may use the shoulder. Sutton has a new 4-mile separated trail. The road is narrow between Kings River and the end of the Byway at mile 135.

The Glenn Highway is a place where geology, culture, and scenery come together to create a majestic and rugged landscape that can be seen only in Alaska. Winters bring the fascinating Northern Lights among snow-capped mountains. In the spring, hawks, eagles, and falcons can be seen gliding over the Glenn Highway. Summers bring endless days of wildflowers and green forests along the Matanuska River Canyon that runs between the Chugach and Talkeetna Mountains, creating beautiful views all the way.

Among the mountains and the unforgettable seasons live a distinct Alaskan culture that has been developing for centuries—beginning with the native Alaskan culture that was altered so much with the arrival of Russian fur traders and, later, gold miners from the lower 48. The history of all of Alaska's cultures can be seen along the Byway in museums and historic places.

THE BYWAY STORY

The Glenn Highway tells archaeological, cultural, historical, natural, recreational, and scenic stories that make it a unique and treasured Byway.

Archaeological

Although pieces of archaeology can be found all over the ancient lands along the Glenn Highway, many of them are so delicate that few people know about them. From studying small tools made of flint and other materials, archaeologists are slowly becoming acquainted with societies that are long forgotten in Alaska. In Knik, south of Wasilla, archaeologists are uncovering a village and many artifacts. The Knik townsite became a Euro-American trading

Alaska

✻ *Glenn Highway*

and supply post in the late 1800s. Archaeologists have uncovered an old blacksmith shop, an assayer's house, and tools used for refining gold. When the townsite has been excavated, the discoveries and artifacts will go on display in a nearby museum.

As you travel the Glenn Highway, you may also want to explore Anthracite Ridge near Sutton. The ridge was formed when a warmer climate existed on the lands that are now Alaska. Ginkgo trees and other warm vegetation were buried here to create the coal resources and the fossils that attract both miners and paleontologists. Bones from a dinosaur known as the Hadrosaur were also found near the Byway at Gunsight Mountain in the Talkeetna Mountains. The dinosaur has been affectionately dubbed "Lizzie."

Cultural

Cultures from all over the world have combined along the Glenn Highway. They join to make the winter a little warmer and communities a little brighter. The native cultures of Alaska changed and developed over many centuries before they were joined by fur traders from Russia and miners from the United States. Amid gold rush history, native tradition, and Russian influence, Alaska has emerged as a diverse state in more than just its natural resources.

Although many different cultures are gathered along the Byway, museums, architecture, and historic districts celebrate the unique history of each culture. To discover the original cultures of Alaska, visit the Anchorage Museum of History and Art or the Alaska Native Heritage Center. Historic villages of Eklutna and Chickaloon also house buildings and places that are reminiscent of days gone by.

Native society was structured around the family unit, and the bigger the family, the better. Families hunted together and when fishing, hunting, or trapping was good, the entire family experienced prosperity. But survival in the arctic was always a challenge. This way of life remained unchanged for many years, until a new culture emerge during the late 1700s.

When people from Russia began to come to Alaska, they brought their religion with them. Their goal was to introduce the native people of Alaska to Christianity, and one of the rules was that the people could accept the religion only of their own free will. Because of this, the Russian priests who lived in Alaska were extremely dedicated to supporting their parishes during the 100 years they were in Alaska. Yet native Alaskans often combined cultural beliefs: native people who converted to Orthodoxy would bury the remains of their dead, but also build a small "spirit house" above the grave. The St. Nicholas Russian Orthodox Church located in Eklutna is an example of the Russian Orthodox influence in Alaska. In fact, Eklutna provides some of the most striking examples of the mix of Russian Orthodoxy and native tradition in its buildings and even the cemetery.

An economic culture began to grow in Alaska during the 1870s. Rumors of coal, timber, and especially gold brought another significant culture to the land. Mining towns sprung up all over the land, and Alaska embarked on another great change. Many of those mining towns became the central cities of Alaska; descendents of gold miners became coal miners. Today, Independence Mine State Historic Park allows visitors to explore the lifestyle of the early gold miners in Alaska.

During the 20th century, people continued to gather in Alaska for relief from the Depression or for military strategy during World War II. It was during wartime that the Glenn Highway was constructed as an attempt to better connect Alaska with the lower 48 states. You can still see roadhouses along the Glenn Highway that offered shelter to early travelers.

Historical

Alaska's history in the United States has been shorter than that of the rest of the lower 48, but it is a romanticized land with history of gold camps, dogsled races, and native Alaskans. The roots of these historical ideas were established long before Alaska became a part of the US. Native people with the courage and endurance to establish their culture in this rugged territory settled here nearly 35,000 years ago. Since then, Alaska has maintained its pristine wildernesses, unique wildlife, and exotic atmosphere.

A people known as the Athabascans came from Asia to be the first inhabitants in the lands where the Glenn Highway is now located. The village of Eklutna is a settlement that has been inhabited since the late 1600s by these people, and the Athabascan languages are still preserved in the names of places along the Glenn Highway. It was not until the 1700s that the land and its people were recorded by Europeans. Explorers James Cook and Vitus Bering opened up European trade between native people in Alaska and their own countries. After the Russian-American Company began to establish missions, trade, and government here in the late 1790s, the people of Russia and Alaska interacted for nearly 100 years, for better or for worse, until another country began to take interest in Alaska.

In 1867, the United States purchased Alaska from Russia and caused a scandal among the American people. They were mortified at the $7.2 million price tag that the government was willing to pay for a frozen wasteland. But with the continued wealth achieved from fur trapping and gold discovered in Alaska, the area's reputation improved in the eyes of Americans, and people from the states began to flock to the territory. The need for roads in Alaska came with the expanding population of miners and trappers; during World War II, Alaska's strategic position also made it a candidate for improved roads. As Alaska's roads improved, communities grew up and were able to have contact with each other. In fact, the Glenn Highway is known for connecting Alaska's history and culture.

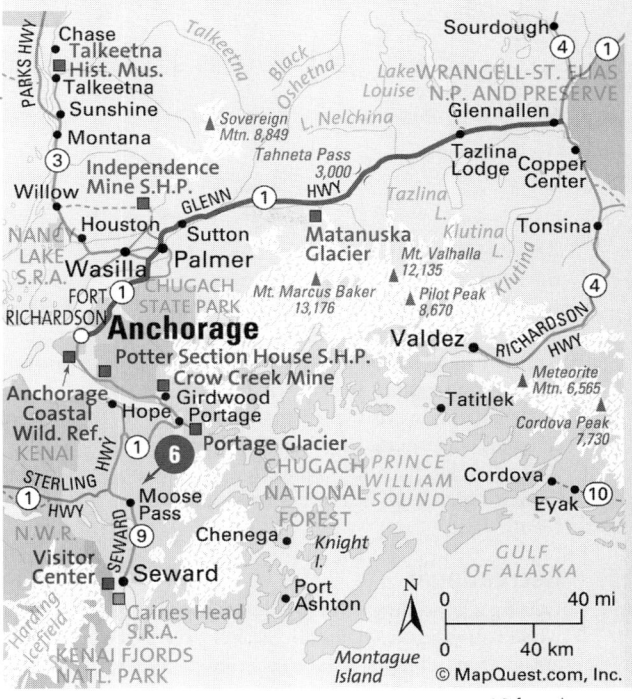

see page A6 for color map

Natural

Dramatic natural events formed the landscape along the Glenn Highway, and many of these events continue today. This is a land where melting glaciers, winds, and rivers are the moving forces. They create the scenery and, in many ways, have determined the history of the Byway. Without the rich soils and, of course, the gold that was found here, Alaska may still be unknown to Americans. Fortunately, even with the coming of settlers and roads, the wildlife and wildlands are preserved in Alaska as the defining features.

Earthquakes and the movement of the Earth's plates thousands of years ago created the Chugach and the Talkeetna mountain ranges, and the rich minerals found in the mountains have been drawing people to Alaska for more than 100 years. It was just off the Glenn Highway where some of Alaska's first gold was discovered. Today, mining is still occurring in the mountains, as geologists search the sediment for fossils and other geological remnants. Rivers, wind, and ice have played a role in the formation of the mountains since the beginning of their existence, moving the rich sediment from one end of the landscape to the other.

Alaska

❋ *Glenn Highway*

Although the Glenn Highway runs through the tundra, this ecosystem is far from a frozen wasteland. You may see salmon and trout swimming in the rivers while a moose wanders by the riverside. Flowers, trees, bushes, and meadow grasses are an array of different colors. Accumulating meltwater forms wetlands and marshes where birds and waterfowl gather. And when all the land is blanketed with snow, spruce, aspen, and other trees create a winter wonderland.

Recreational

Getting a good dose of nature isn't difficult when you visit the Glenn Highway for recreation. From winter sports to summer pastimes, the Byway provides plenty of places where scenery and activity come together. Chugach State Park is accessible from the Byway, and places like the Palmer Hayflats and the Matanuska Glacier provide opportunities to spot wildlife or get a closer look at a glacier. With the Chugach and Talkeetna mountains surrounding the Byway, you have many opportunities for hiking and exploring these ancient landforms.

In a place where winter engulfs a large part of the year, winter recreation has been perfected. The lodges and roadhouses along the Glenn Highway are the perfect place to stop in the winter and enjoy cross-country skiing, snowmobiling, and snowshoeing. You can hardly help enjoying a winter night in Alaska, where the short days lead to extra-long nights. You may want to do some stargazing here or watch for the Northern Lights. You've never seen so many stars!

But even in Alaska, the snow melts and summer activities become available to travelers and residents. Alaska is the Land of the Midnight Sun, where, in summer, the long, sunny days make up for the nights of winter. Many people come just to see the wildflowers and watch for wildlife. During March, April, and early May, the air is filled with birds, migrating and moving. A stop at milepost 118 provides an excellent opportunity for viewing birds of prey. The melting rivers and streams are another source of activity. Of course, the fishing in Alaska is superb, but anglers aren't the only ones who enjoy the rivers; rafters and kayakers find places on Alaska rivers to test their skills. In Anchorage, a biking trail is located along the Byway for cyclists and in-line skaters to make their way from Anchorage to Chugiak. The city of Anchorage holds many diversions, including museums and nature centers. Whether you're drawn to the mountains or to cities, the Glenn Highway is a great way to see it all.

Scenic

Along the Glenn Highway, scenery is just waiting to be noticed out of every car window. Drivers wish they were passengers as they drive among mountain ranges, crystal-clear waterways, and tundra where moose and bear wander. And just when you feel that you've reached the edge of civilization, a historic lodge or village comes into view.

The Byway is bordered by the Chugach Mountain Range from beginning to end. Majestic rock formations rise in between the glaciers that are so prevalent in this area. When the day is clear, you can look to the north and catch a glimpse of Mount McKinley, the highest mountain in the United States. Just past Palmer, Alaska, the Chugach Mountains are joined by the Talkeetna Mountains. Fields of wild irises decorate the Palmer Hayflats and follow the Knik River back to a glacier of the same name. Knik Glacier is located in the shadow of Mount Marcus Baker, one of the highest peaks in the Chugach Mountains.

Glaciers have formed much of Alaska, carving great masses of rock and stone. You can see the Matanuska Glacier from the road and feel the cool air that surrounds it. This huge mass of slow-melting ice displays the blue, gray, and white colors it has collected over the hundreds of years it has been retreating. When glaciers retreat, they leave streams and lakes behind: The Matanuska River is a collection of melted glacier water that runs among a bed of gray silt, creating a braided appearance. In summer, you can see where meltwater goes.

Alaska may not have as many April showers as other places in the nation, but what it doesn't get in rain it makes up in glacial meltwater. The water brings entire fields of wildflowers in the late spring and summer. Flowers of every color and kind decorate the valleys beneath the mountains, inviting travelers to take a closer look or try some nature photography. Wetland areas like the Palmer Hay Flats create views of marshy reeds and willows, where a tundra swan or a Canadian goose may be swimming. All along the Byway, sights of moose or Dall sheep are a reminder that this scenic country still belongs to nature.

HIGHLIGHTS

The Glenn Highway takes you through several Alaskan towns and villages (listed here alphabetically).

- **Anchorage:** The city of Anchorage began as a ramshackle community of rail workers living in tents. The community, settled in 1915, has grown and evolved into the largest city in Alaska, with 260,000 people. For a look at Alaskan culture, Anchorage is the place to be. Explore the Anchorage Museum of History and Art or the Alaska Native Heritage Center for a taste of what Alaska has to offer.

- **Chickaloon Village:** This native community is nestled above the confluence of Moose Creek and the Matanuska River in the Talkeetna Mountains. It is the home of Alaska's first native-maintained school and Katie's Wall, built 60 years ago by Katie Wade to stop the cut slope from eroding. Many of the perennial shrubs she planted are still alive today and bloom brightly in the spring.

- **Eagle River:** This community, within the municipality of Anchorage, is nestled in the foothills of the Chugach Mountains and provides access to the Old Glenn Highway.

- **Eklutna Village:** The Athabascan Village of Eklutna has a museum, a Russian Orthodox church, and a cemetery with spirit houses that provide visitors a look into native life.

- **Glacier View Community:** The Glacier View Community provides several views of the Matanuska Glacier. The Matanuska Glacier Park Campground allows you to walk up next to—or even onto—the glacier.

- **Palmer:** Palmer is the seat of government for the Matanuska Susitna Borough, the home of the Alaska State Fair, the center of colonial history, and the heart of Alaska's breadbasket.

- **Sutton:** This quaint residential community is located in the Talkeetna Mountains. The Alpine Heritage and Cultural Center provides a look into Sutton's past.

THINGS TO SEE AND DO

Driving along the Glenn Highway will certainly keep your senses engaged, but if you yearn to get out of the car and stretch your legs, or if you'd like to make a mini-vacation out of your trip, check out these attractions along the route.

ALASKA NATIVE HERITAGE CENTER. *8800 Heritage Center Dr, Anchorage (99506). Phone 907/330-8000; toll-free 800/315-6608.*

Alaska

❇ *Glenn Highway*

www.alaskanative.net. The Alaska Native Heritage Center brings to life the rich history, culture, music, and art of major Native American peoples found in Alaska, including the Aleut, Athabascan, Eskimo, Tlingits, Haida, and Tshimshian cultures. **$$$$**

ANCHORAGE COASTAL WILDLIFE REFUGE. *333 Raspberry Rd, Anchorage (99518-1599). Phone 907/267-2182. www.state.ak.us/adfg/wildlife/region2/refuge2/acwr.htm.* Known as Potter's Marsh, this refuge supports at least 130 species of birds, plus an array of fish and mammals. **FREE**

ANCHORAGE MUSEUM OF HISTORY AND ART. *121 W 7th Ave, Anchorage (99501). Phone 907/343-6173. www.anchoragemuseum.org.* One of the ten most visited attractions in Alaska. Exhibits focus on the state's art, history, and cultures. **$$**

CHUGACH STATE PARK. *Mile 115 Seward Hwy, Anchorage (99540). Phone 907/345-5014.* Chugach State Park is an accessible wilderness in the backyard of Anchorage. Wildlife viewing and mountain scenery are year-round pleasures, and campers can choose developed campgrounds or secluded backcountry valleys. Nearly 30 trails take you throughout the park to see some of its most enchanting views. Many visitors may want to stop at the Eagle River Nature Center for a guided tour or interpretive program. You may want to explore a few of the park's 50 glaciers on your own. And for extreme adventure, try climbing a mountainside or plunging through river rapids. Whatever the case, the 495,000-acre park offers a wide variety of activities in all seasons.

EKLUTNA FLATS AND PALMER HAY FLATS. *N of Anchorage at the head of the Knik Arm in Cook Inlet. Phone 907/267-2182.* The Eklutna Flats and Palmer Hay Flats are a tidally influenced wetlands area at the confluence of the Knik and Matanuska rivers. This flat open area provides the broadest view of the Matanuska Valley bordered by the Chugach Mountains, a stone's throw to the east. The ancient Talkeetna Mountains rise in the distance. This area is teeming with waterfowl and other migratory birds in spring and fall. You may even spot a moose during the long winter months. The Palmer Hay Flats State Game Refuge comprises a large portion of this area.

INDEPENDENCE MINE STATE HISTORIC PARK. *On Hatcher Pass Rd between Palmer and Willow. Phone 907/269-8400. www.dnr.state.ak.us/parks/units/indmine.htm.* Located in Hatcher Pass in the heart of the Talkeetna Mountains, Independence Mine is a representative of Alaska's hard rock gold mining past. As many as 200 miners worked the mine during the 1920s and 1930s until its closure as a result of World War II. Facilities include a museum, hiking trails, and recreation gold panning. It has been proposed that the old tunnels be retrofitted to allow mine tours in the future.

KEPLER-BRADLEY STATE PARK. *Glenn Hwy, Anchorage (99501). Phone 907/269-8400.* A fisherman's paradise, this popular state park comprises several trout- and grayling-filled lakes. Kepler-Bradley State Park is within easy driving distance of Anchorage. The lakes are located in crevasses in between morraine ridges formed by glaciers. Trails from the park connect to the Mat/Su Borough Crevasse Morraine Trail System.

MATANUSKA GLACIER STATE RECREATION AREA. *Glenn Hwy, Anchorage (99501). Phone 907/269-8400.* This newly redeveloped recreation area showcases the Matanuska Glacier with an up-close view that will be forever etched into travelers' memories.

PLACES TO STAY

If you choose to include an overnight stay in your trip along this Byway, Mobil Travel Guide recommends staying the night at one of the following lodgings.

★★ **ALASKAN LEOPARD BED & BREAKFAST.** *16136 Sandpiper Dr, Anchorage (99501). Phone 907/868-1594; toll-free 877/277-7118. www.alaskanleopard.com.* 4 rooms, 2 story. Hillside chalet with spectacular views of the Anchorage Bowl, Cook Inlet, Mount McKinley, the Kenai Peninsula, and the volcanoes of the Alaska Range. Known for extraordinary breakfasts. $

★★★ **FIFTEEN CHANDELIERS B&B INN.** *14020 Sabine St, Anchorage (99511). Phone 907/345-3032.* 5 rooms, 3 story. European-style Georgian mansion set in a botanical garden. Breakfast is served in a formal dining room with fine china and stemware. $$

★★ **K STREET BED & BREAKFAST.** *1433 K St, Anchorage (99501). Phone 907/279-1443. www.cruising-america.com/kstreetbb/kst.html.* 3 rooms, 2 story. Contemporary cedar-sided home in a residential neighborhood with a garden and solarium. Features homemade breakfast and original Alaskan art. $

★★ **A LOON'S NEST BED & BREAKFAST.** *1455 Hillcrest Dr, Anchorage (99503). Phone 907/279-9884; toll-free 800/786-9884. www.aloonsnest.com.* 2 rooms, 2 story. Frank Lloyd Wright-designed house poised on a bluff overlooking Westchester Lagoon. Features Shaker-style furniture and whirlpool tubs. $
D

★★★ **MAHOGANY MANOR BED & BREAKFAST INN.** *204 E 15th Ave, Anchorage (99501). Phone 907/278-1111; toll-free 888/777-0346. www.mahoganymanor.com.* 6 rooms, 2 story. Luxury-oriented bed-and-breakfast in a secluded environment. All rooms feature private baths, entrances, high-speed Internet connections, and DVD players. $$$

★★★ **THE OSCAR GILL HISTORIC BED & BREAKFAST.** *1344 W 10th Ave, Anchorage (99501). Phone 907/279-1344. www.oscargill.com.* 3 rooms, 2 story. 1913 home located in Delaney Park bordering the Cook Inlet with views of Denali and Sleeping Lady. Cited as one of Alaska's best lodgings. $

★ **PLANET ANCHORAGE BED & BREAKFAST.** *1025 H St, Anchorage (99501). Phone 907/770-6742. www.planetanchorage.com.* 3 rooms, 2 story. 1950s-style home five minutes from downtown Anchorage. Fresh homemade breakfasts with local ingredients. $

★★ **SUSITNA SUNSETS BED & BREAKFAST.** *9901 Conifer St, Anchorage (99507). Phone 907/346-1067. www.susitnasunsets.com.* 3 rooms, 3 story. Features views of Mount McKinley with breakfast served in your room or on one of the decks. Children 10 and over only. $

PLACES TO EAT

A long day of driving is sure to make you hungry. At the end of your journey, take a table at one of the following restaurants.

★★★ **CAMPOBELLO BISTRO.** *601 W 36th Ave, Anchorage (99501). Phone 907/563-2040.* Mediterranean menu. Lunch, dinner. Featuring sophisticated Mediterranean cuisine and an impressive wine list in a midtown location decorated with modern art. $$$

★★ **CLUB PARIS.** *417 W 5th Ave, Anchorage (99501). Phone 907/277-6332. www.clubparisrestaurant.com.* Steak menu. Lunch, dinner. Alaska's oldest steakhouse with an old-fashioned, dark and smoky feel. Known for its filet mignon, which is 4 inches thick. $$$

★★★ **CROW'S NEST RESTAURANT.** *5th Ave and K St, Anchorage (99501). Phone 907/343-2217.* American menu. Closed Sun, Mon. Dinner. Featuring one of the best views in Anchorage, this restaurant is best known for its five-course prix fixe menu and an impressive wine list. $$$

★★ **JEN'S.** *701 W 36th Ave, Anchorage (99501). Phone 907/561-5367. www.jensrestaurant.com.* French menu. Closed Sun. Lunch, dinner. Chef-owned fine-dining restaurant exquisitely decorated with Alaskan art. Menu changes daily. $$$

Alaska

❋ *Glenn Highway*

★★★ **KUMAGORO.** *533 W 4th Ave, Anchorage (99501). Phone 907/272-9905.* Japanese menu. Breakfast, lunch, dinner. The only restaurant in Alaska to feature traditional Japanese breakfast and Shabu Shabu dinners. $$

★★★ **MARX BROTHERS' CAFÉ.** *627 W 3rd Ave, Anchorage (99501). Phone 907/278-2133.* American menu. Closed Sun. Dinner. A local favorite, this café was built in 1916 and features progressive American cuisine with an award-winning wine list. $$$

★★★ **SACKS CAFÉ & RESTAURANT.** *328 G St, Anchorage (99501). Phone 907/274-4022. www.sackscafe.com.* American menu. Lunch, dinner. Award-winning restaurant specializing in eclectic New American cuisine. $$

★★ **SIMON & SEAFORT'S SALOON & GRILL.** *420 L St, Anchorage (99501). Phone 907/274-3502.* American menu. Lunch, dinner. One of Anchorage's most popular restaurants, located a short walk from the Captain Cook Hotel with views of the Cook Inlet from large picture windows. $$

The Seward Highway
❋ ALASKA   AN ALL-AMERICAN ROAD

Quick Facts

LENGTH: 127 miles.

TIME TO ALLOW: 3 to 5 hours.

BEST TIME TO DRIVE: From May to mid-October, salmon fishing is at its peak, and you can see whales along the shore and sheep on the mountainsides. The off-season consists of winter and spring. Avalanches may cause the road to be closed for short periods throughout the winter.

BYWAY TRAVEL INFORMATION: Alaska Public Lands Information Center: 907/271-2737; Alaska Department of Transportation and Public Facilities: 907/465-6975; Chugach National Forest: 907/743-9500; Byway local Web site: www.dot.state.ak.us/stwdplng/scenic/bsewardhwy.html.

SPECIAL CONSIDERATIONS: The only significant seasonal problem facing the Seward Highway is adverse winter conditions. The Alaska Department of Transportation and Public Facilities has made a serious and effective commitment to keeping the Seward Highway passable during the winter months, however, because it is the principal highway serving the Kenai Peninsula.

RESTRICTIONS: Due to extreme conditions during the winter, the road is closed by avalanches an average of five times a year for approximately four hours.

BICYCLE/PEDESTRIAN FACILITIES: Bicyclists can take advantage of existing wide shoulders and many miles of separated bike paths. Pedestrians are accommodated at most of the highway's pullouts and along many of the trails paralleling the route.

The Seward Highway, linking Anchorage with Seward, passes through some of the most spectacular scenery in the country. The landscape varies from the muddy waters of Turnagain Arm to the icy blue glaciers that hang almost to the sea. Wildflowers and waterfalls brighten every corner of the road as it glides below rough mountains that pierce thick, heavy clouds. Only Alaska's Seward Highway can offer this particular mix created by climate, geography, and geology.

The Seward Highway is located in a richly varied and highly diverse corridor. Its character changes over the course of its length. Roadside topography, the proximity of water, the types of views, the levels and types of development, and the width and character of the road are some of the ways in which the Seward Highway expresses different moods and landscapes between Anchorage and Seward. Each of these distinctive landscapes is uniquely spectacular.

For 127 miles, the road winds through a land of remarkable beauty, a land of saltwater bays, frigid blue glaciers, knife-edged ridges, and alpine valleys. From the reflective waters of Turnagain Arm, you rapidly ascend 1,000 feet above sea level to an alpine meadow. Within the hour, you find yourself back at sea level surrounded by fjords, having just passed through a district of rivers and lakes.

Whether you drive for pleasure or you fish, hunt, backpack, camp, or ski, the Seward Highway can take you there. And it's all against a backdrop of spruce forests, wildflowers, and extraordinary wildlife.

Alaska

❋ *The Seward Highway*

THE BYWAY STORY

The Seward Highway tells historical, natural, recreational, and scenic stories that make it a unique and treasured Byway.

Historical

Far removed from the rest of the world sits Alaska, perched above the fast-paced industry of the world below. The route from Resurrection Bay to Alaska's interior has been in existence for thousands of years; even Russian explorers searched the area for gold and fur in the 1700s. Following the same early routes used by native Alaskans, sled dogs, miners, and trains, the Seward Highway has evolved into a modern transportation system.

Natives first used an area along the Seward Highway 9,000 years ago as a hunting camp. In this area, now known as Beluga Point on Turnagain Arm, Tanaina Indians also discovered abundant game in the region over 8,000 years after the first natives inhabited the area. The region finally received its name in 1778 when Captain Cook sailed along the coast in his quest for the Northwest Passage. When shallow water forced him to turn around, he christened the sound Turnagain River. South of Anchorage, Highway 1 now follows the shore of Turnagain Arm.

In 1895, prospectors discovered gold in Hope, Alaska, in the Kenai Peninsula, and the rush began. One miner panned 385 ounces of gold from the river in one day. (Now, fishermen line the stream with hopes of catching salmon.) This gold rush of the late 1800s brought several thousand gold seekers to the area. Suddenly, the tiny towns of Hope and Sunrise grew into booming gold mining towns. Sunrise became the largest town in the Cook Inlet area and was even considered as a potential state capital. Scattered findings of gold all over the Kenai Mountains established the need for improved transportation routes from the ice-free port of Seward to Turnagain Arm.

Today's Byway traces several historic routes that miners used to cross the Kenai Mountains. The route from Seward to Snow River was used by hikers, dog teams, and horse parties. These travelers crossed Kenai Lake and landed at Cooper Landing, or they continued on to Moose Pass. The route from Moose Pass to Tern Lake and Cooper Landing was used when Kenai Lake was impassable, and it was used by northbound travelers from Kenai and Cooper Landing. Johnson Pass was the route of choice from Moose Pass to Sunrise and Hope. The Trail Creek to Placer River route was a direct path from Moose Pass to Portage Valley. This route was later chosen for the Alaska Central Railroad, which was in use by 1909.

By 1910, most miners had left the area in order to follow prospects of gold farther north. Sunrise dwindled into nothing more than a few residences, and mining activity in Hope came almost to a standstill. However, Cooper Landing's economy was soon influenced not by mining but by interest in big-game hunting and fishing.

Today, the mining legacy of the Kenai Peninsula lives on through stories, museum photos, and weathered wood remains scattered throughout the Kenai Mountains. The privately owned townsite of Sunrise is a historic archaeological district. The Hope Historical Society operates a small museum that includes photographs, journals, mine buildings, and equipment from the gold rush.

Natural

As you travel the Seward Highway, watch for wildlife along the highway. You may hear the honking of Canadian geese in the wetlands, the whistle of hoary marmots in the alpine valleys, and the cry of bald eagles in the dense coastal forests. Just south of Anchorage, Potter's Marsh Wildlife Viewing Area offers a temporary home to ducks, geese, and other nesting water birds as they raise their young. Along Turnagain Arm, you may spot Dall sheep as they scale rugged mountainsides or bring their young near the highway to forage. Bald eagles, moose, bears, mountain goats, salmon, and a variety of birds thrive along the highway as well. Many species of wildflowers help beautify the road corridor. Two of the most common and colorful are the blue-purple arctic lupine and the pink-red fireweed.

Spotting Alaska's wildlife isn't always easy. Catching a glimpse of wildlife usually means being in the right place at the right time, but you can increase your chances by taking time to stop and scan hillsides and valleys, using binoculars to search for movement. Knowing where and why animals frequent can increase your chances of seeing them.

Recreational

From the beginning of human habitation in Alaska, people have been aware of the great natural resources of the land. In more recent years, people have come to discover another resource besides good hunting and gold mining: recreation. Although the activities offered on the Byway are unique and diverse, you will find camping, hiking, and picnicking spots in abundance all along the highway.

The section of the Seward Highway adjacent to Turnagain Arm provides scenic vistas across the Arm to the Kenai Mountains. Most of the lands above the highway are within Chugach State Park and provide you with a collection of things to see and ways to see them: windsurfing on the Arm, rock climbing on roadside rock cuts, rafting or canoeing on the Russian River, kite flying at Beluga Point, angling at Bird Creek, and bicycling the highway. Two hundred miles of trails are in the forest alone.

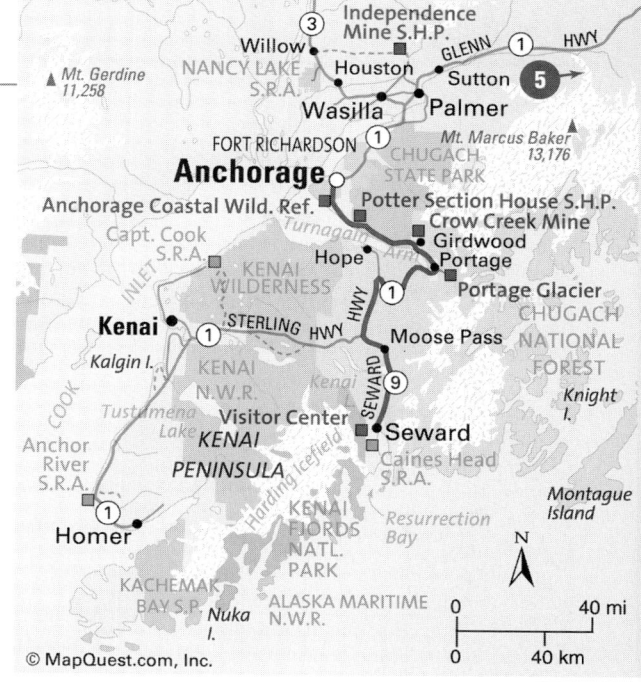

Once a mining town, Girdwood is now home to a world-famous ski resort that offers excellent scenery and plenty of challenges. This town combines the best of today's recreation with classic activities of the past, like panning for gold—try your luck! During the summer, the community celebrates a Forest Fair with arts, crafts, food, and entertainment. Other Byway towns like Hope and Cooper Landing offer havens for fishing. In Anchorage, you can stroll the streets and browse in shops or visitor centers.

Scenic

The trip from Anchorage to Seward is one of the most scenic drives you can take. Frequent pullouts offer vistas of snow-capped mountains, glaciers, wildlife, and wildflowers at almost every turn, and side trips and hiking trails beckon adventurous explorers. With such an impressive menu of vacation selections, you don't want to rush between appetizer and dessert.

Alaska

✤ The Seward Highway

The road up Portage Valley leads into the 5.8 million-acre Chugach National Forest and past three hanging glaciers that are perched in the cleavage of mountain canyons. Portage Glacier pokes its nose through the mountains at the head of a valley that it cut a long time ago. Since 1890, it has receded 1 mile and will be out of view by 2020, so don't procrastinate taking a trip to see it. Last year, the glacier finally withdrew from the lake and stopped calving. Now, only a few bergs float in water that was once brimming with ice. The visitor center offers excellent descriptive displays of glaciers and the best chance to see ice worms, pin-sized critters that burrow into glaciers and eat algae. Temperatures above freezing kill them.

If the many sights along the road to Seward make up the appetizer and main course, a boat trip along the rugged coast of Kenai Fjords National Park offers a high-calorie dessert. You can take a day cruise to see wildlife and tidewater glaciers that calve into the sea. Along the way, you may see orcas breach at boatside or a humpback whale with young swimming placidly along. At Chiswall Islands, thousands of puffins and kittywakes circle the boat. Just when you think you've seen the best, the boat stops at the foot of Holgate Glacier. With the engines cut, the cracking and popping of the 500-foot wall of aquamarine ice thunders through the frigid air like cannons firing. A slab of ice silently slips from the face of the glacier and crashes into the water. Seconds later, the blast reaches your ears. This is no dainty wildflower beside a trickling stream; you're witnessing the raw power of nature that carves valleys through mountains and determines the weather of the entire planet.

HIGHLIGHTS

The Seward Highway is in a richly varied and highly diverse area of Alaska. Over the length of its route, the character of the Byway continually changes with its proximity to water, mountains, and towns. The Seward Highway begins in the town of Seward nestled among the fjords surrounding Resurrection Bay. Nearby Kenai Fjords National Park offers the chance to see puffins, otters, eagles, arctic terns, whales, seals, and other marine life.

- Traveling north, the landscape surrounding the Byway becomes one of alpine meadows dotted with rivers and lakes. During late July and early August, **Ptarmigan Creek Recreation Site,** 23 miles from Seward, is an excellent place to stop and watch the incredible salmon run, when thousands of red salmon can be seen in this creek heading upstream to spawn.

- Farther north, approximately 75 miles from Seward, is **Twentymile Flats,** an expanse of lowlands and intertidal mudflats where three river valleys empty their silt-laden waters into Turnagain Arm and provide unobstructed views of the surrounding mountain peaks and glaciers. The view here is breathtaking, definitely worth stopping and taking in for a few minutes at the very least.

- Another 5 miles along the Byway is Portage Lake. **Portage Glacier,** located on the far side of Portage Lake, is rapidly receding out of the lake and provides an incredible opportunity to watch glacial action on fast-forward. One-hour boat tours are available to better witness the action.

- The remaining portion of the Seward Highway travels along the **Turnagain Arm** and offers you a plethora of things to see, both on and off the water. Turnagain Arm experiences the second highest tides in the world, often up to a 38-foot change in water level. Bore tides, a rare natural phenomenon in which the front of an incoming tide is a moving wall of water from 3 to 5 feet high, can be witnessed during extremely low tides in Turnagain Arm.

- The city of **Anchorage** is located at the northern terminus of the Seward Highway. With its rich history as a city on the edge of one of the final frontiers, Anchorage offers a wealth of historic and cultural sites that you can enjoy, whether you have an hour or a day to spend.

THINGS TO SEE AND DO

Driving along The Seward Highway will certainly keep your senses engaged, but if you yearn to get out of the car and stretch your legs, or if you'd like to make a mini-vacation out of your trip, check out these attractions along the route.

ALASKA SEALIFE CENTER. *301 Railway Ave, Seward (99664). Phone 907/224-6300; toll-free 800/224-2525. www.alaskasealife.org.* The Alaska SeaLife Center offers an unrivaled up-close and personal experience with Gulf of Alaska marine wildlife. Witness 1,500-pound Steller sea lions gliding past underwater viewing windows, puffins diving in a carefully crafted naturalistic habitat, and harbor seals hauled out on rocky beaches. Alaskan king crabs, sea stars, and Pacific octopi also await you, as well as a variety of intertidal creatures and deep-sea fishes. Open daily; closed Thanksgiving, Dec 25. $$$

CHUGACH NATIONAL FOREST. *3301 C St, Anchorage (99503). Phone 907/743-9500. www.fs.fed.us/r10/chugach/.* The Chugach National Forest is the second largest forest in the National Forest System. Roughly the same size as the states of Massachusetts and Rhode Island combined, the Chugach (pronounced CHEW-gatch) is the most northern of national forests, only 500 miles south of the Arctic Circle. One-third of the Chugach is composed of rocks and moving ice. The remainder is a diverse and majestic tapestry of land, water, plants, and animals. The mountains, lakes, and rivers of the Kenai Peninsula; the islands and glaciers of Prince William Sound; and the copious wetlands and birds of the Copper River Delta make this national forest a mecca for adventurers.

CHUGACH STATE PARK. *Mile 115 Seward Hwy, Anchorage (99540). Phone 907/345-5014. www.dnr.state.ak.us/parks/.* Chugach State Park is an accessible wilderness in the backyard of Anchorage. Wildlife viewing and mountain scenery are year-round pleasures, and campers can choose developed campgrounds or secluded backcountry valleys. Nearly 30 trails take hikers throughout the park to see some of its most enchanting views. Many visitors stop at the Eagle River Nature Center for a guided tour or interpretive program. Travelers may want to explore a few of the park's 50 glaciers on their own. And for extreme adventure, try climbing a mountainside or plunging through river rapids. The 495,000-acre park offers a wide variety of activities in all seasons.

KENAI FJORDS NATIONAL PARK. *Seward Hwy, Seward (99664). Phone 907/224-2132. www.nps.gov/kefj/.* Kenai Fjords National Park includes one of the four major ice caps in the United States, the 300-square-mile Harding Icefield, and coastal fjords. Located on the southeastern Kenai Peninsula, the national park is a pristine and rugged land supporting many unaltered natural environments and ecosystems. Here, a rich, varied rain forest is home to tens of thousands of breeding birds, and adjoining marine waters support a multitude of sea lions, sea otters, and seals. The most popular visitor activity at Kenai Fjords is viewing the park from a tour boat. The boats are privately owned, and the many operators offer tours of varying lengths

Alaska

✣ *The Seward Highway*

and features. Authorized commercial guides provide camping, fishing, and kayaking services. Air charters fly over the coast for flight seeing and access to the fjords. Boat tours and charters are available from Seward. In summer, boat tours ply the coast, observing calving glaciers, sea birds, and marine mammals.

PORTAGE GLACIER. *Portage Glacier (99587). Phone 907/783-3242 or -2326. www.fs.fed.us/ rlo/chugach/chugach_pages/bbvc.html.* Many of the world's glaciers are receding. This phenomenon is strikingly evident at Portage Glacier. At Portage, the **Begich-Boggs Visitor Center** used to squarely face the massive blue Portage Glacier directly in front of it. But only a few years after the Forest Service built the visitor facility, Portage Glacier receded—around a corner of Portage Lake and out of view. Now, tourists must view the glacier's face from a tour boat. Visitor center open daily 9 am-6 pm Memorial Day-Labor Day, Sat-Sun 10 am-5 pm the rest of the year.

TURNAGAIN PASS. The drive through Turnagain Pass may be one of the most scenic on the Byway. This is the highest point on the Byway, and wildlife spotting occurs regularly here. Turnagain Pass is located in the south beyond Turnagain Arm. Two large pullouts are easily accessible from the only section of divided highway outside of the Anchorage bowl. Views from the highway here show off the distinctive U-shaped valley created by retreating glaciers. Northbound travelers are treated to spectacular views of Turnagain Arm and Twentymile glaciers as they head down from this 900-foot pass to sea level. This area is especially popular in the winter for skiing and snowmobiling, and in mid-summer for its wildflower displays.

PLACES TO STAY

If you choose to include an overnight stay in your trip along this All-American Road, Mobil Travel Guide recommends the following lodgings.

★★★ **FIFTEEN CHANDELIERS B&B INN.** *14020 Sabine St, Anchorage (99511). Phone 907/345-3032.* 5 rooms, 3 story. European-style Georgian mansion set in a botanical garden. Breakfast is served in a formal dining room with fine china and stemware. $$

★★ **K STREET BED & BREAKFAST.** *1433 K St, Anchorage (99501). Phone 907/279-1443; toll-free 888/KST-BANB. www.cruising-america.com/ kstreetbb/kst.html.* 3 rooms, 2 share bath, 2 story. Complimentary breakfast. Contemporary cedar-sided home in a residential neighborhood with a garden and solarium. Features homemade breakfasts and original Alaskan art. $

★★ **A LOON'S NEST BED & BREAKFAST.** *1455 Hillcrest Dr, Anchorage (99503). Phone 907/279-9884; toll-free 800/786-9884. www.aloonsnest.com.* 2 rooms, 2 story. Complimentary breakfast. Frank Lloyd Wright-designed house poised on a bluff overlooking Westchester Lagoon featuring Shaker-style furniture and whirlpool tubs. $
D

★★★ **THE OSCAR GILL HISTORIC BED & BREAKFAST.** *1344 W 10th Ave, Anchorage (99501). Phone 907/279-1344. www.oscargill.com.* 3 rooms, 2 share bath, 2 story. Complimentary breakfast. Check-in 5-7 pm. 1913 home located in Delaney Park bordering the Cook Inlet with views of Denali and Sleeping Lady. Cited as one of Alaska's best lodgings. $

★ **PLANET ANCHORAGE BED & BREAKFAST.** *1025 H St, Anchorage (99501). Phone 907/770-6742. www.planetanchoragebb.com.* 3 rooms, 2 story. Check-in 5 pm, check-out 11 am. 1950s-style home five minutes from downtown. Fresh homemade breakfasts made with local ingredients. $

★ **SUSITNA SUNSETS BED & BREAKFAST.** *9901 Conifer St, Anchorage (99507). Phone 907/346-1067. www.susitnasunsets.com.* 3 rooms, 3 story. Children 10 and over only. Features views of Mount McKinley with breakfast served in your room or on one of the decks. $

PLACES TO EAT

A long day of driving is sure to make you hungry. At the end of your journey, take a table at one of the following restaurants.

★ **ALPINE BAKERY.** *1 Alyeska Hwy, Girdwood (99587). Phone 907/783-2550.* American menu. Breakfast, lunch, dinner. American- and European-style baked goods and light dinners. $

★ **THE BAKE SHOP.** *The Old Hotel on Olympic Circle, Girdwood (99587). Phone 907/783-2831. www.thebakeshop.com.* American menu. Breakfast, lunch, dinner. Homemade bakery items and desserts. Famous for sourdough pancakes. $

★ **THE DOUBLE MUSKIE INN.** *1 Crow Creek Rd, Girdwood (99587). Phone 907/783-2822.* Cajun menu. Closed Sun. Lunch, dinner. Renowned local restaurant serving Cajun preparations of local ingredients. $$

★ **SUMMIT LAKE LODGE.** *Mile 45.5 Seward Hwy, Moose Pass (99631). Phone 907/244-2031. www.summitlakelodge.com.* American menu. Closed Oct-Apr. Breakfast, lunch, dinner. Family-oriented restaurant with amazing views. $$

★ **RESURRECTION ROADHOUSE.** *Mile 05 exit Glacier Rd, Seward (99503). Phone 907/224-7116. www.sewardwindsong.com.* American menu. Closed mid-Oct-mid-Apr. Lunch, dinner. Known for authentic local specialties. $$

Arroyo Seco Historic Parkway
ROUTE 110 ✹ CALIFORNIA

Quick Facts

LENGTH: 9.45 miles.

TIME TO ALLOW: 1 hour.

BEST TIME TO DRIVE: All year.

BYWAY TRAVEL INFORMATION: Scenic Arroyo Seco: 323/221-8900, extension 310; Byway local Web site: www.arroyoseco.org/asparkway.htm.

SPECIAL CONSIDERATIONS: The Arroyo Seco Parkway is open at all times of the year. Recreational opportunities in the area may be hampered by seasonal rains in the wintertime (November-March), when high water levels and saturated soils make hiking and fishing in the San Gabriel Mountains difficult.

The parkway experiences typical Los Angeles-area commuter congestion during major drive times in the early morning and late afternoon. Baseball games at Dodger Stadium and the Rose Parade on New Year's Day are other seasonal activities that result in predictable congestion.

RESTRICTIONS: Oversized vehicles are prohibited on the Byway. Instead of continuous shoulders, the highway has intermittent "turn-out pockets" for disabled vehicles. Several of the ramps have posted speed limits of 5 mph.

BICYCLE/PEDESTRIAN FACILITIES: Bicycles and pedestrians are not permitted on the Arroyo Seco Parkway. However, several recreational hiking, bicycling, and equestrian trails exist within the naturalized areas of the corridor.

Dedicated on December 30, 1940, the Arroyo Seco Historic Parkway connects Los Angeles and Pasadena through the historic Arts and Crafts landscape of the Arroyo Seco, a compelling native landscape that inspired turn-of-the-century artists and craftsmen associated with the Arroyo culture. Their studios and workshops dotted the banks of this intermittent river. Today, the area's natural and built environment form a seamless cultural landscape, strongly associated with the Arts and Crafts era, that continues to inspire new generations of artists, musicians, writers, architects, and craftsmen.

Conceived in the parkway tradition with its gentle curves, lush landscape, and scenic vistas, the parkway also incorporated the modern elements that laid the groundwork for the California freeway system. Combining ideas reminiscent of the older parkway tradition with those of modern freeway design, the Arroyo Seco Parkway (also called the Pasadena Freeway, State Route 110) was the first divided-lane, high-speed, limited-access road in the urban western United States and was the prototype of the world-renowned Los Angeles freeway system. The parkway was envisioned both as a scenic pleasure road traversing the Arroyo Seco and as a vital traffic conduit linking the expanding cities of Pasadena and Los Angeles.

THE BYWAY STORY

The Arroyo Seco Historic Parkway tells cultural, historical, natural, and recreational stories that make it a unique and treasured Byway.

California

ROUTE 110 ✸ Arroyo Seco Historic Parkway

Cultural

The Arroyo Seco was the center for the Arts and Crafts movement on the West Coast and is one of four internationally recognized centers of the movement in America. The Arts and Crafts movement started in the United Kingdom between the late 1850s and early 1860s and is characterized by a disregard for industrialization, with followers of the movement building their own houses out of as many natural materials as possible and handcrafting as much of their environment as possible.

By the late 1890s, the movement had worked its way over to America, having significant influence on the Arroyo culture throughout the first two decades of the 20th century. The movement gave rise to thriving enterprises, including furniture design and manufacturing, home plans and kits, ceramics, glasswork, metalwork, and textiles. The influence of the Arts and Crafts movement on the Arroyo Seco culture is most evident in the architecture of many of the structures along the Byway. Bungalows along the Byway are built of all natural materials and feature wide porches and long roof overhangs. Additionally, almost all of the buildings feature native Arroyo cobblestone trim, collected from the river of the valley.

The Arroyo Seco Parkway Scenic Byway, in addition to the many private homes and businesses reflecting the Arts and Crafts movement, contains a number of museums, parks, and other sites devoted to or reflecting the movement. The Lummis House and Gardens, once home to Charles Lummis, recognized as the father of the Arroyo culture, offers tours and educational workshops on the Arts and Crafts movement. The Gamble House, located in Pasadena, is an internationally recognized landmark of the California Craftsman style of architecture related to the movement. The Highland Park Historic District is comprised of buildings from the first two decades of the 20th century and is the largest historic district in Los Angeles. The Oaklawn Waiting Station is another product of the movement, featuring enormous boulders of native Arroyo rock, a hallmark of regional Craftsman design.

Historical

The Arroyo Seco Historic Parkway was the first parkway in California, the first freeway in the west, and the prototype of the world-famous Los Angeles freeway system. Its significance in California's highway history is highlighted by its designation as an American Civil Engineering Landmark. The Arroyo Seco Historic Parkway is also California's first and only California state historic parkway and is nationally recognized as one of the most significant roadways of the 20th century.

The megalopolis of Los Angeles actually began as just a small settlement of a colony of settlers from Mexico. The Arroyo Seco Historic Parkway lies nearly adjacent to that original settlement, El Pueblo del Nuestra Signora, La Rena de Los Angeles. The site contains more than 20 historic buildings, many of which can be viewed or are now museums.

Natural

While located in the second largest city in the United States, the Arroyo Seco Historic Parkway is an urban oasis with natural areas, diverse parklands, and views of the Angeles National Forest in the snow-peaked San Gabriel Mountains to the north. Much of the Arroyo Seco remains in a highly naturalized state, dramatically contrasting with the hustle and bustle of nearby downtown Los Angeles. The Arroyo Seco remains an example of the natural and unique landscape that drew artists, craftsmen, writers, and intellectuals to the area.

Arroyo Seco, Spanish for "dry stream," is geographically the most prominent feature of the northeastern Los Angeles landscape. The great, long canyon of the Arroyo Seco extends from the foot of the San Gabriel Mountains north of Pasadena, southward along the western edge of South Pasadena. The canyon then continues south through Highland Park until it joins the Los Angeles River not far from Elysian Park.

The Arroyo Seco Historic Parkway, of its own merits a natural escape from urbandom, is also lined with a number of parks. Debs Park, managed by the National Audubon Society, and Mount Washington provide concentrated native habitat for the area's diverse bird population. Other notable escapes from the concrete jungle are Arroyo Seco Park, Elysian Park, and Sycamore Grove Park.

The Los Angeles River Center lies at the confluence of the Arroyo Seco and the Los Angeles River. The center features exhibits, lectures, regional hikes, and outings, all originating from the River Center. Additionally, the center provides space for environmental groups working with natural resources in the corridor, such as Northeast Trees; the Mountains, Rivers and Conservation Authority; and the National Park Service.

Recreational

In the 1920s, under the urging of Charles Lummis, Pasadena and Los Angeles recognized the opportunities of the Arroyo Seco to provide recreational access to a growing metropolitan area. The lands along the Arroyo Seco Historic Parkway represent a distinct and direct urban link to the wilderness area in the San Gabriel Mountains. You can hike the Byway corridor from the city of Los Angeles to the top of Mount Wilson along public lands. The rugged native landscape that inspired so many painters, architects, and craftsmen is still enjoyed today by residents and tourists alike. Active recreation, like hiking, swimming, horseback riding, bicycling, fishing, tennis, and golf, is matched by more passive pursuits like bird-watching, painting, and stargazing.

The Arroyo Seco lies in the heart of Los Angeles, a recreational melting pot. The Byway itself features Dodger Stadium, allowing you to partake of America's favorite pastime. For golfers, courses are abundant in the area, including Arroyo Seco's own course. Downtown Los Angeles, only a block from the Byway, has days worth of activities, from basketball or exhibits at the Staples Center to provocative contemplation at the Museum of Contemporary Art. Hollywood, with its many studios, is only a few minutes' drive away. Anaheim, home to Disneyland, Knott's Berry Farm, and countless other recreational sources, is only 30 miles down the highway. Your visit to the Byway is only the beginning of a recreational wonderland.

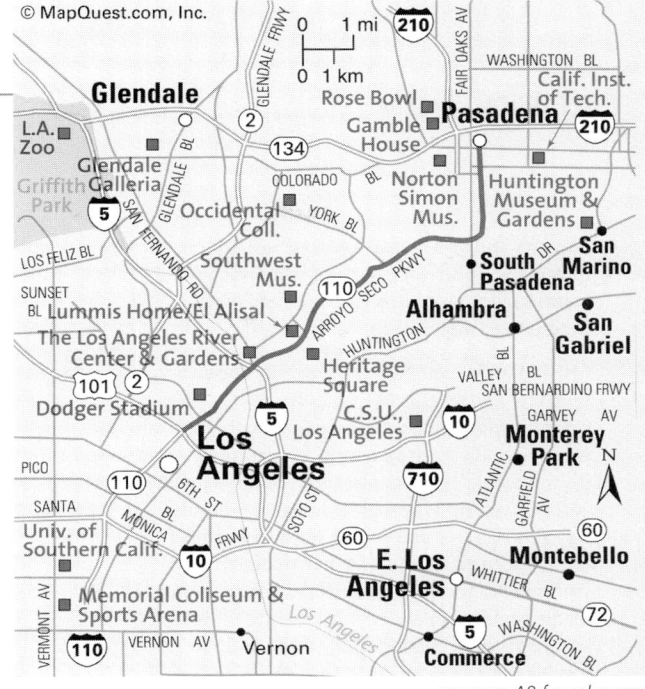

see page A8 for color map

THINGS TO SEE AND DO

Driving along the Arroyo Seco Historic Parkway will certainly keep your senses engaged, but if you yearn to get out of the car and stretch your legs, or if you'd like to make a mini-vacation out of your trip, check out these attractions along the route.

THE ARROYO SECO TRAIL. *Ventura St and Windsor Ave, Altadena (91001).* This 7.5-mile trail leads through a thick forest along the Arroyo Seco River in the foothills near Pasadena. The first part of the trail is a paved fire road, with easy biking for even less-experienced riders. As it winds farther north, however, the trail

27

California

ROUTE 110 ❋ *Arroyo Seco Historic Parkway*

narrows and you'll cross the river—expect to carry your bike across the rocky riverbed. Continue into the Angeles National Forest for a longer ride. **FREE**

CHINATOWN. *900 N Broadway, Los Angeles (90012). Phone 213/680-0243. www.chinatownla.com.* Because this Chinatown was originally built as a tourist attraction, it's not as big or authentic as its better-known counterpart up Highway 1, in San Francisco. But you still feel like you've stepped out of the LA scene and into another world when you wander through it, especially because many of the buildings have that distinctive Chinese look with their tiled roofs. Dine at a dim-sum restaurant, check out the curio shops selling jade and gold jewelry, eye the Chinese treasures available at antique dealers, learn about natural remedies at herb shops, and more. Before leaving, toss a few coins in the wishing well in the central plaza on Broadway—especially if you're looking for love, good health, or wealth.

DODGER STADIUM. *1000 Elysian Park Ave, Los Angeles (90012). Phone 323/224-1500 or 323/224-1HIT. www.losangeles.dodgers.mlb.com.* This more than 40-year-old stadium is the home of Major League Baseball's Los Angeles Dodgers.

❋ **EL PUEBLO DE LOS ANGELES HISTORIC MONUMENT AND OLVERA STREET.** *125 Paseo de la Plaza, Los Angeles (90012). Phone 213/628-3562. www.ci.la.ca.us/elp/.* If you're looking to dispel the myth that nothing in Los Angeles is older than the newest strip mall, El Pueblo and Olvera Street are the answer. El Pueblo is where it all began. Here, you'll find 27 historic buildings, four of which are open to the public free of charge as historic museums: Avila Adobe is the oldest house in the city, dating back to 1818; Sepulveda House dates back to 1887 and is home to the monument's visitor center; the Fire House Museum, built in 1884, was in service as a fire station for 13 years before evolving into a saloon and a boarding house; and the Masonic Hall, built in 1858, is the oldest building south of the plaza. A big part of the fun is Olvera Street, dating to 1877 and now a Mexican marketplace where you can find everything from cheap tourist-trap shops to authentic Mexican clothing and food. As you walk through the narrow street, with mariachi bands playing and the smell of salsa in the air, you'll swear you've been transported south of the border. Open daily. **FREE**

ELYSIAN PARK. *1880 Academy Dr, Los Angeles (90012). Phone 213/222-9136. www.laavenue.com/elysian.htm.* This park covers 600 acres, with beautiful landscaping. Picnicking, playgrounds, tennis courts, and ball fields beckon play of many kinds. Open daily. **FREE**

THE GAMBLE HOUSE. *4 Westmoreland Pl, Pasadena (91103). Phone 626/793-3334. www.gamblehouse.org.* Exemplary of the mature California bungalow designs of American architects Greene and Greene (1908); interiors of teakwood, mahogany, maple, and cedar; gardens. One-hour guided tour. Open Thurs-Sun afternoons; closed holidays. **$$$**

KIDSPACE. *390 S El Molino Ave, Pasadena (91101). Phone 626/449-9144. www.kidspace-museum.org.* This hands-on museum for kids includes a TV studio, indoor beach, computer center, theater, and build-it area. Open Tues-Sun. **$$**

LUMMIS HOME AND GARDEN STATE HISTORICAL MONUMENT. *200 E Ave 43, Los Angeles (90042). Phone 323/222-0546.* Charles Lummis, the noted writer, photographer, historian, and archaeologist, spent 14 years (1896-1910) building this L-shaped home out of concrete and granite boulders. One look at this residential piece of art, now the headquarters for the Historical Society of Southern California, and you sense that this eccentric man had a keen interest in pueblos and missions (indeed, he founded the Southwest Museum). Lummis named the house El Elisal, the Spanish word for sycamore, after the large tree that once grew beside it. Many drought-tolerant plants native to southern California flourish in the gardens, offering a lesson in regional horticulture. Tours are available. Open Fri-Sun noon-4 pm; closed holidays.

◪ NORTON SIMON MUSEUM OF ART. *411 W Colorado Blvd, Pasadena (91105). Phone 626/449-6840. www.nortonsimon.org.* Many art lovers will tell you that this stellar museum in Pasadena outclasses the better-known, more-hyped Getty in Los Angeles. In this 85,000-square-foot facility, you'll be awed by one of the world's finest private collections of European, American, and Asian art spanning more than 2,000 years. Paintings, sculptures, works on paper, photography—it has it all. Of particular note are rare etchings by Rembrandt and Goya, along with a collection of Picasso graphics. Much of what you'll see belonged to the museum's wealthy namesake, who died in 1993. A wildly successful entrepreneur, his company's holdings included Avis Car Rental, Hunt-Wesson Foods, and McCall's Publishing. Open Mon, Wed-Thurs noon-6 pm, Fri to 9 pm, Sat-Sun to 6 pm; closed Tues; also Jan 1, Thanksgiving, Dec 25. $$

PACIFIC ASIA MUSEUM. *46 N Los Robles Ave, Pasadena (91101). Phone 626/449-2742. www.pacificasiamuseum.org.* This museum offers changing exhibits of traditional and contemporary Asian and Pacific Basin art.

Chinese Imperial Palace-style building and Chinese courtyard garden, research library, and bookstore. Tours are available. Open Wed-Thurs, Sat-Sun 10 am-5 pm, Fri 10 am-8 pm. $$

THE ROSE BOWL. *1001 Rose Bowl Dr, Pasadena (91103). Phone 626/577-3100. www.rosebowlstadium.com.* One of the country's most famous football stadiums, the Rose Bowl seats more than 98,000. Home of the UCLA Bruins football team, this stadium is also the scene of the annual Rose Bowl and other events throughout the year.

SOUTHWEST MUSEUM. *234 Museum Dr, Los Angeles (90065). Phone 323/221-2164. www.southwestmuseum.org.* The oldest museum in Los Angeles (1907), the Southwest Museum offers immense insight into the life and culture of Native Americans. Its 17,000 square feet of exhibit space features four main exhibit halls in which you learn about the native people of the Southwest, California, the Great Plains, and the Northwest Coast. See a Cheyenne tepee, prehistoric painted pottery, basketry, and much more. The museum recently merged with the Autry Museum of Western Heritage, forming the Autry National Center of the American West, which also includes the Institute for the Study of the American West. Open Tues-Sun, 10 am-5 pm; closed holidays. $$

PLACES TO STAY

If you choose to include an overnight stay in your trip along this Byway, Mobil Travel Guide recommends the following lodgings.

Los Angeles

★★★ **MILLENNIUM BILTMORE HOTEL LOS ANGELES.** *506 S Grand Ave, Los Angeles (90071). Phone 213/624-1011; toll-free 800/245-8673. www.thebiltmore.com.* 683 rooms, 12 story. Check-out noon,

California

ROUTE 110 ✸ *Arroyo Seco Historic Parkway*

check-in. TV; cable (premium), VCR available. In-room modem link. Restaurant, bar. Room service 24 hours. In-house fitness room, massage, sauna. Indoor pool, whirlpool. Valet parking. Business center. Luxury level. $$

★★★ OMNI LA HOTEL CALIFORNIA PLAZA.
251 S Olive St, Los Angeles (90012). Phone 213/617-3300; toll-free 800/442-5251. www.omnihotels.com. Located in the heart of downtown Los Angeles atop Bunker Hill, this hotel is part of a plaza complex with an outdoor courtyard displaying contemporary sculptures. The Museum of Contemporary Art is next door. 454 rooms, 17 story. Check-out noon, check-in 3 pm. TV; cable (premium), VCR available. In-room modem link. Restaurant, bar. Room service 24 hours. Babysitting services available. In-house fitness room, spa, massage, sauna. Outdoor pool, poolside service. Valet parking. Business center. Concierge. Luxury level. $$

★★★ WILSHIRE GRAND HOTEL AND CENTRE.
930 Wilshire Blvd, Los Angeles (90017). Phone 213/688-7777; toll-free 888/773-2888. www.wilshiregrand.com. 900 rooms, 16 story. Check-out noon. TV; cable (premium). In-room modem link. Minibars. Restaurant, bar. Heated pool, whirlpool, poolside service. Barber, beauty shop. Garage parking $24. Business center. Convention center/facilities. Concierge. $$

Pasadena

★★★ HILTON PASADENA.
168 S Los Robles Ave, Pasadena (91101). Phone 626/577-1000; toll-free 800/445-8667. www.hilton.com. At the foothills of the San Gabriel Mountains, this hotel is in a great location for both business and pleasure travel. 285 rooms, 13 story. Four-day minimum during Rose Parade. Check-out 1 pm. TV; cable (premium). In-room modem link. Restaurant, bar. Room service. In-house fitness room. Pool, whirlpool, poolside service. Business center. Concierge. $

★★★★ THE RITZ-CARLTON HUNTINGTON HOTEL AND SPA.
S Oak Knoll Ave, Pasadena (91106). Phone 626/568-3900; toll-free 800/241-3333. www.ritzcarlton.com. The Ritz-Carlton Huntington Hotel and Spa has been painting a rosy picture for lucky guests since 1907. This historic hotel, acquired by Ritz-Carlton in 1991, is nestled at the foothills of the San Gabriel Mountains on 23 beautiful acres. Its relaxed, rural setting defies its location in Pasadena, near Los Angeles. Oriental carpets, crystal chandeliers, and antiques comprise the resolutely classic interiors. The guest rooms reflect the great tradition of this hotel while incorporating modern necessities. Dining at the Terrace Restaurant is a treat, from its alfresco setting with a view of the Picture Bridge to its appetizing dishes. The Grill specializes in seafood and meats in a casual environment, while the lounge and pool bar entertain day and night. From refreshing spa treatments and bike rentals to tee times and tennis lessons, this resort has it covered. 392 rooms, 3-8 story. Pet accepted, some restrictions; fee. Check-out noon, check-in 3 pm. TV; cable (premium), VCR available. Restaurant, bar; entertainment. Room service 24 hours. Spa. Pool, whirlpool, poolside service. Lighted tennis. Lawn games. Bicycle rental. Valet parking. Business center. Concierge. Luxury level. $$$

★★★ THE WESTIN PASADENA.
191 N Los Robles Ave, Pasadena (91101). Phone 626/792-2727; toll-free 800/222-8733. www.westin.com/pasadena. This luxurious hotel is adjacent to City Hall in the center of the San Gabriel Valley. 350 rooms, 12 story. Check-out noon. TV; cable (premium). Some

balconies. Refrigerators. Microwaves available. Valet services. Restaurant, bar; entertainment Tues-Sat. Room service 24 hours. In-house fitness room, massage, sauna, steam room. Heated pool, whirlpool, poolside service. Garage parking $6, valet $11. Airport transportation. Business services available. Convention facilities. Concierge. Luxury level. City hall adjacent. $
[D] [SC]

★★★ **ARTIST'S INN BED & BREAKFAST.** *1038 Magnolia St, South Pasadena (91030). Phone 626/799-5668; toll-free 888/799-5668. www.artistsinns.com.* This quaint 1890s Victorian-style inn is located near Old Town Pasadena. Each guest room is beautifully appointed, reflecting the work of an artist or an art period. 10 rooms, 1 with shower only, 2 story. Children over 9 years only. Complimentary full breakfast; afternoon refreshments. Check-out 11 am, check-in 3-6 pm. TV available. Some fireplaces. Antiques. Totally nonsmoking. $$

PLACES TO EAT

A long day of driving is sure to make you hungry. At the end of your journey, take a table at one of the following restaurants.

Los Angeles

★★★ **CICADA.** *617 S Olive St, Los Angeles (90014). Phone 213/488-9488. www.cicadarestaurant.com.* Thirty-foot ceilings, icy black walls, and carved wood abound at this modern Italian landmark inside the historic Oviatt building. Italian menu. Closed Sun. Lunch, dinner. Bar; entertainment: jazz. Casual attire. Reservations required. Totally nonsmoking. $$

★★ **SEOUL JUNG.** *930 Wilshire Blvd, Los Angeles (90017). Phone 213/688-7880. www.wilshire-grand.com.* Located in the Wilshire Grand Hotel. Korean menu. Lunch, dinner. Bar. Valet parking. Totally nonsmoking. $$
[D]

★★★ **WATER GRILL.** *544 S Grand Ave, Los Angeles (90071). Phone 213/891-0900. www.watergrill.com.* Rated one of LA's best restaurants, this longstanding favorite serves flawlessly prepared seafood. Options include prix fixe, à la carte, and raw bar samplings. The Art Deco setting models a luxury liner that transmits a just-right tone, given the pricey seafood and fine wine list. Consequently, Water Grill is the place to take a business colleague or romantic partner you aim to impress with your refinement. Its downtown location makes it a good pre-theater option. Seafood menu. Closed major holidays. Lunch, dinner. Bar. Jacket requested. Reservations required. Valet parking. $$$
[D]

Pasadena

★★ **BECKHAM GRILL.** *77 W Walnut St, Pasadena (91103). Phone 626/796-3399. www.beckhamgrill.com.* Seafood menu. Closed most major holidays. Lunch, dinner. Bar. Valet parking. Outdoor seating. $$
[D] [SC]

★★ **CAFE SANTORINI.** *64-70 W Union St, Pasadena (91103). Phone 626/564-4200. www.cafesantorini.com.* Italian, Mediterranean menu. Closed some major holidays. Lunch, dinner. Bar. Outdoor seating. $
[D]

★ **CROCODILE CAFÉ.** *140 S Lake Ave, Pasadena (91101). Phone 626/449-9900. www.crocodilecafe.com.* California, eclectic menu. Closed Thanksgiving, Dec 25. Lunch, dinner. Bar. Outdoor seating. $$
[D]

★ **MAISON AKIRA.** *713 E Green St, Pasadena (91101). Phone 626/796-9501. www.maison-akira.com.* Specializes in miso-marinated Chilean sea bass, baby rack of lamb. Lunch (except Sun), dinner. Reservations accepted. $$$
[D]

California

ROUTE 110 ✽ *Arroyo Seco Historic Parkway*

★★ **MI PIACE.** *25 E Colorado Blvd, Pasadena (91105). Phone 626/795-3131.* Italian menu. Lunch, dinner. Bar. Casual attire. Valet parking. Outdoor seating. Totally nonsmoking. $$
[D]

★★ **MIYAKO.** *139 S Los Robles Ave, Pasadena (91101) Phone 626/795-7005.* Japanese menu. Closed Mon; July 4, Thanksgiving, Dec 25. Lunch, dinner. Bar. Boat dinners. Totally nonsmoking. $$

★★★ **OYE.** *69 N Raymond Ave, Pasadena (91103). Phone 626/796-3286.* This upscale restaurant seats 120 in its beautiful dining room but feels very comfortable and provides a casual dining experience. Asian-Cuban menu. Closed some major holidays. Dinner. Bar. Wine list. Valet parking. Reservations accepted. Supper club atmosphere; tropical décor. Totally nonsmoking. $$

★★★ **RAYMOND.** *1250 S Fair Oaks Ave, Pasadena (91105). Phone 626/441-3136. www.theraymond.com.* American menu. Closed Mon; Jan 1, July 4, Dec 25. Lunch; dinner; Sat, Sun brunch. Menu changes weekly. Bar. Wine cellar. Own desserts. Patio dining. Reservations accepted. Turn-of-the-century caretaker's cottage; wood floors, lace curtains, fireplace. $$$
[D]

★★ **SALADANG SONG.** *383 S Fair Oaks Ave, Pasadena (91105). Phone 626/793-5200.* Thai menu. Closed some major holidays. Breakfast, lunch, dinner. Casual attire. Totally nonsmoking. $$
[D]

★★★ **SHIRO.** *1505 Mission St, South Pasadena (91030). Phone 626/799-4774.* The 1950s-style décor features retro tableware, murals, and a bar serving tropical drinks. Continental menu changes daily. Closed Mon; major holidays; also three weeks in Sept. Dinner. Totally nonsmoking. $$
[D]

★★ **TWIN PALMS.** *101 W Green St, Pasadena (91105). Phone 626/577-2567. www.twin-palms.com.* California coastal menu. Extensive salad selection. Closed Dec 25. Lunch, dinner, Sun brunch. Bar; entertainment. In a converted warehouse; California resort atmosphere. Outdoor seating. $$$
[D]

★★★ **XIOMARA.** *69 N Raymond Ave, Pasadena (91103). Phone 626/796-2520.* If you're up for crazily inventive yet harmonious and pleasant new flavor combinations, visit this Asian-Latin fusion temple. Bring your Spanish skills to alleviate communication problems with the authentic staff. Continental menu. Closed Dec 25. Lunch (weekdays only), dinner. Bar. Valet parking. Outdoor seating. Reservations accepted. Bistro atmosphere. $$
[D]

★★★ **YUJEAN KANG'S.** *67 N Raymond Ave, Pasadena (91103). Phone 626/585-0855.* Chinese menu. Closed Thanksgiving. Lunch, dinner. Totally nonsmoking. $$
[D]

Big Sur Coast Highway
ROUTE 1 ✤ CALIFORNIA
AN ALL-AMERICAN ROAD

Quick Facts

LENGTH: 72 miles.

TIME TO ALLOW: 3 to 5 hours.

BEST TIME TO DRIVE: Spring, summer, and fall. High season is during June, July, and August.

BYWAY TRAVEL INFORMATION: Monterey Travel and Tourism Alliance: 831/626-1424; Monterey Peninsula Visitor and Convention Bureau: 831/372-9323.

SPECIAL CONSIDERATIONS: Fill your gas tank in Carmel before heading south or in San Simeon before heading north on Route 1, because you'll encounter few gas stations along the way. The road is narrow and curvy, and in some places it has narrow shoulders and sharp drop-offs to the ocean far below. Large, long vehicles may have trouble with this winding road. Drive with care and watch for pedestrians and bicyclists.

RESTRICTIONS: The road is open all year, except for occasional mudslides during severe rainstorms.

BICYCLE/PEDESTRIAN FACILITIES: This Byway is a major attraction to pedestrians and cyclists. You'll find many shoulders along the way (although in some areas, they're narrow with sharp drop-offs) and plenty of room where all can share.

Route 1 from Carmel south to the San Luis Obispo County line follows some of the most spectacular and highly scenic shoreline found along California's coast. Views include rugged canyons and steep sea cliffs, granite shorelines, sea lions and other marine life, windswept cypress trees, and majestic redwood forests.

This Byway also provides you with a lesson in California's rich Mission-era and natural history. The primary goal of the Byway is to preserve California's delicate and pristine coastal ecosystem for its natives, visitors, and future generations, while still providing opportunities to experience its wonder.

Travel the route that hugs the California coast, providing access to austere, windswept cypress trees, fog-shrouded cliffs, and the crashing surf of the Pacific Ocean.

THE BYWAY STORY

The Big Sur Coast Highway tells cultural, historical, natural, recreational, and scenic stories that make it a unique and treasured Byway.

Cultural

The Big Sur is one example of an area whose culture is largely shaped by the region's geography. The awe-inspiring scenic beauty of the Big Sur has lured and inspired countless artists, authors, and poets. The literary works of Henry Miller are filled with vivid descriptions of the Big Sur, while the artwork of Emil White and others attempts to portray the breathtaking scenery of the Big Sur's rocky coast and coastal mountains.

California

ROUTE 1 ❋ Big Sur Coast Highway

The Carmel area and the Salinas valley, less rugged but no less scenic or inspiring, have also had a vital role to play in the area's culture. The area has been home to many artists, none more famous than John Steinbeck, whose novels vividly describe life in the fertile Salinas valley. Although Steinbeck is the most famous, the area has also been home to Clint Eastwood, photographer Ansel Adams, and poet Robinson Jeffers.

Historical

Written histories regarding the region now known as the Big Sur began to appear in the mid-1500s, when a Portuguese ship passed by the area's coastline. New groups of European explorers approached the area throughout the late 1500s and early 1600s, many anchoring for a time in Monterey Bay. However, it wasn't until 1770 that the first permanent settlement was established, when a Spanish group started a mission in Carmel. The Spaniards first called the area south of the Carmel settlement El Pais Grande del Sur, or "the Big Country of the South." These same Spanish settlers were quick to introduce themselves and their culture to the area natives, who had lived in the region for centuries.

For centuries before the Europeans discovered the Big Sur, the Esselen Indians had thrived in the area as hunters and gathers, using land and sea animals and plants in the woodlands and coastal plains between Point Sur and Lopez Point. By the early 18th century, other Spanish missions followed the Carmel Mission. The missions had the dual purpose of claiming the land for Spain and teaching the natives the Europeans' message of Christianity. In the late 1700s, the Spanish missionaries and soldiers forced many of the Esselen and other native peoples to leave their villages and move into the missions. Smallpox, cholera, and other European diseases almost completely wiped out the Esselen people when they came in contact with foreign settlers. Those who were left mixed with other natives in the missions so that they ceased to maintain a separate existence. As a result, very little is known today about their way of life.

A colorful variety of settlers of various nationalities began to take notice of the scenic Big Sur area and its inviting foothills. The Spanish and Mexican history also heavily influenced the culture and history of the area. Monterey was soon an important port, bringing even more people to the area.

Until the late 1800s, a small, rough trail served as the best overland route to Monterey from the Big Sur. Eventually, the trail widened into a road of sorts, which was still frequently lost in landslides. This widening allowed the journey to Monterey to be made in just 11 hours, as opposed to the three or four days it had taken previously. After many years of difficult passage over poor roads between Big Sur and the rest of central California, Route 1 was completed in 1937. By its completion, 15 years of labor and $9 million had been expended.

Natural

The allure of the Big Sur Coast Highway comes not just from the sea and the mountains, but also from the convergence of the sea with the mountains. Many other destinations around the country feature beautiful mountains, and countless others offer beaches from which to enjoy the ocean. The Big Sur, however, is one of the few places in America where these two dominant features converge so dramatically. Travelers from around the world visit the Big Sur to experience its breathtaking scenery.

The Byway enables you to experience the Pacific Ocean in its most natural, prehistoric state. The endless blue horizon, as seen from the Byway, is most often void of any man-made floating vessels, unlike most other coastlines. Travelers are more likely, in fact, to witness a massive whale surfacing for air or some sea otters playing than to see a freighter waiting to port. Additionally, the Big Sur offers you the unique experience of enjoying the enchanting sounds of the sea, unhindered by any other noise. Many people find that time escapes them as they park on one of the many turnouts and take in the sounds of the sea.

The San Lucia coastal mountain range offers the other side of the Big Sur's natural beauty. The range is a natural paradise of cypress and redwood forests, waterfalls, and meadows full of colorful wildflowers, such as lupines and poppies. The mountains also host one of the Byway's most unique natural elements: the giant redwood tree. The redwoods stretch along a narrow strip of land from the Big Sur area to the southwest corner of Oregon; redwood trees thrive in the specific climate along this area and are not native to any other region in the world. Many of the oldest of the trees are around 2,000 years old. The tallest redwoods have reached heights of 350 feet. Most redwoods average to 50 to 250 feet in height. Such heights require solid foundations, with many of the giant trees' diameters spanning 10 to 15 feet.

The convergence of the Pacific Ocean with the San Lucia Mountains of the Big Sur coastline is the source of the inviting, often overwhelming scenery of the Big Sur. The ocean has helped to carve out the tantalizing craggy rock inlets along the corridor. The highway hugs steep, rocky cliffs on the east side of the road, while blunt drops to the west fall straight to the sea. The solid land mass of the shoreline holds strong as waves of the mighty Pacific push against its cliffs and crash against its rocks. The Big Sur offers a fulfilling blend of natural sights and sounds unlike anywhere else.

Recreational

While Big Sur's beaches hardly resemble the vast stretches of sun-baked sand that dot Southern California's coastline, they do offer you a wide variety of recreational possibilities. Even during the summer, Big Sur's beaches are subject to generally cool weather. Sunny days are sporadic because a blanket of seasonal fog often hugs the coastline, dropping the temperature in the process. To be prepared, bring a change of warm clothes. Also, bring a pair of sturdy shoes—getting to Big Sur's beaches requires at least a short hike.

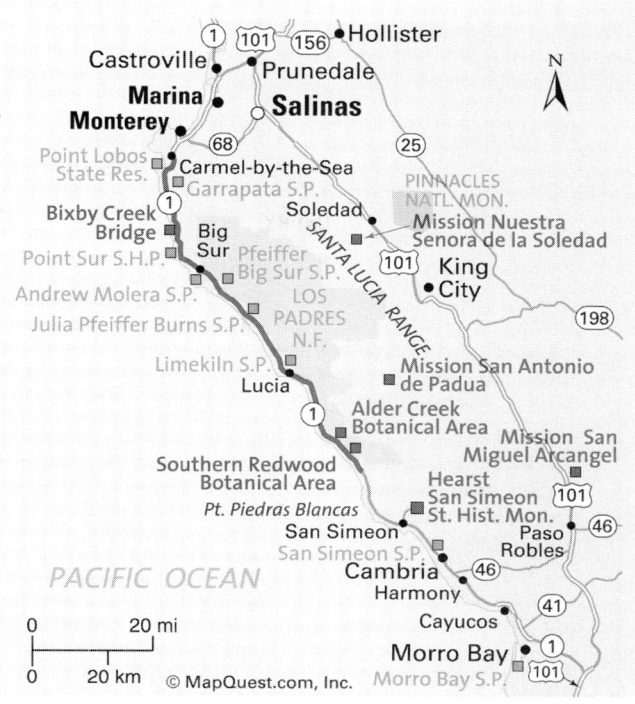

Private property and Big Sur's steep terrain make most of its coastline inaccessible to the public. Fortunately, however, several state park and US Forest Service beaches are open to the public all year. These beaches are recommended due to easy access and breathtaking scenery. Located 23 miles south of Carmel, **Andrew Molera State Park** is the largest state park on the Big Sur coast. A wide, scenic, mile-long path leads to a sandy beach that's sheltered from the wind by a large bluff to the north. The path itself is as much a delight as the beach, taking you through a meadow filled with wildflowers and sycamore trees and offering fine views of the coastal mountain range to the east. The path parallels the Big Sur River, which enters the sea adjacent to Molera's beach.

Although **Pfeiffer Beach** is Big Sur's most popular coastal access point, this beach is hard to find

California

ROUTE 1 ✸ Big Sur Coast Highway

if you've never been to it before. The trick is locating unmarked Sycamore Canyon Road. Here's a tip: Sycamore Canyon Road is the only paved, ungated road west of Route 1 between the Big Sur post office and Pfeiffer Big Sur State Park. After you find the turnout, make a very sharp turn and follow the road for about 2 miles until it ends. Drive carefully—this is a narrow and winding road and is unsuitable for trailer traffic. From a large parking area at the end of the road, a short, well-marked path leads to the beach. Cliffs tower above this breathtaking stretch of sand, and a large arch-shaped rock formation just offshore makes for some dazzling sunsets.

Just a mile south of the US Forest Service Station in Pacific Valley and 14 miles north of the San Luis Obispo County line lies **Sand Dollar Beach**. From a large parking lot across Route 1 from Plaskett Creek Campground, a well-built stairway leads to a crescent-shaped beach that's protected from the wind by bluffs. Sand Dollar offers visitors the widest expanse of sand along the Big Sur Coast and, possibly, the mildest weather. Standing on the beach and looking northeast, towering 5,155-foot **Cone Peak** is visible. For an interesting side trip, visit **Jade Cove**, which is located 2 miles south of Sand Dollar Beach. Big Sur's south coast is famous for its jade reserves, and Jade Cove is a popular spot for beachcombers and rockhounds.

Scenic

The Big Sur Coast Highway affords you fantastic views of one of the nation's most scenic coastlines. (Keep in mind that the scenery can be overwhelming, and you may struggle to keep your eyes on the narrow, winding road.) At certain points along the Byway, the only way to get any closer to the Pacific is to get in it! Traveling Route 1 offers you ample opportunity for experiencing the mighty ocean pounding against the pristine coastline, with waves crashing against the rocks and cliffs. Scenic overlooks are plentiful along the Byway, providing you with breathtaking views from safe turnouts.

If the vast blue waters of the Pacific aren't enough for you, direct your eyes inland, taking in the beautiful coastal hills and mountains. The inland side delights your eyes with its cypress and redwood forests, impressing you with trees towering over the road. Other areas feature mountain meadows, ablaze in colorful wildflowers. Each season offers its own unique scenic experience. The spring months are a wonderful time to experience the Big Sur's deep green colors and colorful wildflowers that brighten the grassy hillsides. Autumn in Big Sur country brings with it new fall colors. The sycamores, cottonwoods, and maples display golden yellows and oranges, while the leaves of the poison oak turn a deep red. The winter months of December through March are the best time to spot a gray whale, migrating to and from the warm waters of Baja. Whenever the season, the Big Sur showcases nature at its best.

HIGHLIGHTS

The Big Sur Coast Highway runs along Route 1 from north of San Simeon to Carmel. If you're traveling the opposite direction, simply follow the list from the bottom up.

- **Ragged Point** marks the official entrance to the Big Sur Coast Highway. Ragged Point has incredible views in every direction and features a restaurant, gas station, and hotel.

- Not far after Ragged Point, the Byway enters **Los Padres National Forest.**

- Continuing North, the Byway travels past the **Southern Redwood Botanical Area,** and then the **Alder Creek Botanical Area.**

- **Lucia,** consisting of a restaurant and small motel, is the next major point of interest along the corridor.

- From Lucia, the Byway passes several state parks, including **Limekiln** and **Julia Pfeiffer Burns state parks.**

- Following the Julia Pfeiffer Burns State Park, the corridor soon enters the expansive Big Sur area. The **Big Sur** area consists of several inns, restaurants, and other shops scattered along the corridor.

- Another important point of interest near the Big Sur area is the **Point Sur State Historic Park,** home to the historic Point Sur Lighthouse.
- Historic **Bixby Bridge** lies farther north of Point Sur.
- From Bixby Bridge, the Byway continues north to its ending point in **Carmel.**

THINGS TO SEE AND DO

Driving along the Big Sur Coast Highway will certainly keep your senses engaged, but if you yearn to get out of the car and stretch your legs, or if you'd like to make a mini-vacation out of your trip, check out these attractions along the route.

BIXBY BRIDGE. The Bixby Bridge, completed in 1932, is a marvel of engineering and one of the ten highest single span bridges in the world. The bridge spans a large canyon along the Big Sur coastline. The weather conditions can have a noticeable impact on the bridge's appearance: clouds may partially hide it, or the sun may reflect off of the gleaming white structural supports. That quality, combined with the massive appearance of the bridge, brings countless people to photograph the bridge. **FREE**

CARMEL MISSION AND BASILICA. *3080 Rio Rd, Carmel (93923). Phone 831/624-1271. www.carmelmission.org.* The Carmel Mission, located on Rio Road off of Route 1, was the second of California's historical missions, built in 1771. At that time, Father Junipero Serra founded the Basilica of Mission San Carlos Borromeo de Carmelo, one of only two basilicas on the West Coast. It is considered the jewel of California missions, and it was Father Serra's favorite. He is buried near the altar. Mission San Carlos Borromeo de Carmelo has been a haven for artists and writers for over a century. Open Mon-Sat 9:30 am-4:30 pm, Sun 10:30 am-4:30 pm. **$**

JULIA PFEIFFER BURNS STATE PARK. *Big Sur Station #1, Big Sur (93920). Phone 831/667-2315. www.parks.ca.gov.* Julia Pfeiffer Burns State Park stretches from the Big Sur coastline into nearby 3,000-foot ridges. The park features redwood, tan oak, madrone, chaparral, and an 80-foot waterfall that drops from granite cliffs into the ocean from the Overlook Trail. A panoramic view of the ocean and miles of rugged coastline is available from the higher elevations along the trails east of Route 1. The park also has a 1,680-acre underwater reserve which protects a spectacular assortment of marine life. Special-use permits allow experienced scuba divers to explore the reserve. Seals, sea lions, and sea otters can be seen in the park's cove. Hikers can discover the park's backcountry via several trail systems. Open daily dawn-dusk. **$$**

MONTEREY BAY AQUARIUM. *886 Cannery Row, Monterey (93940). Phone 831/648-4888. www.mbayaq.org.* The Monterey Bay Aquarium contains more than a hundred galleries and exhibits, each re-creating some of the bay's many habitats. The world-class aquarium contains more than 6,500 live creatures, like jellyfish,

California

ROUTE 1 ❋ Big Sur Coast Highway

sharks, octopus, and giant ocean sunfish. Many exhibits allow the visitor to interact and even touch the sea creatures. The aquarium includes a towering three-story kelp forest, hands-on touch pools, a walk-through aviary, and the enchanting exhibit of playful sea otters. The outer Bay Wing features a depiction of life in the open ocean, while the "Mysteries of the Deep" exhibit offers a peek into the deepest of the undersea Monterey Canyon. Videos, special programs, and a host of hands-on activities bring the entire family closer to sea life than ever before. Open daily 9:30 am-6 pm Memorial Day-Labor Day; 10 am-6 pm the rest of the year; closed Dec 25. $$$$

POINT LOBOS STATE RESERVE. *Hwy 1, Carmel (93921). Phone 831/624-4909. pt-lobos.parks.state.ca.us.* Deriving its name from the offshore rocks at Punta de los Lobos Marinos (Point of the Sea Wolves) where the sound of the sea lions carries inland, the reserve has often been called the crown jewel of the State Park System. Point Lobos State Reserve offers outstanding recreational opportunities, such as sightseeing, photography, painting, nature study, picnicking, SCUBA diving, and running. In addition to the spectacular beauty, nearly every aspect of its resources is of scientific interest. You'll see rare plant communities, endangered archeological sites, unique geological formations, and incredibly rich flora and fauna of both land and sea. The Reserve contains headlands, coves, and rolling meadows. The offshore area forms one of the richest underwater habitats in the world, popular with divers. Wildlife includes seals, sea lions, sea otters, and migrating gray whales (from December to May). Thousands of seabirds also make the reserve their home. Hiking trails follow the shoreline and lead to hidden coves. The area used to be the home of a turn-of-the-century whaling and abalone industry. A small cabin from that era still remains on Whaler's Cove, near Carmel. Open 9 am-5 pm; longer hours in the summer. $$

POINT SUR STATE HISTORIC PARK. *On Rte 1, 19 miles S of Carmel and Monterey and 1/4 mile N of Point Sur Naval Facility. Phone 831/625-4419. www.pointsur.org.* Point Sur State Historic Park is the home of the historic Point Sur Light Station and an active US Coast Guard light station. The park sits 361 feet above the surf on a large volcanic rock. Point Sur has been a navigational landmark throughout history, and the nearby coastline has been the site of several notable shipwrecks, both before and after the installation of the lighthouse. Point Sur is on the National Register of Historic Places, and is a California State Historic Landmark. From the highway you can see the majestic stone buildings of the Point Sur Light Station that have been part of the Big Sur coast for almost 100 years. Lighthouses and lightships were an important part of coastal navigation. The facilities were established for the safety of seagoing vessels moving up and down the Big Sur coast. First lit on August 1, 1889, it has remained in continuous operation. Four lighthouse keepers and their families lived at the site until 1974, when the light station was automated. Call for specific hours and tour times. Tours. $

PLACES TO STAY

If you choose to include an overnight stay in your trip along this All-American Road, Mobil Travel Guide recommends the following lodgings.

Big Sur

★★★★ **POST RANCH INN.** *Rte 1, Big Sur (93920). Phone 831/667-2200; toll-free 800/527-2200. www.postranchinn.com.* Perched on the tip of a cliff overlooking the dramatic coastline of Big Sur, this inn brings new meaning to living on the edge. This unique hideaway offers an experience far from the ordinary. Designed to live in harmony with the majestic natural setting, the architecture resembles a collection of sophisticated treehouses. Clean lines and simple interiors create an uncluttered appearance and state of mind. Floor-to-ceiling windows open to awe-inspiring views and enhance the subtle beauty of the accommodations, while two-sided fireplaces are the ultimate luxury, allowing guests to enjoy the warm glow from the bed or the bath. No televisions or alarm clocks disrupt the gentle rhythm of this place, where yoga and tai chi reawaken the soul and the spa soothes the spirit. The Sierra Mar restaurant (see) is a triumph of California cuisine, and the extensive wine list is a perfect accompaniment to the superb dishes. 30 rooms, 2 story. Adults only. Complimentary continental breakfast. Check-out 1 pm, check-in 4 pm. TV; cable (premium). Fireplaces. Restaurant. In-house fitness room; spa, massage. Heated outdoor pool, whirlpool. Free wine tasting Sat. Mountain views. $$$$

★★★ **VENTANA INN & SPA.** *Rte 1, Big Sur (93920). Phone 831/667-2331; toll-free 800/628-6500. www.ventanainn.com.* The views are breathtaking at this inn overlooking the Pacific's dramatic cliffs. All rooms and suites are divided between 12 buildings tucked into the 240-acre landscape. The Allegria Spa reconnects guests with nature and offers classes and guided hikes. 60 rooms, 1-2 story. Complimentary continental breakfast; afternoon refreshments. Check-out noon, check-in 4 pm. TV, VCR available. In-room modem link. Fireplaces. Refrigerators, wet bars; some whirlpools. Balconies. In-house fitness room, spa, massage, sauna. Heated outdoor pool, whirlpool. Dining room. Bar. Concierge. Hiking. Horseback riding. Sun deck. $$$$

Carmel

★★ **CANDLE LIGHT INN.** *San Carlos, between 4th and 5th aves, Carmel (93921). Phone 831/624-6451; toll-free 800/433-4732. www.ibts-candlelight.com.* 20 rooms, 4 kitchen units, 2 story. No A/C. June-Oct weekends 2-day minimum. Complimentary continental breakfast. Check-out noon. TV. Whirlpool. Business services available. Refrigerators; some fireplaces; microwaves available. Totally nonsmoking. $

★★★ **CARRIAGE HOUSE INN.** *Junipero between 7th and 8th aves, Carmel (93921). Phone 831/625-2585; toll-free 800/433-4732. www.ibts-carriagehouse.com.* 13 rooms, 2 story. No A/C. Weekends 2-day minimum. Complimentary continental breakfast; evening refreshments. Check-out noon, check-in 3 pm. TV; cable (premium), VCR (movies). In-room modem link. Refrigerators, wet bars, fireplaces; some in-room whirlpools. Antique furnishings. Totally nonsmoking. $$

★ **LOBOS LODGE.** *Ocean Ave and Monte Verde St, Carmel (93921). Phone 831/624-3874. www.loboslodge.com.* 28 rooms, 1-3 story. Complimentary continental breakfast. Check-out noon. TV; cable (premium). In-room modem link. Fireplaces. Beach four blocks. $

★★ **NORMANDY INN.** *124 E Bearskin Rd, Carmel (93921). Phone 831/624-3825; toll-free 800/843-3825. www.normandyinncarmel.com.* 41 rooms, 2 story. Complimentary continental breakfast. Check-out 11 am, check-in 3 pm. TV. Refrigerators available. Heated pool. $

★★★★ **QUAIL LODGE RESORT AND GOLF COURSE.** *8205 Valley Greens Dr, Carmel (93923). Phone 831/624-2888; toll-free 888/828-8787. www.quaillodge.com.* Quail Lodge Resort and Golf Club is a magnet for active travelers seeking the total resort experience. Set on 850 acres on the sunny side of the Carmel Valley, the grounds are a lovely mix of rolling hills, lakes, and gardens. It is no wonder that golf is a favorite pursuit here, with a fantastic 18-hole course designed by Robert Muir-Graves and a 7-acre

California

ROUTE 1 ✳ Big Sur Coast Highway

driving range. The Carmel River gently snakes along the course, making it a particularly scenic round. Four tennis courts and two outdoor pools tempt others, while the spa alleviates aches and pains with its wonderful assortment of facials, massages, and hydrotherapy with Vichy showers. The rooms and suites are attractively appointed and cradle guests in comfort. All preferences are suited at the three restaurants, and The Covey stands out for its charming lakeside setting, gourmet cuisine, and extensive wine list. 97 units, 2 story. Summer weekends 2-day minimum; golf plan Sun-Thurs. Resort fee $15 per day. Complimentary continental breakfast. Check-out noon. TV; cable (premium), VCR available. In-room modem link. Some fireplaces. Pool, whirlpool, poolside service. Restaurants, bars; entertainment. Room service. In-house fitness room, spa, massage, steam room. Tennis. 18-hole golf, greens fee $140-$175. Hiking, bicycling. Airport transportation. Concierge. $$$

Monterey

★★★ **DOUBLETREE HOTEL.** *2 Portola Plz, Monterey (93940). Phone 831/649-4511; toll-free 800/222-8733. www.doubletree.com.* This hotel is a short drive from Pebble Beach, great golf courses, fine restaurants, and many shops and galleries. 380 rooms, 10 suites, 7 story. No A/C. Check-out noon, check-in 3 pm. TV; cable (premium). In-room modem link. Restaurant, bar. Room service. Babysitting services available. In-house fitness room, massage, steam room. Outdoor pool, whirlpool. Valet, self-parking. Business center. Concierge. $$

★★★ **HOTEL PACIFIC.** *300 Pacific St, Monterey (93940). Phone 831/373-5700; toll-free 800/554-5542. www.hotelpacific.com.* Enjoy modern interiors, fountains, and gardens, all done in a Spanish-style motif. 105 rooms, 2-3 story. Complimentary continental breakfast, evening refreshments. Check-out noon, check-in 4 pm. TV; cable (premium), VCR (movies). Refrigerators, fireplaces, wet bars. Whirlpool. Valet parking. Concierge. Totally nonsmoking. $$

★★★ **JABBERWOCK BED AND BREAKFAST.** *598 Laine St, Monterey (93940). Phone 831/372-4777; toll-free 888/428-7253. www.jabberwockinn.com.* This quiet bed-and-breakfast is only four blocks from Cannery Row, six blocks from the aquarium, and a 20-minute walk from Fisherman's Wharf. 7 rooms, 2 share bath, 3 story. No A/C. No room phones. Closed Dec 24-25. Complimentary breakfast. Check-out noon, check-in 3 pm. Some fireplaces. Whirlpool. 1/2-acre gardens; waterfalls. Former convent. Totally nonsmoking. $$

★★★ **OLD MONTEREY INN.** *500 Martin St, Monterey (93940). Phone 831/375-8284; toll-free 800/350-2344. www.oldmontereyinn.com.* Perfect for golfers visiting nearby courses or those wanting a romantic escape, this historic inn is set amidst striking gardens. Extra in-room comforts abound with featherbeds, down comforters, terry robes, and candles. A pleasant breakfast and sunset wine hour make this a first-rate escape. 10 rooms. No A/C. Complimentary continental breakfast. Check-out noon, check-in 3 pm. TV; cable (premium), VCR (movies). In-room modem link. Many fireplaces. Totally nonsmoking. $$$

★★ **SAND DOLLAR INN.** *755 Abrego St, Monterey (93940). Phone 831/372-7551; toll-free 800/982-1986. www.sanddollarinn.com.* 63 rooms, 3 story. Check-out noon, check-in 3 pm. Complimentary continental breakfast. TV; cable (premium). In-room modem link. Laundry services. Outdoor pool, whirlpool. $

PLACES TO EAT

A long day of driving is sure to make you hungry. At the end of your journey, take a table at one of the following restaurants.

Big Sur

★★★★ **CIELO BIG SUR.** *Rte 1, Big Sur (93920). Phone 831/667-4242; toll-free 800/628-6500. www.ventanainn.com/dining/.* Cielo is a magical place. Set on the cliffs of Route 1, the restaurant affords breathtaking mountain views and heart-stopping peeks at the white-capped, deep-blue ocean below. With nature's bounty on such magnificent display, outdoor dining on the wide, rustic, elegant patio is the way to go. If seats outside aren't available, the dining room is warm and cozy, with tall windows, a large stone fireplace, wood-beamed ceilings, and a bird's-eye view of the sparkling new exhibition kitchen, where you'll witness pristine California ingredients being transformed into sumptuous plates of new American fare. California, Mediterranean menu. Lunch, dinner. Bar. Outdoor seating (lunch). Totally nonsmoking. $$$
D

★★ **NEPENTHE.** *Rte 1, Big Sur (93920). Phone 831/667-2345. www.nepenthebigsur.com.* American, California menu. Lunch, dinner. Bar. No A/C. Outdoor seating. Forty-mile view of the Pacific coastline. Family-owned. $$$
D

★★★★ **SIERRA MAR RESTAURANT.** *Rte 1, Big Sur (93920). Phone 831/667-2800. www.postranchinn.com.* Perched high over the Pacific Ocean on the Pacific Coast Highway is this highly acclaimed restaurant, an elegant but comfortable space appointed with wood and chrome and, of course, surrounded by magnificent views of cliffs, mountains, and the wide ocean below. It's tough to compete with such incredible natural beauty, but the food at Sierra Mar does a winning job of it. Innovative and modern but grounded in precise French technique, the four-course prix fixe menu changes daily and utilizes seasonal organic products. You'll find seafood, lamb, and beef alongside luxurious ingredients like oysters, truffles, foie gras, and caviar. The restaurant has one of the most extensive wine cellars in North America, giving you many options for glass-clinking toasts. Eclectic California cuisine. Menu changes daily. Lunch, dinner. Bar. Outdoor seating (lunch). Totally nonsmoking. $$$
D

Carmel

★★★ **ABALONETTI SEAFOOD TRATTORIA.** *57 Fisherman's Wharf, Carmel (93921). Phone 831/373-1851. www.restauranteur.com/abalonetti/.* Italian, seafood menu. Closed Dec 25. Lunch, dinner. Bar. No A/C. Children's menu. Outdoor seating. Reservations accepted. Exhibition kitchen. Harbor view. Totally nonsmoking. $$
D

★★★ **ANTON AND MICHEL.** *Mission St, Carmel (93921). Phone 831/624-2406; toll-free 866/244-0645. www.carmelsbest.com/antonmichel/.* Continental menu. Closed the first week of Jan. Lunch, dinner. Bar. Reservations accepted. Garden view from the main dining room. Totally nonsmoking. $$$
D

★★★ **CASANOVA.** *5th Ave and Mission, Carmel (93921). Phone 831/625-0501. www.casanovarestaurant.com.* Southern French, northern Italian menu. Closed Dec 25. Lunch, dinner, Sun brunch. Bar. No A/C. Reservations accepted. Outdoor seating. Totally nonsmoking. $$$
D

California

ROUTE 1 ❋ Big Sur Coast Highway

★ **COTTAGE RESTAURANT.** *Lincoln St, Carmel (93921). Phone 831/625-6260. www.cottagerestaurant.com.* American menu. Closed Dec 25. Breakfast, lunch, dinner (Thurs-Sat only). No A/C. Children's menu. Casual attire. Totally nonsmoking. **$$**
D

★★ **FLYING FISH GRILL.** *Carmel Plz, Carmel (93921). Phone 831/625-1962.* Seafood menu. Closed Tues; July 4, Thanksgiving, Dec 25. Dinner. Reservations accepted. Pacific Rim décor; fish motif includes artwork, papier mâché flying fish decorations. **$$**

★★ **MISSION RANCH.** *26270 Dolores, Carmel (93923). Phone 831/625-9040; toll-free 800/538-8221. www.missionranchcarmel.com.* American menu. Closed Dec 25. Dinner, Sun brunch. Bar. Piano. Children's menu. Casual attire. Outdoor seating. Totally nonsmoking. **$$$**
D

★★ **ROCKY POINT.** *Hwy 1, Carmel (93922). Phone 831/624-2933. www.rocky-point.com.* American, seafood, steak menu. Breakfast, lunch, dinner. Bar. Casual attire. Spectacular views from every table with outdoor seating available. A famous point for whale-watching. Totally nonsmoking. **$$**

Monterey

★★★ **CIBO RISTORANTE ITALIANO.** *301 Alvarado St, Monterey (93940). Phone 831/649-8151. www.cibo.com.* This simple yet elegant California-style restaurant offers a perfect setting for innovative interpretations of classical Sicilian cooking. Considered one of the best places for live jazz on Monterey Bay, Cibo is located in the heart of historic downtown. Italian menu. Closed Thanksgiving, Dec 25. Dinner. Bar; entertainment. Modern Italian décor. Totally nonsmoking. **$$$**
D

★★★ **FRESH CREAM.** *99 Pacific St, Bldg 100 C, Monterey (93940). Phone 831/375-9798. www.freshcream.com.* This restaurant overlooks Monterey Harbor. Stunning views, elegant décor, and impeccable service set the mood for romantic dining. French menu. Closed Easter, Dec 25. Dinner. Reservations accepted; required weekends. Bar. Five dining rooms, all with harbor views. Totally nonsmoking. **$$$**
D

★★ **MONTRIO BISTRO.** *414 Calle Principal, Monterey (93940). Phone 831/648-8880. www.montrio.com.* Mediterranean menu. Closed July 4, Thanksgiving, Dec 25. Lunch (except Sun), dinner. Bar. Children's menu. Reservations accepted. Eclectic décor in a former firehouse (1910); the open kitchen features wood-burning rotisserie. Totally nonsmoking. **$$**
D

★★ **RAPPA'S SEAFOOD.** *101 Fisherman's Wharf, Monterey (93940). Phone 831/372-7562. www.rappas.com.* Seafood menu. Closed Thanksgiving, Dec 25. Bar. Lunch, dinner. Casual dining. Scenic view of the bay. Family-owned. Totally nonsmoking. **$$$**

★★★ **TARPY'S ROADHOUSE.** *2999 Monterey-Salinas Hwy, Monterey (93940). Phone 831/647-1444. www.tarpys.com.* American country menu. Closed July 4, Thanksgiving, Dec 25. Lunch, dinner, Sun brunch. Bar. Children's menu. Outdoor seating. Reservations accepted. Located in a historic country stone house; the dining area is a former wine-tasting room. Fireplaces. **$$$**
D

Death Valley Scenic Byway
✳ CALIFORNIA

Quick Facts

LENGTH: 81.5 miles.

TIME TO ALLOW: 3 hours.

BEST TIME TO DRIVE: Winter and spring. Spring is the high season.

BYWAY TRAVEL INFORMATION: Byway local Web site: www.nps.gov/deva.

SPECIAL CONSIDERATIONS: Be aware of extreme heat, lack of water, and occasional flash floods. Gas is available at Panamint Springs, Stovepipe Wells, and Furnace Creek.

RESTRICTIONS: Route 190 is fully paved and open year-round. Road conditions are posted at Furnace Creek and Stovepipe Wells and are available from the park's Web site. Access to Death Valley National Park can be limited by winter snowstorms, when traveling from the west over the Sierra Nevada in California on Routes 108 and 120 and on Route 160 from Las Vegas to the east in Nevada. During the year, occasional flash flooding can occur and wash out parts of the roads in the park. Death Valley National Park charges an entrance fee.

BICYCLE/PEDESTRIAN FACILITIES: Death Valley Scenic Byway accommodates bicycles.

Death Valley National Park contains the hottest, driest, lowest point in North America. It has 3.3 million acres of spectacular desert scenery, interesting and rare desert wildlife, complex geology, undisturbed wilderness, and sites of historical and cultural interest.

Located in one of the most remote parts of California, travelers from all over the world use the Death Valley Scenic Byway (Route 190) as the gateway to Death Valley. International visitors see Death Valley as part of the grand tour of California—over 75 percent of the summer visitors in this area come from abroad. Not only does this destination attract tourists from everywhere; scientists and researchers also come to study and explore the park's unique resources.

THE BYWAY STORY

The Death Valley Scenic Byway tells archaeological, historical, natural, recreational, and scenic stories that make it a unique and treasured Byway.

Archaeological

Archaeologists have found traces of distinct prehistoric cultures in Death Valley National Park. The first known inhabitants of Death Valley lived there some 7,000 years ago and were known as the Nevares Spring Culture. After another 6,000 years and many climatic changes, a new group of people entered the valley. This group came to be known as the Desert Shoshone and has been in the valley ever since.

California

❋ Death Valley Scenic Byway

The Desert Shoshone were distinguished by their production of superior arrowheads, as well as their skills to make pottery. Their ingenuity led to constructing pits for storing mesquite beans, which were later ground and processed for the seed. The Desert Shoshone moved about the Death Valley region, hunting sheep, deer, and rabbits when the animals were abundant. During other seasons, the people harvested plants and seeds. The Desert Shoshone had this wilderness to themselves until 1849, when emigrants from the east began to arrive.

Historical

For centuries, the native Desert Shoshone were the lone inhabitants of the Death Valley wilderness. Starting in 1849, that all changed with the arrival of various waves of emigrants from the east. Early pioneers were soon followed by the '49ers, headed for the California gold fields. Many stayed to mine for other minerals in the Death Valley area, but eventually, even these inhabitants went elsewhere, leaving their mines and towns to waste away.

A tale of the valley's history must include one brief but important period that started when some of the '49ers, who were heading for the California gold fields, took an ill-advised detour through Death Valley. This began the boom-and-bust era of Death Valley, a period that involved more bust than boom. Borax, the "white gold of the desert," was the only significant "gold" found in Death Valley.

Eventually, the prospectors lost hope of finding gold in the desert. Likewise, the miners eventually deserted their borax mines, leaving behind relics and deserted towns. In the 1870s, for example, Darwin was a thriving mining town. Now, the historical city has but a few residences, a post office, and a phone booth. Rhyolite, once the largest town in the Death Valley area during the mining boom, is now home to a train depot, a jail, a two-story schoolhouse, the ruins of a three-story bank building, and a house built completely of bottles. Skidoo was one of the last gold mining camps in Death Valley. This ghost town is a marvel of mining engineering that existed from 1906 to 1922. Additionally, Twenty Mule Team Canyon displays an amazing number of old prospector tunnels.

Natural

Death Valley Scenic Byway, from the west entrance of Death Valley National Park to the east edge of the park, is one of the most unique and dramatic routes in the western United States. The nation's largest park unit outside of Alaska, Death Valley covers more than 3.3 million acres. Because of the faulting in Death Valley, the vertical rise from the lowest point to the top of Telescope Peak is one of the greatest (11,049 feet) in the United States. Traveling on Route 190 from the west end of the park from Towne Pass to some 282 feet below sea level (the lowest spot in North America), this trip is highlighted by rugged natural beauty. You're afforded 80-mile views that include bare mountain slopes towering above huge alluvial fans. Other highlights along the Byway are salt-encrusted salinas created by evaporated water basins that accumulate salts, borates, and other minerals. Wind-swept sands across the valley floor form ever-changing patterns. Desert varnish, shiny black iron, and manganese oxide, which cover the cobbles, make an interesting mosaic of pavement.

With an average of 1 1/2 inches of rain a year and average high temperatures nearing 120 degrees during the summer, this region is one of the driest and hottest environments in the Western hemisphere. Passing from the lowest point to the highest summit, you traverse four major plant zones, each determined by climate and elevation. The diversity of plants along this drive ranges from Piñon pine and juniper in the upper elevations to the valley's mesquite, desert holly, and cacti. This complex ecosystem includes kangaroo rats, sidewinder rattlesnakes, burrowing owls, and bighorn sheep. What fascinates many travelers is how plants and animals can survive in this

see page A10 for color map

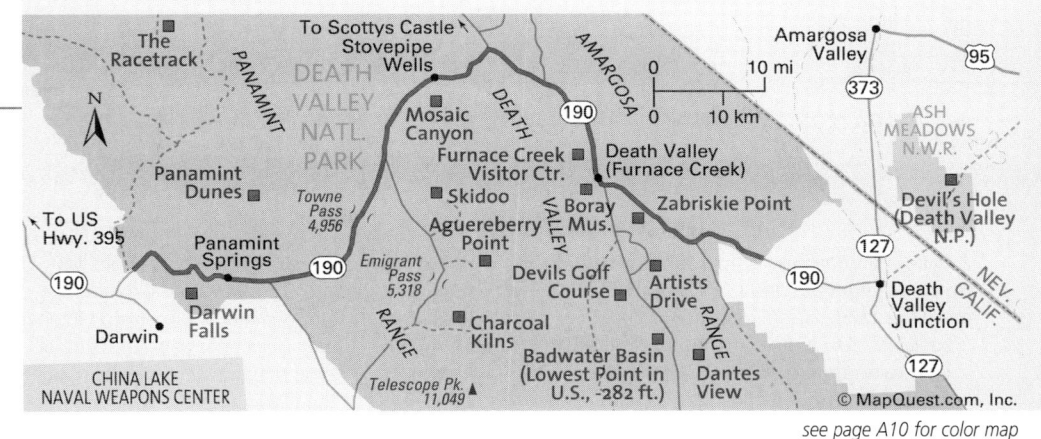

harsh environment. Thousands of years of adaptation in the plant and animal species make this drive a fascinating experience.

Recreational

One of the best ways to discover Death Valley National Park is to get out of the car and take a hike. Due to the extreme elevation changes and climate, however, many of the hikes within Death Valley may be too difficult for the average visitor, but several very easy to moderate hikes are accessible to just about everyone. When you do go for a hike, remember to drink 2 quarts of water. Sunglasses and a hat will help, too, because the sun often glares throughout the park. Stop by the Death Valley Visitor Center in Furnace Creek for specifics on hikes; park rangers in the office will help you choose appropriate hikes to suit your abilities.

Scenic

Death Valley Scenic Byway is one of the most unique and dynamic routes in the western US. Death Valley National Park's scenic diversity includes deep rugged canyons, sand dunes, and, surprisingly, even fragile wetlands. The desert is also surrounded by high rising mountain ranges, adding dramatic contrast to the scenic variety.

Toward the western end of the Death Valley Scenic Byway, you climb to the turnoff for Father Crowley Point, located at the top of the Argus Mountain Range. The short drive to this observation point provides spectacular views overlooking the Panamint Valley and the complex geology of the Panamint Mountain Range. This observation point is the perfect location to view the setting sun on Telescope Peak. You can also peer down into Rainbow Canyon, a steep and colorful canyon draining into the Panamint Valley.

HIGHLIGHTS

Consider taking this scenic tour of Death Valley, beginning in the early morning:

- Enter **Death Valley National Park** on Route 190 about 3 miles northeast of **Death Valley Junction.** Remember that there is a $10 entrance fee into the park, but the pass is good for an entire week.

- Traveling north along Route 190, you'll notice that you're following along the **Furnace Creek Wash.** There may or may not be any water, but watch for thunderstorms—water rises fast in this area!

- When you stop at **Zabriskie Point,** about 8 miles past the entrance, you'll enter the heart of Death Valley—**Furnace Creek.** Spend time here discovering the many interpretive trails and museums. This area is full of history and is a recommended base camp for visiting Death Valley. Visitor services are sparse in the park, so stock up while you're here. Stop at the **Furnace Creek Visitor Center** to orient yourself to the park and the area around you.

- After spending the heat of the day relaxing and learning indoors, take an afternoon drive farther north along Route 190 to Harmony Borax Works and Salt Creek. Catch the sunset near the sand dunes, and then back into Furnace Creek or on to **Stovepipe Wells Village,** where a hotel and campground are available.

45

California

✺ Death Valley Scenic Byway

- Take a day to explore the southern end of the park, including Badwater Devil's Golf Course, Artist's Drive, and Gold Canyon. In the summer, take a detour through Emigrant Canyon and on up the road to see the **Charcoal Kilns**. Parts of the roads to these sites are not paved, so a four-wheel-drive, high-clearance vehicle is recommended. Or you can head north to **Scotty's Castle** for a great tour. After visiting the castle, head toward Beatty, Nevada, for a tour of **Rhyolite Ghost Town**.
- As you wind up your tour, continue touring the sites of Death Valley National Park, head to Las Vegas, Nevada, or continue west to the Eastern Sierra State Scenic Byway (California Route 395) that connects to the Tioga Road/Big Oak Flat Road and Yosemite National Park.

THINGS TO SEE AND DO

Driving along the Death Valley Scenic Byway will certainly keep your senses engaged, but if you yearn to get out of the car and stretch your legs, or if you'd like to make a mini-vacation out of your trip, check out these attractions along the route.

✪ DEATH VALLEY NATIONAL PARK.

Death Valley National Park (92328). Phone 760/786-2331. www.nps.gov/deva/. Here, approximately 300 miles northeast of Los Angeles, are more than 5,200 square miles of rugged desert, peaks, and depressions—an unusual and colorful geography. The park is one vast geological museum, revealing secrets of ages gone by. Millions of years ago, this was part of the Pacific Ocean; violent uplifts of the earth occurred, creating mountains and then ranges and draining water to the west. Today, 200 square miles of the valley are at or below sea level. The lowest point on the continent (282 feet below sea level) is here; Telescope Peak, at 11,049 feet, towers directly above it. The valley itself is about 140 miles long and 4 to 16 miles wide. The average rainfall is less than 2 inches a year. From October to May, the climate is very pleasant. In summer, it's extremely hot; a maximum temperature of 134 degrees in the shade has been recorded. If considered all together, this is the lowest, hottest, and driest area in North America.

The visitor center at Furnace Creek is open daily. Primitive camping is available, as are guided walks, evening programs, and talks (November–April). **Note:** Venturing off paved roads in this area in the summer months can be very dangerous. Obey all National Park Service signs and regulations. Make sure that your vehicle has plenty of gas and oil. Carry water when you explore this park, especially in hot weather. $$

- **Badwater:** At 279 feet below sea level, this is near the lowest spot on the North American continent; look for the sea level sign.
- **Charcoal Kilns:** Beehive-shaped stone structures formerly used to make charcoal for nearby mines are a sight to see. Note that the last mile of the access road is unpaved.
- **Dante's View:** This area (at 5,475 feet) offers a view of Death Valley, with a steep drop to 279 feet below sea level at Badwater.

- **Devil's Golf Course:** Vast beds of rugged salt crystals. Greens fee $40, pro, driving range.
- **Golden Canyon:** Offers a display of color ranging from deep red to rich gold. A 1-mile trail provides access.
- **Natural Bridge:** A bridge spanning a rugged canyon in the Black Mountains; 1-mile walking trail.
- **Rhyolite Ghost Town:** www.nps.gov/deva/rhyolite.htm. This was the largest town in the mining history of Death Valley in the early 1900s, when 5,000 to 10,000 people lived here. The town bloomed from 1905 to 1910; by 1911, it was a ghost town. One structure still left standing from that era is the bottle house, constructed of between 12,000 and 50,000 beer and liquor bottles, depending on who does the estimating.
- **Sand Dunes:** Sand blown by the wind into dunes 5 to 100 feet high.
- **Scotty's Castle:** www.nps.gov/deva/scottys1.htm. A desert mansion (circa 1922-1931), designed and built to be viewed as a work of art as well as a house. The furnishings are typical of the period; many were especially designed and hand-crafted for this house. Costumed interpreters lead living-history tours; tickets are sold on a first-come, first-served basis and often sell out. $$
- **Telescope Peak:** The highest point in the Panamint Range (11,049 feet). A 14-mile round-trip hiking trail leads to the peak; it's inaccessible in the winter months.
- **Ubehebe Crater:** A colorful crater left by a volcanic steam explosion.
- **Visitor Center at Furnace Creek:** Stop here before continuing on for an orientation film, day-trip suggestions, help in organizing sightseeing routes, and important information about camping areas and road conditions.
- **Zabriskie Point:** View of Death Valley and the Panamint Range from the rugged badlands of the Black Mountains.

PLACES TO STAY

If you choose to include an overnight stay in your trip along this Byway, Mobil Travel Guide recommends the following lodgings.

★★ **FURNACE CREEK INN.** *Hwy 190, Death Valley National Park, Furnace Creek (92328). Phone 760/786-2345; toll-free 800/236-7916. www.furnacecreekresort.com.* This elegant and charming resort features the lowest golf course in the world. 66 rooms, 4 story. Check-out noon. TV. Private patios, balconies. Many refrigerators. Restaurant, bar. In-house fitness room, sauna. Natural thermal spring water pool, poolside service. Golf privileges. Lighted tennis. Lawn games. Concierge. 1920s and 1930s décor; native stone in many areas. $

★★★ **FURNACE CREEK RANCH.** *Hwy 190, Death Valley National Park, Furnace Creek (92328). Phone 760/786-2345; toll-free 800/236-7916. www.furnacecreekresort.com.* 224 rooms, 1-2 story. Check-out noon, check-in 4 pm. TV. Natural thermal spring water pool. Playground. Dining rooms. Bar. Grocery. Coin laundry. Package store. Lighted tennis. Golf, greens fee $40, pro, driving range. Volleyball, basketball courts. Museum. Some refrigerators. $

★ **STOVEPIPE WELLS VILLAGE.** *Hwy 190, Death Valley National Park, Furnace Creek (92328). Phone 760/786-2387. www.stovepipewells.com.* 83 rooms, 5 buildings. No room phones. Pet accepted; $20 refundable. Check-out 11 am. Heated pool. Restaurant, bar. Landing strip. Panoramic view of the mountains, desert, and dunes. ¢

California

✻ *Death Valley Scenic Byway*

★★★ **CARRIAGE INN.** *901 N China Lake Blvd, Ridgecrest (93555). Phone 760/446-7910; toll-free 800/772-8527. www.carriageinn.biz.* 162 rooms, 1 story. TV; cable (premium). In-room modem link. Restaurants, bar. Offers a mix of luxury suites and poolside cabanas in a full-service hotel environment. $$

★★ **HERITAGE INN & SUITES.** *1050 N Norma St, Ridgecrest (93555). Phone 760/446-6543; toll-free 800/843-0693.* 169 rooms, 2 story. TV. Restaurant. Pool. Business center. Large, well-appointed hotel geared toward business travelers and tourists. $$

PLACES TO EAT

A long day of driving is sure to make you hungry. At the end of your journey, take a table at one of the following restaurants.

★ **THE 19TH HOLE.** *Hwy 190, Death Valley National Park, Furnace Creek (92328). Phone 760/786-2345. www.furnacecreekresort.com.* American menu. Lunch, dinner. Located on a site overlooking the world's lowest golf course, this establishment also offers drive-through service for golf carts. $

★★★ **INN DINING ROOM.** *Hwy 190, Death Valley National Park, Furnace Creek (92328). Phone 760/786-2361. www.furnacecreekresort.com.* Continental menu. Breakfast, lunch (Oct-May only), dinner. Bar. Own baking. Valet parking. Jacket required. 1930s décor; beamed ceilings. Totally nonsmoking. $$$
D

★ **CHARLIE'S PUB & GRILL.** *901 N China Lake Blvd, Ridgecrest (93555). Phone 800/772-8527. www.carriageinn.biz.* American menu. Lunch, dinner. Serving family-style food in a unique décor of aircrew memorabilia that was donated from squadrons around the world. $

★ **FARRIS RESTAURANT.** *1050 N Norma St, Ridgecrest (93555). Phone 800/843-0693.* American menu. Lunch, dinner. A favorite dining spot of locals, the Farris Restaurant offers regional American cuisine in a comfortable atmosphere. $

San Luis Obispo North Coast Byway
ROUTE 1 ✺ CALIFORNIA
AN ALL-AMERICAN ROAD
A continuation of the Big Sur Coast Highway.

Quick Facts

LENGTH: 57 miles.

TIME TO ALLOW: 2 hours or more.

BEST TIME TO DRIVE: Year-round.

SPECIAL CONSIDERATIONS: Temporary seasonal closures are expected each year north of San Luis Obispo County. These closures occur most often along the rugged Big Sur Coast during heavy rainfall months.

BICYCLE/PEDESTRIAN FACILITIES: The Byway corridor offers incredible opportunities for hiking and bicycling; many cyclists even ride the entire stretch of Route 1 between San Luis Obispo and Monterey. Bike lanes exist from the city of San Luis Obispo to Hearst Castle, but in many areas of the Byway, bike lanes and shoulders are absent. Trails along portions of the Byway allow you to stroll leisurely and enjoy the great scenery and sunset views the Byway offers.

Route 1 in north San Luis Obispo County winds past and through some of the finest views in the western United States. The Byway blends the rural beauty associated with much of Route 1 in the northern portion of the state with the convenience and amenities found in the more heavily populated southern sections of California.

Whether you're taking your first trip on the Byway or you're an adventuring local making one of many repeat visits, this stretch of Route 1 is sure to enrich your spirit and engage your imagination. Navigating along this coastal Byway will surely reconnect your soul to natural and historical treasures that lurk within sight and close proximity.

THE BYWAY STORY

The San Luis Obispo North Coast Byway tells historical, natural, recreational, and scenic stories that make it a unique and treasured Byway.

Historical

From historical points in the city of San Luis Obispo to Hearst Castle in San Simeon, the San Luis Obispo North Coast Scenic Byway is rich in history.

The city of San Luis Obispo has its beginnings in the 1772 founding of the Mission San Luis Obispo de Tolosa by Father Junípero Serra; it was named for the Franciscan saint known as Louis, Bishop of Toulouse (France). Built on a knoll beside a sparkling creek, the mission became the hub of a growing settlement, serving as the center of both the community and the county. Mission San Luis Obispo is considered by many to be the most beautiful of all California missions.

California

ROUTE 1 ❋ San Luis Obispo North Coast Byway

During the 1880s, the Southern Pacific Railroad built a railroad south from San Jose. After a five-year delay, the railroad came to San Luis Obispo in 1894. Construction of the railroad helped bring both industry and variety to the small community and changed the face of the city. Remnants of the historical railroad system remain at the Ramona Railroad Depot and the San Luis Obispo Railroad Museum. The museum collects, restores, displays, and operates historic railroad equipment.

Hearst Castle, a California State Historical Monument, is just off of the Byway, north of Cambria. The castle, a living monument to the area's early 20th-century history, was built by publisher William Randolph Hearst, who entertained the rich and famous here. He intended it to be an elaborate getaway, complete with fine art and architecture. This historic treasure now provides a look into the windows of the past; it one of the most heavily visited facilities in the California State Park System.

Natural
The San Luis Obispo North Coast Byway's prominent resource is the ocean, including its sea life and nationally recognized bays: Morro Bay, Morro Estuary, and Monterey Bay. The bays and ocean along the route often afford travelers views of otters, seals, sea lions, and whales. Morro Estuary serves a critical environmental function of the Pacific Coast by supporting many species of migratory birds protected by international treaties.

One of the most remarkable recent activities along this stretch of Route 1 is the establishment of breeding colonies of elephant seals near Piedras Blancas Point. As you drive, elephant seal colonies are easily viewable from the Byway. In addition, the California Department of Transportation, working closely with Hearst Ranch Corporation, has provided excellent vista points and informational kiosks about the seals, which are the largest of all pinnipeds and can exceed 2 tons in weight and 10 feet in length. Like many marine mammals, elephant seals were hunted to near extinction in the 19th century and, until recently, the huge seals lived in isolated areas far from humans. Then, in 1990, they started colonizing the unspoiled beaches and coves just south of Point Piedras Blancas.

The San Luis Obispo North Coast Byway also bisects lush valleys and rural farmland. The Byway skirts the Morros Peaks and the Santa Lucia coastal mountain range and goes through the state's southernmost native Monterey pine forest. Equally important is the fertile land of the area, a significant natural resource for farming, which is one of the important industries of central and northern California.

Recreational
The San Luis Obispo corridor is blessed with pristine opportunities for outdoor recreation. Visitors may hike, cycle, surf, ride horses, watch birds, wind surf, hang glide, kayak, and fly kites, among many other activities. The excellent climate of the area allows for year-round recreation.

The Byway's close proximity to countless cycling routes makes it a desirable destination for cyclists. The highway itself generally has generous shoulders and makes for a great bike ride, allowing you to move along at a pace that gives you more time to take in the beauty of the route.

Perhaps the best way to take in the immense scenic opportunities of the Byway is to hike or ride horses right along the coastline. Coastal access adjacent to the southern boundary of the Monterey Bay National Marine Sanctuary, for example, gives you the opportunity to experience the magnificence of the Pacific Ocean. The area also offers horse enthusiasts the opportunity to explore miles of coastline along the Byway. You can bring your own horses or utilize one of the local outfitters who rent horses for rides along the Byway.

The Harmony Coast contains unique opportunities to explore rocky coastal inlets by kayak. Just north of the California beach community of Cayucos on rural Route 1, rocky sections support some of the state's richest and most extensive tide pool habitat areas. Kayaking allows for in-depth exploration of these intriguing natural habitats.

Scenic

Many travelers have daydreamed of traveling along a peaceful coastal road, with the blue waters of the ocean washing the beach or crashing craggy rock walls on one side and serene hills, farmland, and mountain peaks on the other side. The San Luis Obispo North Coast Byway turns these daydreams into reality.

The Byway travels along a coastline containing rocky headlands, hundreds of coves, dozens of uncrowded beaches, and clean blue water stretching to the distant horizon. The air above the Byway is without pollution, and the horizon is free of giant oil tankers and freight ships that inhibit similar coastal drives. The Byway takes you past wide coastal terraces, sandy shores and dune areas, rocky inshore areas, and sheer granite cliffs and bluffs high above the sea.

The harbors and bays found along the Byway have undoubtedly served as inspiration for artistic seascape paintings. Morro Bay, a working fishing village and a protected harbor, is also home to the Morro Bay Estuary and Morro Rock. Morro Rock, abruptly rising over 500 feet above the bay, provides a dreamy backdrop for activities in the clean harbor. Other scenic bays along the route include Estero Bay, San Simeon Bay, and the southern portion of part of the Monterey Bay National Marine Sanctuary.

The spectacular shoreline of the San Luis Obispo North Coast Byway is backed by a series of coastal terraces that rise to the foothills and then to the high ridges of the Santa Lucia Range. The land is covered with open rangelands, including coastal prairie grasslands, oak savannas, pine forest meadows,

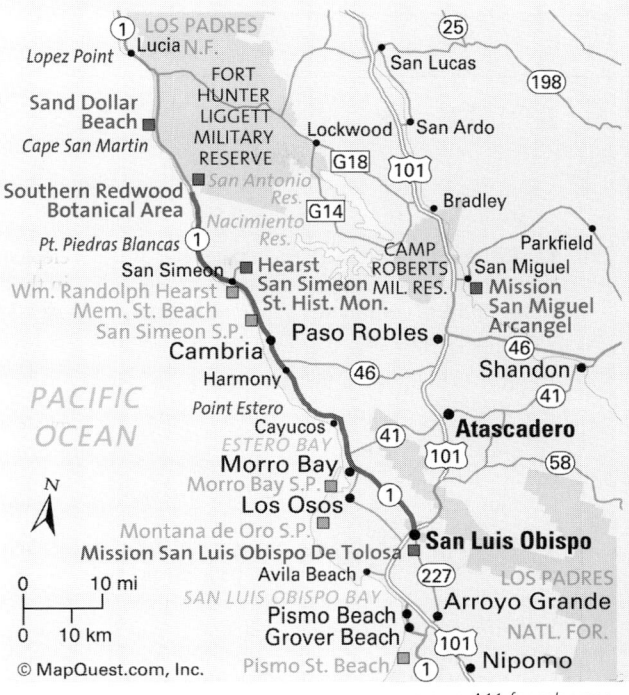

see page A11 for color map

and grassland-covered upland slopes. In spring, these areas are mantled in the lush green of new growth, followed by vibrant displays of orange California poppy, purple lupine, and other colorful native wildflowers. Later in the year, these same grasslands are toasted to a golden brown, providing rich contrast to the somber and dark evergreen forests around Cambria. Softly sculptured hills ring the city, with a series of steep, conical peaks, called morros. Morros are the remains of ancient volcanoes jutting up from the valley floor.

THINGS TO SEE AND DO

Driving along the San Luis Obispo North Coast will certainly keep your senses engaged, but if you yearn to get out of the car and stretch your legs, or if you'd like to make a mini-vacation out of your trip, check out these attractions along the route.

AH LOUIS STORE. *800 Palm St, San Luis Obispo (93401). Phone 805/543-4332.* A leader of the Chinese community, Ah Louis was an extraordinary man who achieved prominence at a time when Asians were given few opportunities. The two-story building, dating to 1874, served as

California

ROUTE 1 ❈ San Luis Obispo North Coast Byway

the Chinese bank, post office, and general merchandise store and was the cornerstone of the Chinese community. Open Mon-Sat; closed holidays.

HEARST SAN SIMEON STATE HISTORICAL MONUMENT. *750 Hearst Castle Rd, San Simeon (93452). 805/927-2020. 800/444-4445. www.heartcastle.com.* In the Santa Lucia Mountains of California on a hilltop overlooking the Pacific Ocean, craftsmen labored nearly 28 years to create a magnificent estate of 165 rooms and 127 acres of gardens, terraces, pools, and walkways. Rooms were furnished with a magnificent collection of Spanish and Italian antiques and art. Called La Cuesta Encantada (the Enchanted Hill), it is better known as Hearst Castle, once the home of newspaper publisher, art collector, and builder William Randolph Hearst. Day tours take approximately one hour and 45 minutes; evening tours take approximately two hours and 15 minutes. The main house itself, La Casa Grande, is a grand setting for Hearst's collection of European antiques and art pieces. It was also a most fitting site for hosting the many influential guests who stayed at Hearst's 250,000-acre San Simeon ranch. Guests included President Calvin Coolidge, Winston Churchill, George Bernard Shaw, Charles Lindbergh, Charlie Chaplin, and a diverse array of luminaries from show business and the publishing industry. Open daily; closed Jan 1, Thanksgiving, and Dec 25. Five tours daily. **$$-$$$$**

MADONNARI ITALIAN STREET PAINTING FESTIVAL. *751 Palm St, San Luis Obispo (93401). Phone 805/781-2777. www.rain.org/~imadonna.* Local artists decorate the streets around the mission with chalk drawings. Also music, Italian cuisine, and an open-air market. Held at the Mission San Luis Obispo de Tolosa in Sept.

MISSION SAN LUIS OBISPO DE TOLOSA. *751 Palm St, San Luis Obispo (93401). Phone 805/543-6850. www.missionsanluisobispo.org.* Fifth of the California missions, founded in 1772, this mission still serves as the parish church. Eight-room museum contains extensive Chumash collection and artifacts from early settlers. First olive orchard in California was planted here; two original trees still stand. Open daily 9 am-4 pm; closed holidays. **FREE**

MONTANA DE ORO STATE PARK. *350 Pecho Valley Rd, Los Osos (93402). Phone 805/528-0513. www.parks.ca.gov.* Spectacular scenery along 7 miles of shoreline, with tide pools, beaches, and camping. Hiking trails up 1,350-foot Valencia Peak. Popular for whale-watching and viewing harbor seals and sea otters along the shore. **$$$**

MORRO BAY AQUARIUM. *595 Embarcadero, Morro Bay (93442). Phone 805/772-7647. www.morrobay.com/morrobayaquarium/index.html.* Displays 300 live marine specimens, including seals, sharks, and harbor seals. Open daily. **$**

MORRO BAY STATE PARK. *Morro Bay (93442). Phone 805/772-7434. www.parks.ca.gov.* Approximately 2,400 acres on Morro Bay. Fishing, boating; 18-hole golf course (fee), picnicking, hiking, tent and trailer camping (showers; water and electric hookups).

MORRO ROCK. *Morro Bay, Morro Bay (93442). Phone 805/772-4467. www.morrobay.com/rock.htm.* A 576-foot-high volcanic boulder often called the Gibraltar of the Pacific, is now a bird sanctuary. Drive to the base of the rock for optimal viewing. Open daily.

MOZART FESTIVAL. *1160 Marsh St, San Luis Obispo (93401). Phone 805/781-3008. www.mozartfestival.com.* Recitals, chamber music, orchestra concerts, and choral music. Held at various locations throughout the county, including Mission San Luis Obispo de Tolosa and Cal Poly State University campus. Held in late July-early Aug.

MUSEUM OF NATURAL HISTORY. *State Park Rd, Morro Bay (93442). Phone 805/772-2694. www.morrobaymuseum.org.* Films, slide shows, displays; nature walks. Open daily 10 am-5 pm; closed Jan 1, Thanksgiving, Dec 25. **$**

PERFORMING ARTS CENTER SAN LUIS OBISPO. *Grand Ave, San Luis Obispo (93407). Phone 805/756-2787. www.pacslo.org.* This 91,500-square-foot center offers professional dance, theater, music, and other performances all year. The 1,350-seat Harmon Concert Hall is JBL Professional's exclusive North American test and demonstration site. Ticket prices vary by event; call or check the Web site for the current performance schedule.

RENAISSANCE FESTIVAL. *1087 Santa Rosa St, San Luis Obispo (93408). Phone 707/864-5706; toll-free 800-688-1477. www.hisrev.org/slo.html.* Celebration of the Renaissance; period costumes, food booths, entertainment, arts and crafts. Held in July.

SAN LUIS OBISPO CHILDREN'S MUSEUM. *1010 Nipomo St, San Luis Obispo (93401). Phone 805/544-KIDS.* A hands-on museum for children in preschool through elementary school (must be accompanied by an adult); houses many interactive exhibits; themes change monthly. Open Tues-Sun; closed holidays. **$$**

SAN LUIS OBISPO COUNTY MUSEUM AND HISTORY CENTER. *696 Monterey St, San Luis Obispo (93401). Phone 805/543-0638. www.slochs.org.* Local history exhibits; decorative arts. Open Wed-Sun 10 am-4 pm; closed holidays. **FREE**

SHAKESPEARE PRESS MUSEUM. *Cal Poly's Graphic Communication Building, California Polytechnic State University, San Luis Obispo (93401). Phone 805/756-1108. www.grc.calpoly.edu/pages/shakes.html.* Collection of 19th-century printing presses, type, and related equipment; demonstrations for prearranged tours. Open Mon, Wed; closed holidays. **FREE**

SLO INTERNATIONAL FILM FESTIVAL. *817 Palm St, San Luis Obispo (93401). Phone 805/546-3456. www.slofilmfest.org.* Showcases the history and art of filmmaking. Screenings of new releases and classics are held over four days in November.

PLACES TO STAY

If you choose to include an overnight stay in your trip along this All-American Road, Mobil Travel Guide recommends the following lodgings.

Cambria

★★★ **BURTON DRIVE INN.** *4022 Burton Dr, Cambria (93428). Phone 805/927-5125; toll-free 800/572-7442. www.burtondriveinn.com.* A bright blue entrance welcomes you to this inn located in the center of town. All units are spacious at 600 square feet each. 10 rooms, 2 story. No A/C. Complimentary continental breakfast. Check-out 11 am, check-in 2 pm. TV; cable (premium). Totally nonsmoking. **¢**

★ **CAMBRIA SHORES INN.** *6276 Moonstone Beach Dr, Cambria (93428). Phone 805/927-8644; toll-free 800/433-9179. www.cambriashores.com.* 24 rooms. No A/C. Pet accepted, some restrictions; fee. Complimentary continental breakfast. Check-out 11 am. TV. **$**

California

ROUTE 1 ❋ San Luis Obispo North Coast Byway

★★ **CASTLE INN BY THE SEA.** 6620 Moonstone Beach Dr, Cambria (93428). Phone 805/927-8605. www.cambria-online.com/CastleInnbytheSea. 31 rooms. Complimentary continental breakfast. Check-out 11 am. TV. Outdoor pool, whirlpool. ¢

★ **SAN SIMEON PINES RESORT.** 7200 Moonstone Beach Dr, Cambria (93428). Phone 805/927-4648; toll-free 866/927-4648. www.sspines.com. 60 rooms, 1-2 story. No A/C. Complimentary continental breakfast. Check-out 11 am. TV. Outdoor pool. Golf. Lawn games. Hiking. $

★★★ **SQUIBB HOUSE.** 4063 Burton Dr, Cambria (93428). Phone 805/927-9600; toll-free 866/927-9600. www.squibbhouse.com. This yellow Italianate structure has been painstakingly restored to its original 1877 splendor. You'll find the same handcrafted pine furniture in your room in the 100-year-old Shop Next Door. 5 rooms, 2 story. No A/C. No room phones. Complimentary continental breakfast. Check-out 11 am, check-in 3-6 pm. Antiques. Wine tasting. Totally nonsmoking. $$

Cayucos

★★★ **BEACHWALKER INN.** 501 S Ocean Ave, Cayucos (93430). Phone 805/995-2133; toll-free 800/750-2133. www.beachwalkerinn.com. The individually designed rooms of this inn are cozy, but don't miss this quaint town's beaches, magnificent gardens, and other attractions, including water sports, golf, whale- and seal-watching, and wineries. 24 rooms, 2 story. No A/C. Complimentary continental breakfast. Check-out 11 am, check-in 2 pm. TV; cable (premium), VCR available (movies). Opposite beach. Totally nonsmoking. $$

Morro Bay

★ **BAY VIEW LODGE.** 225 Harbor St, Morro Bay (93442). Phone 805/772-2771. 22 rooms, 2 story. No A/C. Check-out 11 am. TV; cable (premium), VCR (movies fee). Fireplaces. Laundry services. Bay 1 block. $

★★★ **INN AT MORRO BAY.** 60 State Park Rd, Morro Bay (93442). Phone 805/772-5651; toll-free 800/321-9566. www.innatmorrobay.com. Nestled in Morro State Park, this inn offers a wide variety of activities, including golf and the Blue Herron Rookery. 98 rooms, 2 story. No A/C. Check-out noon. TV; cable (premium). Restaurant, bar; entertainment. Health club privileges. Massage. Outdoor pool, poolside service. Guest bicycles. On Morro Bay. ¢

★★ **LA SERENA INN.** 990 Morro Ave, Morro Bay (93442). Phone 805/772-5665; toll-free 800/248-1511. www.laserenainn.com. 37 rooms, 3 story. Complimentary continental breakfast. Check-out 11 am. TV; cable (premium). In-room modem link. Sauna. $

San Luis Obispo

★★★ **APPLE FARM.** 2015 Monterey St, San Luis Obispo (93401). Phone 805/544-2040; toll-free 800/255-2040. www.applefarm.com. This delightful inn successfully combines country Victorian charm with modern conveniences. Guest rooms are charmingly furnished with fireplaces, canopy beds, and window seats. 69 rooms, 3 story. Check-out noon. TV. In-room modem link. Fireplaces. Restaurant. Pool, whirlpool. Free airport transportation. Bakery, millhouse. $

★★★ **GARDEN STREET INN.** *1212 Garden St, San Luis Obispo (93401). Phone 805/545-9802. www.gardenstreetinn.com.* Built in 1887 and beautifully restored in 1990, this Italianate/Queen Anne home is remarkable. Guest rooms are spacious and handsomely appointed with lovely wall coverings and antiques. 13 rooms, 2 story. Children over 16 years only. Complimentary breakfast. Check-out 11 am, check-in 3-7 pm. Free airport transportation. Totally nonsmoking. $$

★★ **MADONNA INN.** *100 Madonna Rd, San Luis Obispo (93405). Phone 805/543-3000; toll-free 800/543-9666. www.madonnainn.com.* 109 rooms, 1-4 story. Some A/C. No elevator. Check-out noon. TV; cable (premium). Restaurant, dining room, bar; entertainment. Free airport transportation. Individually decorated rooms, each in a motif of a different nation or period. On a hill with mountain views. Totally nonsmoking. $$

★★★ **SANDS SUITES & MOTEL.** *1930 Monterey St, San Luis Obispo (93401). Phone 805/554-0500; toll-free 800/441-4657. www.sandssuites.com.* 70 rooms, 1-2 story. Pet accepted; fee. Complimentary continental breakfast. Check-out 11 am. TV; VCR (free movies). In-room modem link. Laundry services. Outdoor pool, whirlpool. Free airport transportation. ¢

★ **VILLA.** *1670 Monterey St, San Luis Obispo (93401). Phone 805/543-8071. www.villamotelslo.com.* 14 rooms, 1-2 story. Complimentary continental breakfast. Check-out 11 am. TV; cable (premium). ¢

San Simeon

★★ **BEST WESTERN CAVALIER OCEANFRONT RESORT.** *9415 Hearst Dr, San Simeon (93452). Phone 805/927-4688; toll-free 800/826-8168. www.cavalierresort.com.* 90 rooms, 2 story. No A/C. Pet accepted. Check-out noon. TV; cable (premium), VCR available. In-room modem link. Fireplaces. Restaurant, bar. Room service. In-house fitness room. Outdoor pool, whirlpool. $

PLACES TO EAT

A long day of driving is sure to make you hungry. At the end of your journey, take a table at one of the following restaurants.

Cambria

★★ **ROBIN'S RESTAURANT.** *4095 Burton Dr, Cambria (93428). Phone 805/927-5007. www.robinsrestaurant.com.* Asian, vegetarian menu. Closed Thanksgiving, Dec 25. Lunch, dinner. Outdoor seating. Garden. Totally nonsmoking. $$

★★ **THE BRAMBLES DINNER HOUSE.** *4005 Burton Dr, Cambria (93428). Phone 805/927-4716. www.bramblesdinnerhouse.com.* Continental menu. Dinner, Sun brunch. Bar. Children's menu. Victorian décor; antiques. Outdoor seating. Totally nonsmoking. $$

Morro Bay

★★★ **GALLEY.** *899 Embarcadero, Morro Bay (93442). Phone 805/772-2806.* This dining spot features the freshest locally caught seafood in Morro Bay and is consistently chosen as a favorite of locals and visitors alike. Seafood menu. Closed late Nov-Dec 25. Lunch, dinner. Children's menu. Totally nonsmoking. $$$

55

California

ROUTE 1 ❋ San Luis Obispo North Coast Byway

★★ **ROSE'S LANDING.** *725 Embarcadero, Morro Bay (93442).* Phone *805/772-4441.* Seafood, steak menu. Lunch, dinner. Bar. Entertainment. Children's menu. Outdoor seating. **$$**
[D]

San Luis Obispo

★ **APPLE FARM.** *2015 Monterey St, San Luis Obispo (93401). 805/554-6100; toll-free 800/255-2040. www.applefarm.com.* American menu. Breakfast, lunch, dinner. Outdoor seating. Totally nonsmoking. **$$**
[D]

★★ **CAFÉ ROMA.** *1020 Railroad Ave, San Luis Obispo (93401). 805/541-6800.* Italian menu. Closed Sun, major holidays. Lunch, dinner. Bar. Outdoor seating. Totally nonsmoking. **$$**
[D]

★ **IZZY ORTEGA'S.** *1850 Monterey St, San Luis Obispo (93401). 805/543-3333.* Mexican menu. Closed Jan 1, Thanksgiving, Dec 24-25. Lunch, dinner. Bar. Children's menu. Outdoor seating. Totally nonsmoking. **$**
[D]

Tioga Road/ Big Oak Flat Road
❋ CALIFORNIA

Quick Facts

LENGTH: 64 miles.

TIME TO ALLOW: 3 hours.

BEST TIME TO DRIVE: Mid- to late May through mid-November. Summer is the high season.

BYWAY TRAVEL INFORMATION: Yosemite National Park: 209/372-0200.

SPECIAL CONSIDERATIONS: The maximum speed limit is 45 mph along the Byway. You'll find limited fueling opportunities.

RESTRICTIONS: Tioga Road is closed during the winter from Crane Flat Junction to Lee Vining due to snowfall. Call Yosemite National Park for updated road and weather information. Yosemite National Park charges an entrance fee.

BICYCLE/PEDESTRIAN FACILITIES: The Byway is well traveled by pedestrians and bicyclists. National Park entrance fees are reduced when entering on foot, bicycle, or motorcycle.

Tioga Road/Big Oak Flat Road offers one of the most spectacular passages over the Sierra Nevada, making it the highest automobile pass in California, boasting an elevation change of over 1 mile from west to east. Along the route, views include towering granite peaks, pristine lakes, wildflower-covered meadows, and lush evergreen forests with Giant Sequoia groves. Tuolumne meadows offers visitors a chance to see how ancient glaciers created this serene and rugged landscape.

The Byway provides motorists with an opportunity to experience this scenery from a vehicle. For hiking enthusiasts, it offers some of the most beautiful High Sierra backcountry trails.

THE BYWAY STORY

The Tioga Road/Big Oak Flat Road tells historical, natural, recreational, and scenic stories that make it a unique and treasured Byway.

Historical

The area now encompassed by Yosemite National Park was once home to various nations of Native Americans. By the mid-1800s, when American explorers first caught sight of the area, the natives were primarily of Southern Miwok ancestry and called themselves the Ahwaneechee. The word "Yosemite" is in fact derived from the Ahwanaeechee word for grizzly bear, *uzumati*. These earliest inhabitants of Yosemite soon found themselves at odds with the new settlers of the area. The Gold Rush of 1849 brought thousands of settlers to Yosemite, many crossing over the Sierra Nevada in search of their dreams.

California

Tioga Road/Big Oak Flat Road

Conflict between the natives and the new settlers followed, and eventually, California authorized the organization of the Mariposa Battalion to gather the Ahwaneechee and relocate them to various other locations in the state. Thus the Yosemite valley opened for tourism, which today brings more than 4 million visitors annually.

The many new visitors to the beautiful area did not come without impact, so citizens began a campaign to preserve the area. On June 30, 1864, President Abraham Lincoln signed a bill granting Yosemite Valley and the Mariposa Grove of Giant Sequoias to the state of California as an inalienable public trust. This marked the first time in history that the federal government set aside scenic lands simply to protect them and to allow for their enjoyment by all people. This act also paved the way for the establishment of the nation's first national park, Yellowstone, in 1872. Later, a concerned and energetic conservationist, John Muir, brought about the creation of Yosemite National Park on October 1, 1890.

Natural

The Tioga Road crosses right through the middle of an area known worldwide for its unique natural features. Yosemite National Park includes three major natural features: forested mountains and bald granite domes, mountain meadows, and the Earth's largest living thing—the giant sequoia tree. Two hundred miles of roads help travelers enjoy all these features, whether by car or by the free shuttle buses offered in some areas. To get to know the real Yosemite, however, you must leave your car and take a few steps on a trail.

The Mountains and Granite Domes of the Sierra Nevada began to take shape about 500 million years ago, when the region lay beneath an ancient sea. The seabed consisted of thick layers of sediment, which eventually were folded, twisted, and thrust above sea level. At the same time, molten rock welled up from the earth and slowly cooled beneath the layers of sediment, forming granite. Over millions of years, erosion wore away most of the overlying rock, exposing the granite. While this continued, water and then glaciers shaped and carved the face of Yosemite, leaving massive peaks and bare granite domes. Today, the park ranges from 2,000 feet to more than 13,000 feet above sea level.

The meadows of Yosemite are natural wonders in their own right. They are the most diverse parts of Yosemite's ecosystem, providing food and shelter for nearly all the wildlife living in the park. In the summer, the meadows and lakes are busy with life, as the plants and animals take advantage of the short warm season to grow, reproduce, and store food. The meadows are also unique because they are immense fields of bliss recessed and secluded in the middle of towering granite mountains. The more popular and accessible meadows are found in Yosemite Valley, Tuolumne Meadows, and Wawona. The middle and upper elevations of the park also contain secluded, perfect mountain meadows.

The mighty sequoia is the largest living thing on Earth. Yosemite is one of the few locations where the sequoias can be found, growing in any of three sequoia groves. Mariposa Grove, 35 miles south of Yosemite Valley, is the largest of the groves. The oldest of the sequoia trees have been dated at over 2,700 years old. The greatest of the trees have trunk diameters of over 30 feet! Although the more slender redwood trees along California's coast surpass the sequoia in height, the much more robust sequoia is no shorty, with the highest measuring over 300 feet tall.

Recreational

For more than a century, Yosemite National Park has been a premier destination for recreation. Its unique natural qualities and breathtaking scenery provide the perfect backdrop for outdoor recreational activities. Put hiking on top of your to-do list, because just a bit of hiking can take you to sites more rewarding than sites just off of the highway.

The summer season, although short along the Sierra Nevada, offers the most accommodating environment for recreation. Hiking, enjoying the scenery, fishing, camping, wildlife viewing, mountain and rock climbing, backpacking, and photography are some activities available in the park. Yosemite's wilderness offers experiences for both seasoned hikers and novices. About 800 miles of trails offer a variety of climate, elevation, and spectacular scenery.

In the winter, Yosemite's high country is a serene, white wonderland. The land is covered by deep, undisturbed snow, creating a landscape far different than the summer's. The winter months in Yosemite are seeing increased amounts of mountaineering activities. Meanwhile, cross-country skiing and snowshoeing have grown in popularity and open up a new world for backpackers. Whether you visit in the winter or summer, Yosemite offers an unparalleled chance to get away from it all.

Scenic

The Tioga Road traverses an area in which the most memorable features are remembered not only for their superb natural beauty but also for their unmatched size. Massive granite domes and cliffs take your breath away. Sequoia trees have branches that are larger than the largest of other tree species, while the park's famous waterfalls are remembered for their size and spectacle. For ages, Yosemite has lured and inspired painters, photographers, and writers. Yet most find that no work of art can adequately provide the sense of amazement and serenity granted to Yosemite's visitors.

Spring provides the best time to see Yosemite's waterfalls, as the spring thaw brings with it an abundance of runoff water to fall from cliffs and peaks. Peak runoff typically occurs in May or June, with some waterfalls (including Yosemite Falls) often dwindling to only a trickle or even becoming completely dry by August. Yosemite Falls are the highest in the park at 2,452 feet and are the fifth highest falls in the world. You can walk to Lower Yosemite Fall (320 feet) in just a few minutes. A hike to the top of Upper Yosemite Fall (1,430 feet) is a strenuous, all-day hike. Other famous falls include the Bridaveil Falls (620 feet), Nevada Falls (594 feet), Ribbon Falls (1,612 feet), Staircase Falls (1,300 feet), and Horsetail Falls (1,000 feet). Horsetail Falls, on the east side of El Capitán, is famous for appearing to be on fire when it reflects the orange glow of sunset in mid-February.

The Tioga Road passes through an area of rugged mountain scenery mixed with sublime mountain meadows. The road continues through an area featuring sparkling mountain lakes; bare granite domes; and lofty, forested mountain peaks. Some of the best views are available on the many scenic overlooks along the road, while hiking is sometimes necessary to view that perfect mountainscape.

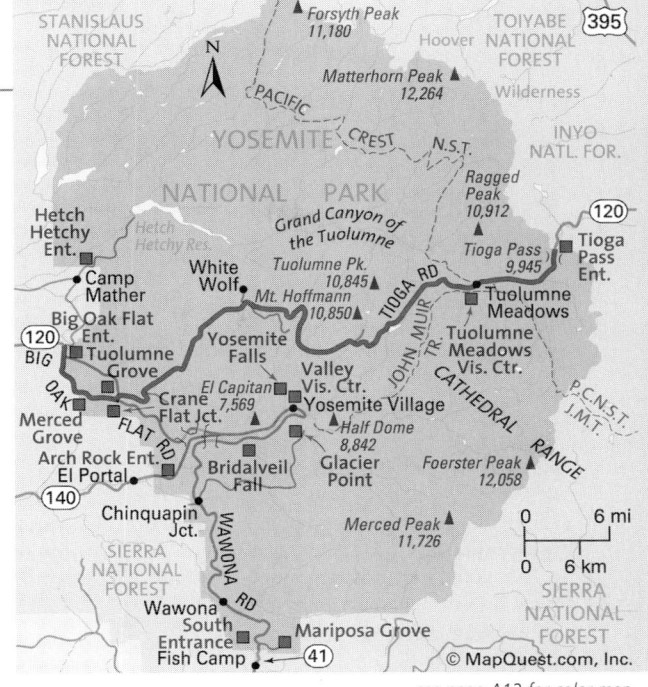

see page A12 for color map

California

❋ *Tioga Road/Big Oak Flat Road*

HIGHLIGHTS

Consider taking this tour of Yosemite National Park:

- Begin on the east end by ascending the **Tioga Pass** and entering the park. Be sure to have the entrance fee handy ($20 for a passenger car). This fee entitles you to seven days of entry into the park, coming and going as you please during that time.
- Enjoy the drive as you approach **Tuolumne Meadows.** Expect to spend several hours learning and exploring through tours and tram rides. You can also take advantage of the concessions offered by the park.
- Fifteen to twenty miles past Tuolumne Meadows, look to the south and notice **Tenaya Lake.** Look up to the north, and you see the towering peaks of **Mount Hoffmann** and **Tuolumne.** One of these peaks is just 5 feet shorter than the other; can you tell which one is which? Continue along the Tioga Road throughout most of the park, a fantastic drive.
- As you approach the junction of the Tioga and Big Oak Flat Roads, chances are, you'll want to get out and enjoy the sights. The Junction at Crane Flat is a good stopping place. To the north is **Tuolumne Grove,** a short hike onto a pretty grove of sequoia trees with a self-guided nature trail. A little down the road and to the south is **Merced Grove.** The trail into Merced is more difficult than at Tuolumne but just as enjoyable.
- As you near the end of the Byway at the **Big Oak Flat Entrance Station,** be sure to stop and gather information about Yosemite. As you exit the park, you may wish to turn to the north and take a side trip up to **Hetch Hetchy Reservoir.** This is an especially great idea if you like the outdoors and backcountry trails. Fishing is available at the reservoir.
- After a visit to the reservoir, turn back toward Big Oak Flat Road and head down into the **Yosemite Valley,** about 40 miles to the south.

Stop at the visitors center for up-to-date information about activities and sights, including the famous **Half Dome, El Capitán,** and **Bridalveil Falls.** Hotels and restaurants are plentiful here, which makes the area an excellent place to stay the night.

- Continue south along Highway 41 (Wawona Road) into **Wawona.** Although smaller than Yosemite Valley, plenty of amenities are still to be found here, including the **Pioneer Museum and Visitors Center.** If you visit at the right time of the year (summer), hop on the free shuttle bus at the Wawona store, which will take you 7 miles away to the **Mariposa Grove.** The grove is famous for the "drive-through trees," the giant sequoias. Although cars no longer drive through these trees, feel free to explore by foot or tram (for a fee). Toward the top of the grove, a small museum and gift shop help orient you.
- The tour ends as you head south and out the South Entrance toward Fish Camp and into the **Sierra National Forest,** which is a whole new treasure to discover.

THINGS TO SEE AND DO

Driving along the Tioga Road/Big Oak Flat Road will certainly keep your senses engaged, but if you yearn to get out of the car and stretch your legs, or if you'd like to make a mini-vacation out of your trip, check out these attractions along the route.

BADGER PASS SKI AREA. *23 miles from Yosemite Valley on Glacier Point Rd. Phone 209/372-1000. www.badgerpass.com.* One triple, three double chairlifts, cable tow; patrol, rentals; snack stand, sun deck, nursery (minimum age 3 years); instruction (over 4 years old). Cross-country skiing. Ice skating (fee) in Yosemite Valley; scheduled competitions. Naturalists conduct snowshoe tours (fee) in the Badger Pass area. Open mid-Dec-mid-Apr, daily 9 am-4:30 pm, weather permitting. $$$$

☆ YOSEMITE NATIONAL PARK.

Yosemite National Park (95389). Phone 209/372-0200. www.nps.gov/yose/. John Muir, the naturalist who was instrumental in the founding of this national park, wrote that here are "the most songful in the world . . . the noblest forests, the loftiest granite domes, the deepest ice sculptured canyons." An area of 1,169 square miles, it is a park of lofty waterfalls, sheer cliffs, high wilderness country, alpine meadows, lakes, snowfields, trails, streams, and river beaches. There are magnificent waterfalls during spring and early summer. Yosemite's granite domes are unsurpassed in number and diversity. Camping reservations are taken by NPRS, the National Park Reservation System for Yosemite Valley (phone toll-free 800/436-7275) and other campgrounds. Boating and fishing; no motors permitted; state license, inland waters stamp, and trout stamp are required. Hiking and backpacking on 840 miles of maintained trails. Wilderness permits are required for all overnight backcountry trips. Advance reservations for permits may be made up to 24 weeks in advance; phone 209/372-0740. Swimming is prohibited at Hetch Hetchy Reservoir and in some areas of the Tuolumne River watershed. Swimming pools are maintained at Camp Curry, Yosemite Lodge, and Wawona. $$$$

- **Giant sequoias:** Located principally in three groves. Mariposa Grove is near the south entrance to the park; toured on foot or by 50-passenger trams (May-early October; fee). Merced and Tuolumne groves are near Crane Flat, northwest of Yosemite Valley. The Grizzly Giant in Mariposa Grove is estimated to be 2,700 years old and is 209 feet high and 34.7 feet in diameter at its base.

- **Glacier Point:** Offers one of the best panoramic views in Yosemite. From here, the crest of the Sierra Nevada can be viewed, as well as Yosemite Valley, 3,214 feet below. Across the valley are Yosemite Falls, Royal Arches, North Dome, Basket Dome, Mount Watkins, and Washington Column; up the Merced Canyon are Vernal and Nevada falls; Half Dome, Grizzly Peak, Liberty Cap, and the towering peaks along the Sierran crest and the Clark Range mark the skyline. Note that the road is closed in winter.

- **High Country:** Tioga Road crosses the park and provides the threshold to a vast wilderness accessible via horseback or on foot to mountain peaks, passes, and lakes. Tuolumne Meadows is the major trailhead for this activity; one of the most beautiful and largest of the subalpine meadows in the High Sierra, 55 miles from Yosemite Valley by way of the Byway. Organized group horse and hiking trips start from Tuolumne Meadows (except in winter), follow the High Sierra Loop, and fan out to mountain lakes and peaks. Each night's stop is at a High Sierra Camp; the pace allows plenty of time to explore at each camp.

- **The Indian Cultural Museum:** Located in the building west of the Valley visitor center, the museum portrays the cultural history of the Ahwaneechee Indians.

California

❋ *Tioga Road/Big Oak Flat Road*

- **Indian Village (Ahwahnee):** This reconstructed Miwok-Paiute Village behind the Visitor Center has a self-guided trail.
- **The Nature Center at Happy Isles:** Exhibits on ecology and natural history. Open summer, daily.
- **Pioneer Yosemite History Center:** A few miles from Mariposa Grove in Wawona. The center has a covered bridge, historic buildings, wagons, and other exhibits. Living-history program in summer.
- **Visitor Center:** *Phone 209/372-0265.* Orientation slide program on Yosemite (open daily). Exhibits on geology and ecology; naturalist-conducted walks and evening programs offered throughout the year on varying seasonal schedules. Native American cultural demonstrators. Open summer, daily.
- ★ **Waterfalls:** Reaching their greatest proportions in mid-May, they may, in dry years, dwindle to trickles or disappear completely by late summer. The Upper Yosemite Fall drops 1,430 feet; the lower fall drops 320 feet.

YOSEMITE MOUNTAIN-SUGAR PINE RAILROAD. *56001 Hwy 41, Fish Camp (93624). Phone 559/683-7273. www.ymsprr.com.* Four-mile historic narrow gauge steam train excursion through scenic Sierra National Forest. Picnic area. Museum; gift shops. Logger steam train (open mid-May-Sept, daily; early May and Oct, weekends). Jenny Railcars (open Mar-Oct, daily). Evening steam train, outdoor barbecue, live entertainment. Open late May-early Oct, Sat evenings; reservations advised. **$$$$**

PLACES TO STAY

If you choose to include an overnight stay in your trip along this Byway, Mobil Travel Guide recommends the following lodgings.

★★ **PINES RESORT.** *54449 Rd 432, Bass Lake (93604). Phone 559/642-3121; toll-free 800/350-7463. www.basslake.com.* 104 rooms, 2 story. Weekends, holidays 2-3 day minimum. Complimentary continental breakfast. Check-out 11 am. TV; cable (premium), VCR (movies available). Balconies, refrigerators, microwaves. Coin laundry. Restaurant, bar; entertainment Fri, Sat. Room service. Split-level units on lake. Pool, whirlpool, poolside service. Tennis. Cross-country ski 5 miles. **$$**

★★ **CEDAR LODGE.** *9966 Hwy 140, El Portal (95318). Phone 209/379-2612; toll-free 800/321-5261. www.yosemite-motels.com/cedarlodge/.* 211 rooms, 1-2 story. Holidays 2-day minimum. Check-out 11 am. TV; cable (premium), VCR available (movies). Restaurant adjacent. Bar. Meeting rooms. Business services available. In-room modem link. Two pools, one indoor; whirlpool. Many refrigerators, microwaves; some in-room whirlpools. Some balconies. Picnic tables, grills. On the river. **$**

★ **YOSEMITE VIEW LODGE.** *11156 Hwy 140, El Portal (95318). Phone 209/379-2681; toll-free 800/321-5261. www.yosemite-motels.com/yosemiteviewlodge/.* 280 kitchen units, 2-3 story. Ski plans; holidays 2-day minimum. Pet accepted; fee. TV; cable (premium). Restaurant, bar. Meeting rooms. Business services available. Grocery store. Coin laundry. Two pools, one indoor; whirlpool. Many in-room whirlpools, fireplaces. Refrigerators, microwaves. Many balconies. On the river. **$**

★★★ **TENAYA LODGE AT YOSEMITE.** *1122 Hwy 41, Fish Camp (93623). Phone 559/683-6555; toll-free 888/514-2167. www.tenayalodge.com.* At this deluxe mountain resort, you can enjoy the beauty of Yosemite National Park by horse or by foot. Enjoy such activities as shooting the rapids, bird-watching, biking, and even a moonlight train ride. 244 rooms, 20 suites, 3-4 story. Package plans. Pet accepted, some restrictions. Check-out noon, check-in 3 pm. TV; cable (premium), VCR available. In-room

AMERICA'S BYWAYS - WEST COAST

modem link. Bathroom phones, minibars. Valet services, coin laundry. Dining room. Room service. Supervised children's activities, ages 3-12. In-house fitness room, massage, sauna, steam room. Game room. Two pools, indoor pool, whirlpool. Cross-country ski on site. Bicycle rentals. Concierge. On the river; water sports. Southwestern, Native American décor; rustic with an elegant touch. June-Sept Western jamboree cookouts, wagon rides. Guided hikes and tours. Totally nonsmoking. $$

★★ **GROVELAND HOTEL AT YOSEMITE NATIONAL PARK.** *18767 Main St, Groveland (95321). Phone 209/962-4000; toll-free 800/273-3314. www.groveland.com.* 17 rooms, 3 suites, 2 separate two-story buildings (one is California Monterey Colonial Adobe). Pet accepted. Complimentary innkeeper breakfast. Check-out noon, check-in 2 pm. TV in common room, bar, some rooms; cable, VCR available (movies). In-room modem link. Fireplace in suites. In-room whirlpool. Restaurant, bar. Room service. Picnic tables. Business services available. Concierge. Built in 1849; European antiques. Totally nonsmoking. $

★ **YOSEMITE RIVERSIDE INN.** *11399 Cherry Lake Rd, Groveland (95321). Phone 209/962-7408; toll-free 800/626-7408. www.yosemiteriversideinn.com.* 18 rooms, 2 kitchen units. No room phones. Complimentary continental breakfast. Check-out 11 am. TV. Balconies, refrigerators available. Pool privileges. Picnic tables. On a stream. $

★ **BEST VALUE MARIPOSA LODGE.** *5052 Hwy 140, Mariposa (95338). Phone 209/966-3607; toll-free 800/341-8000. www.mariposalodge.com.* 44 rooms, 13 rooms with shower only. Pet accepted, some restrictions; fee. Check-out 11 am. TV; cable (premium), VCR available. Outdoor pool, whirlpool. Barber, beauty shop. In-room modem link. Restaurant adjacent. Free airport transportation. Gazebo. ¢

★ **COMFORT INN.** *4994 Bullion St, Mariposa (95338). Phone 209/966-4344; toll-free 800/228-5150. www.comfortinn.com.* 61 rooms, 2-3 story. Complimentary continental breakfast. Check-out 11 am. TV; cable (premium). Restaurant nearby. Meeting rooms. Business services available. In-room modem link. Outdoor pool, whirlpool. ¢

★ **LITTLE VALLEY INN BED & BREAKFAST.** *3483 Brooks Rd, Mariposa (95338). Phone 209/742-6204; toll-free 800/889-5444. www.littlevalley.com.* 5 rooms, 1 cabin. No room phones. Complimentary full breakfast. Check-out noon, check-in 4 pm. TV, VCR (movies). Concierge. Smoking on deck only. $

★★ **MINERS INN MOTEL.** *5181 Hwy 49 N, Mariposa (95338). Phone 209/742-7777; toll-free 888/646-2244.* 78 rooms, 2 story. Pet accepted; fee. Check-out 11 am. TV; cable (premium). In-room modem link. Fireplaces. Restaurant, bar; entertainment Fri, Sat. Outdoor pool, whirlpool. ¢

★★★ **THE AHWAHNEE.** *Yosemite National Park Resort (95389). Phone 559/252-4848. www.yosemitepark.com.* Built in 1927, this National Historic Landmark boasts striking beamed ceilings, a massive stone hearth, and beautifully appointed rooms. The hotel offers a perfect balance of refinement, grandness, and hospitality. 123 rooms, 4 suites, 24 cottages, 6 story. No A/C in cottages. Check-out noon. TV; VCR available. Some balconies, fireplaces. Restaurant (reservation required), bar; entertainment. Room service. Outdoor pool. Tennis. Free valet parking. Meeting rooms. Concierge. Stone building with natural wood interior, Native American décor. Tire chains may be required by the Park Service to reach the lodge Nov-Mar. $$$

California

❋ *Tioga Road/Big Oak Flat Road*

★ **WAWONA.** *Yosemite National Park (95389). Phone 559/252-4848. www.yosemitepark.com.* 104 rooms, 50 with bath, 1-2 story. No A/C. No room phones. Check-out 11 am. TV in lounge; VCR. Outdoor pool. Dining room. Meeting room. Tennis. Nine-hole golf, greens fee $13.75-$22, putting green. Free airport transportation. Saddle trips, stagecoach rides. Historic summer hotel. ¢

★★ **YOSEMITE LODGE.** *Yosemite National Park (95389). Phone 559/252-4848. www.yosemitepark.com.* 226 rooms, 2 story. No A/C. Check-out 11 am. Outdoor pool; lifeguard. Supervised children's activities (June-Aug), over age 3. Restaurant, bar. Room service. Concierge. Barber, beauty shop. Meeting rooms. Valley tours. ¢

PLACES TO EAT

A long day of driving is sure to make you hungry. At the end of your journey, take a table at one of the following restaurants.

★★ **NARROW GAUGE INN.** *48571 Hwy 41, Fish Camp (93623). Phone 559/683-7720. www.narrowgaugeinn.com.* American menu. Dinner. Located in historic Fish Camp, this restaurant offers unique local cuisine in a rustic environment filled with antiques and a nightly fire in the fireplace. $$

★★ **THE VICTORIAN ROOM.** *18767 Main St, Groveland (95321). Phone 209/962-4000. www.groveland.com/dining.htm.* California menu. Dinner. Bar. Outdoor seating. Victorian décor. Totally nonsmoking. $$

★★ **WHOA NELLIE DELI.** *22 Vista Point Rd, Lee Vining (93541). Phone 760/647-1088. www.thesierraweb.com/tiogagasmart.* Eclectic menu. Breakfast, lunch, dinner. Located in the Tioga Gas Mart is this shockingly gourmet restaurant, where chef Matt Toomey serves unique, progressive California cuisine. $

★★ **CHARLES STREET DINNER HOUSE.** *5043 Charles, Mariposa (95338). Phone 209/966-2366. www.charlesstreetdinnerhouse.com.* Steak, seafood menu. Closed Mon, Tues; Thanksgiving, Dec 24-25; also Jan. Dinner. Beer. Reservations accepted. Own desserts. 19th-century house. $$$

★ **CHARLIE'S PUB & GRILL.** *901 N China Lake Blvd, Ridgecrest (93555). Phone 800/772-8527. www.carriageinn.biz.* American menu. Lunch, dinner. Serving family-style food in a unique décor of aircrew memorabilia that was donated from squadrons around the world. $

Volcanic Legacy Scenic Byway

❄ CALIFORNIA AN ALL-AMERICAN ROAD
Part of a multistate Byway; see also OR.

Quick Facts

LENGTH: 360 miles.

TIME TO ALLOW: 1 day.

BEST TIME TO DRIVE: Summer and fall provide for the best travel conditions. The winter months offer beautiful snowscapes. High season is June to September.

BYWAY TRAVEL INFORMATION: Siskiyou County Visitor's Bureau: 888/66-BYWAY; Volcanic Legacy National Scenic Byway Information: 866/772-9929; Byway local Web site: www.volcaniclegacybyway.org.

RESTRICTIONS: The geometry of this Byway makes it the most restrictive of the routes with respect to large vehicles, including recreational vehicles (RVs) and tour buses. Tour buses are allowed on the Byway, subject to specific permitting by the park. All route segments of the Volcanic Legacy Scenic Byway are open to traffic year-round, with the exception of the roadway within Lassen Volcanic National Park. Portions of this road are subject to seasonal closures, typically from November through June. Other portions of the route may be subject to periodic temporary closures or restrictions due to inclement weather and maintenance. Small fees are collected at Lassen Volcanic National Park and Lava Beds National Monument.

BICYCLE/PEDESTRIAN FACILITIES: Bicyclists and pedestrians are permitted along the corridor route segments with the exception of I-5. Pedestrians are, however, discouraged from using some portions of the roadway, particularly in Lassen Volcanic National Park, due to the lack of sufficient shoulder area along the existing roadways. In several areas, particularly the National Park Service and Forest Service lands, trails leading off the Byway are used by bicyclists and pedestrians for recreation, as well as to travel to points of interest.

California's Volcanic Legacy Scenic Byway stretches from Mount Lassen in northern California to the California-Oregon border. From the border, the Byway continues north to Oregon's Crater Lake, making this Byway America's volcano-to-volcano highway. The volcanic activity of the past has created unique geological formations, such as wavy lava flows and lava tube caves. Surrounding this volcanic landscape is a wide diversity of scenery. The Byway travels through or near dense forests, broad wetlands and habitat areas, pastoral grasslands, farms and ranches, and well-managed timber resource lands.

The Volcanic Legacy Scenic Byway offers even more benefits than just the fascinating volcanic geology and scenery. Each season offers a different array of outdoor recreational opportunities. The beautiful green forests and mountains along the Byway are home to hiking trails, including the nationally recognized Pacific Crest Trail; ski slopes; and great fishing and kayaking in clear, cool mountain streams and lakes. Traveling the Byway, you can also enjoy viewing the hundreds of species of wildlife along the way.

THE BYWAY STORY

The Volcanic Legacy Scenic Byway tells historical, natural, recreational, and scenic stories that make it a unique and treasured Byway.

Historical

Although the name may not imply it, the Volcanic Legacy Scenic Byway contains not only natural and scenic qualities, but also rich historical qualities. Much of the historical significance of the Byway arises from its

California

✷ Volcanic Legacy Scenic Byway

Native American roots, and the Byway is dotted with historic mining and logging towns. Many features along the Byway are listed as historical landmarks.

Captain Jack's Stronghold, a national monument located in the Lava Beds National Monument, is historically significant because it was the site of the Modoc War. During the Modoc War of 1872-1873, the Modoc Tribe took advantage of the unique geography of their homelands. Under the guidance of their leader, Kintuashk, who came to be known as Captain Jack, the Modoc people took refuge in a natural lava fortress. The site of the fortress is now known as Captain Jack's Stronghold. From this secure base, Captain Jack and his group of 53 fighting men and their families held off US Army forces, which numbered up to ten times more than Kintuashk's tribe. However, the tribe was still able to hold off the Army forces for five months.

Mount Shasta is another site of historical significance along this Byway. The major history of the mountain lies in its geological greatness. It also has a spiritual history. Native Americans of the area believed Mount Shasta to be the abode of the Great Spirit. Out of respect, the natives never ascended past the timberline. A long history of mythology surrounds the mountain, including legends of Lemurians, Atlanteans, secret commonwealth citizens, dwarfs, fairies, Bigfoot, and space beings that materialize at will. Mount Shasta draws visitors from all over the world, some seeking spiritual insight, others the experience of the beauty and natural wonders that Mother Nature has to offer here in this unique alpine region. The upper elevation of Mount Shasta Wilderness was designated in 1976 as a National Natural Historic Landmark.

The Volcanic Legacy Scenic Byway is dotted with historic towns, many of which began as logging communities. McCloud is one example, being a company-built mill town, still revealing its colorful railroad and logging history. The Heritage Junction Museum in the city offers exhibits displaying 100 years worth of historical artifacts and photographs depicting the region. The still-functioning McCloud Railway is also evidence of the logging history of the town. Likewise, the town of Weed was also a logging town, built in 1897. The Weed Historic Lumber Museum helps to reveal the part Weed played in the logging industry of the time. Other historical towns along the Byway include Westwood, one of the largest company towns in the West during the early to mid-1900s, and Mount Shasta City.

Unfortunately, not all of the history along the Byway is bright. The Tulelake Relocation Center was one of ten American concentration camps established during World War II to incarcerate 110,000 persons of Japanese ancestry. The majority of these people were American citizens. A large monument of basalt rock and concrete along the north side of State Highway 139 commemorates the relocation center. The monument, dedicated in 1979, incorporates multiple levels of rock walls, a concrete apron, and a state historical marker. The Tule Lake Relocation Center is located off the Byway about 10 miles from the town of Tule Lake. The new Tule Lake Museum in the town of Tule Lake has a restored camp building and watch tower on display, as well as information about the relocation center.

Natural

The Volcanic Legacy Scenic Byway includes some of the most spectacular natural wonders in the nation and takes you around magnificent Mount Shasta, a solitary peak rising to a height of 14,162 feet. The Byway allows you to experience the effects of the geological and volcanic history of the region. These geological and volcanic natural wonders are reason enough to travel the Byway, but the Byway also contains an abundance of natural wildlife and vegetative habitats.

This Byway traverses two major geological areas. Lassen Volcanic National Park is located in the southern portion of the Byway. The park contains Lassen Peak, one of the largest plug dome volcanoes in the world. Lassen Peak was a major source of the many geological formations of the area. Lava Beds National Monument, located along the northern part of the Byway, near California's border with Oregon, is the site of the largest concentration of lava tube caves in the world. To finish this exciting volcano-to-volcano journey, continue north on Highway 97 to Crater Lake National Park.

The Volcanic Legacy Scenic Byway stretches across the convergence of the Nevada Mountains with the Great Basin. This convergence provides a vast diversity of habitats. The diversity allows for a significantly higher number of plant and animal species than most other regions of the West, with habitat for more than 360 species of animals and more than 1,000 plant species. The many state parks, recreation areas, and wildlife reserves along the Byway provide the best opportunities to observe these natural living resources. At the refuges, such as the Lower Klamath National Wildlife Refuge, visitors can view the largest concentration of bald eagles in the lower 48 states during the winter, and the largest annual concentration of waterfowl in North America.

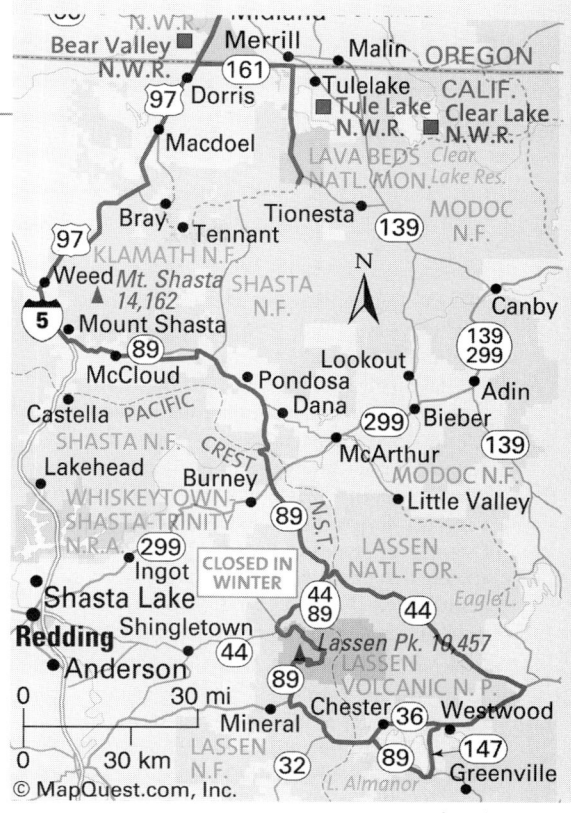

see page A13 for color map

Recreational

The Volcanic Legacy Scenic Byway's length and vast diversity of landscapes provide a wide variety of year-round recreational opportunities. You can tour a lighted lava tube or spelunk on your own at Lava Beds National Monument, see bubbling mud pots and steam vents at Lassen Volcanic National Park, or drive to an elevation of 7,900 feet on Mount Shasta to view the surrounding landscape. The Byway offers hikes through national forest lands that cover much of the area along the Byway. Crisp lakes, streams, and rivers offer great fishing, boating, swimming, or quiet contemplation. Also available are cross country skiing, snowshoeing, and snowmobiling in the winter months. If that isn't enough, hang gliding and parasailing are popular in the Hat Creek area of Lassen National Forest.

California

❋ *Volcanic Legacy Scenic Byway*

Scenic
The volcanic landscape of the Volcanic Legacy Scenic Byway includes distinctive features of mountain lakes and streams, three volcanoes (all nationally recognized), lava flows, and lava tube caves. You can experience these volcanic features through attractions at Crater Lake National Park (in Oregon), Lava Beds National Monument, and Lassen Volcanic National Park. However, the volcanic landscape is visible throughout the entire Byway. The Byway offers extended views of majestic volcano peaks, an abundance of beautiful forest vistas, and up-close views of crisp mountain lakes and streams.

Perhaps the most captivating of the Volcanic Legacy Scenic Byway's picturesque qualities are its vast volcano mountain peaks. Mount Shasta is the tallest of the peaks. Others include Lassen Peak and Mount Scott on the rim of Crater Lake. The immensity of the peaks allows them to be viewed from hundreds of miles away. The Byway circles around Mount Shasta, providing views from every angle. The majority of peaks along the Byway are above the timberline and provide views of broad snowfields and craggy rock outcroppings. At lower elevations, broad grassy meadows with extensive wildflowers offer outstanding foreground settings for views of the more distant peaks.

THINGS TO SEE AND DO
Driving along the Volcanic Legacy Scenic Byway will certainly keep your senses engaged, but if you yearn to get out of the car and stretch your legs, or if you'd like to make a mini-vacation out of your trip, check out these attractions along the route.

LAKE ALMANOR. *Chester (96020). Phone 530/258-2426. www.chesterlakealmanor.com.* Located about 20 miles southeast of Lassen Peak, Lake Almanor is a favorite vacation destination and summer-home spot for residents of north-central California. Tucked between Lassen and Plumas national forests, the lake and the surrounding area offer a mix of recreational opportunities from golf to fishing, as well as a number of resorts and quaint lakeside towns. In winter, the area attracts snowmobilers and cross-country skiers.

LAKE SISKIYOU. *4239 W A Barr Rd, Mount Shasta (96067). www.lakesis.com.* Box Canyon Dam impounds the Sacramento River, creating a 430-acre lake for fishing and swimming.

❋ **LASSEN VOLCANIC NATIONAL PARK.** *44 miles E of Redding via CA 44; 51 miles E of Red Bluff via CA 36, 89. Phone 530/595-4444. www.nps.gov/lavo/.* This 165-square-mile park was created to preserve the area that includes the 10,457-foot Lassen Peak, a volcano last active in 1921. Lassen Park, in the southernmost part of the Cascade Range, contains glacial lakes, virgin forests, mountain meadows, and snow-fed streams. Hydrothermal features, the Devastated Area, and Chaos Jumbles can be seen from Lassen Park Road. Boiling mud pots and fumaroles (steam vents) can be seen a short distance off the road at Sulphur Works. At Butte Lake, colorful masses of lava and volcanic ash blend with the forests, meadows, and streams. The peak is named for Peter Lassen, a Danish pioneer who used it as a landmark in guiding immigrant trains into the northern Sacramento Valley.

After being denuded in 1915 by a mudflow and a hot blast, the Devastated Area is slowly being reclaimed by small trees and flowers. The Chaos Crags, a group of lava plugs, were

AMERICA'S BYWAYS - WEST COAST

formed some 1,100 years ago. Bumpass Hell, a colorful area of mud pots, boiling pools, and steam vents, is a 3-mile round-trip hike from Lassen Park Road. Clouds of steam and sulfurous gases pour from vents in the thermal areas. Nearby is Lake Helen, named for Helen Tanner Brodt, the first white woman to climb Lassen Peak, in 1864.

At the northwest entrance is a visitor center (late June-Labor Day, daily) where you can find information about the park's human, natural, and geological history. There are guided walks during the summer, self-guided nature trails, and evening talks at some campgrounds. Camping (fee) is available at eight campgrounds; there's a two-week limit except at Lost Creek and Summit Lake campgrounds, which impose a seven-day limit; check at a ranger station for regulations. Lassen Park Road is usually open mid-June-mid-Oct, weather permitting. The Sulphur Works entrance to the south and the Manzanita Lake entrance to the northwest are open during the winter months for winter sports. There are facilities for the disabled, including a visitor center, comfort station, and amphitheater at Manzanita Lake.

★ **LAVA BEDS NATIONAL MONUMENT.** *30 miles SW of Tulelake, off CA 139. Phone 530/667-2282. www.nps.gov/labe/.* Seventy-two square miles of volcanic formations are preserved here in the extreme northeastern part of the state. Centuries ago, rivers of molten lava flowed here. In cooling, they formed a strange and fantastic region. Cinder cones dot the landscape, one rising 476 feet from its base. Winding trenches mark the collapsed roofs of lava tubes, an indicator of the 380 caves beneath the surface. Throughout the area are masses of lava hardened into weird shapes. Spatter cones may be seen where vents in the lava formed vertical tubelike channels, some only 3 feet in diameter but reaching downward 100 feet. Outstanding caves include Sentinel Cave, named for a lava formation in its passageway; Catacombs Cave, with passageways resembling Rome's catacombs; and Skull Cave,

with a broad entry cavern reaching approximately 80 feet in diameter. (The name comes from the many skulls of mountain sheep that were found here.) The National Park Service provides ladders and trails in the 24 caves that are easily accessible to the public.

One of the most costly Native American campaigns in history took place in this rugged, otherworldly setting. The Modoc War of 1872-1873 saw a small band of Native Americans revolt against reservation life and fight a series of battles with US troops. Although they were obliged to care for their families and live off the country, the Modocs held off an army almost ten times their number for more than five months.

There is a campground at Indian Well (fee, water available mid-May-Labor Day), and there are picnic areas at Fleener Chimneys and Captain Jacks Stronghold (no water). Guided walks, audiovisual programs, cave trips, and campfire programs are held daily, mid-June-Labor Day. Park headquarters has a visitor center (daily). No gasoline is available in the park, so fill your gas tank before entering. Per vehicle **$**.

MOUNT SHASTA. *E of I-5, in Shasta-Trinity National Forest (96067). Phone 530/926-4865; toll-free 800/926-4865. www.mtshastachamber.com.* This perpetually snow-covered double peak volcano towers to 14,162 feet. Five glaciers persist on the slopes, feeding the McCloud and Sacramento rivers. A scenic drive on the Everitt Memorial Highway climbs from the city of Mount Shasta up the slope to 7,840 feet for a magnificent view. White pine, the famous Shasta lily, and majestic stands of red fir are found at various elevations.

SISSON MUSEUM. *1 N Old State Rd, Mount Shasta (96067). Phone 530/926-5508.* Features exhibits on area history, opportunities for mountain climbing, a fish hatchery, and exhibits of local Native American culture. Open daily; closed Easter, Dec 25, also Jan-Feb. Also visit the **annual quilt show** (late June-early July). **FREE**

California

❋ *Volcanic Legacy Scenic Byway*

SHASTA SUNSET DINNER TRAIN. *28 Main St, McCloud (96057). Phone 530/964-2142; toll-free 800/733-2141. www.shastasunset.com.* The Shasta Sunset Dinner Train takes the same route that the lumber-heavy McCloud Railway did in the late 19th century, departing from the historic station in McCloud, soaring over the southern foothills of 14,162-foot Mount Shasta, and then coming back again. The three-hour ride is filled with breathtaking views as the vintage gold-finished cars (which were originally built in 1916 for the Illinois Central Railroad and are now lavish inside and out) climb inclines and switchbacks and cross trestles and bridges. The dinner menu changes monthly, but it is best described as continental with a regional spin; the extensive wine list emphasizes California labels. There are also sightseeing excursions on open-air railcars and luncheon trips. **$$$$**

STATE FISH HATCHERY. *1 N Old Stage Rd, Mount Shasta (96067). Phone 530/926-2215.* The State Fish Hatchery raises trout and has been in continuous operation since 1888. You can take a self-guided tour of trout ponds. Picnic tables, rest rooms. Open daily. **FREE**

PLACES TO STAY

If you choose to include an overnight stay in your trip along this All-American Road, Mobil Travel Guide recommends the following lodgings.

★★ **BIDWELL HOUSE BED AND BREAKFAST.** *1 Main St, Chester (96020). Phone 530/258-3338. www.bidwellhouse.com.* 14 rooms, 1 cottage, 2 story. No A/C. Room phones available. Holidays 2-day minimum. Complimentary full breakfast. Check-out 11 am, check-in 3-6 pm. TV available. Game room. Some fireplaces. Antiques. Built in 1901. Flower and vegetable gardens. Totally nonsmoking. ¢

★ **MCCLOUD HOTEL BED AND BREAKFAST.** *408 Main St, McCloud (96057). Phone 530/964-2822; toll-free 800/964-2823. www.mccloudhotel.com.* 16 rooms, 2 story. No room phones. Adults only. Complimentary full breakfast. Check-out 11 am, check-in 3-7 pm. TV in common room. Massage. Concierge. Built in 1915. Totally nonsmoking. ¢

★ **BEST WESTERN TREE HOUSE MOTOR INN.** *111 Morgan Way, Mount Shasta (96067). Phone 530/926-3101; toll-free 800/780-7234. www.bestwestern.com.* 95 rooms, 2-3 story. Pet accepted. Complimentary full breakfast. Check-out noon. TV. In-room modem link. Restaurant, bar. Indoor pool, whirlpool. Downhill, cross-country ski 10 miles. Meeting rooms. Business center. View of Mount Shasta. ¢

★ **FINLANDIA MOTEL.** *1612 S Mt Shasta Blvd, Mount Shasta (96067). Phone 530/926-5596.* 25 rooms, 3 kitchen units, 1-2 story. Pet accepted. Check-out 11 am. TV. Downhill ski 9 miles; cross-country ski 8 miles. ¢

★ **MOUNT SHASTA RESORT.** *1000 Siskiyou Lake Blvd, Mount Shasta (96067). Phone 530/926-3030; toll-free 800/958-3363. www.mountshastaresort.com.* 50 cottages, 2 story. Weekends, holidays 2-3-day minimum. Check-out 11 am, check-in 3 pm. TV. In-room modem link. Refrigerators, microwaves, fireplaces. Restaurant, bar. Spa. 18-hole golf, greens fee $42. Lighted tennis, pro. Downhill, cross-country ski 10 miles. Tobogganing. Camping. Business services. Totally nonsmoking. **$**

★ **STRAWBERRY VALLEY INN.** *1142 S Mt Shasta Blvd, Mount Shasta (96067). Phone 530/926-2052. www.strawberryvalleyinn.com.* 25 rooms, 7 suites. Some with A/C. Ski plans. Complimentary continental breakfast. Check-out 11 am. TV. In-room modem link. Restaurant nearby. Downhill, cross-country ski 10 miles. Totally nonsmoking. ¢

★ **SWISS HOLIDAY LODGE.** *2400 S Mt Shasta Blvd, Mount Shasta (96067). Phone 530/926-3446.* 21 air-cooled rooms, 2 story. Pet accepted; fee. Complimentary continental breakfast. Check-out 11 am. TV; cable (premium). Outdoor pool, whirlpool. Refrigerators available. Picnic tables, grills. Downhill, cross-country ski 10 miles. View of Mount Shasta. Totally nonsmoking. ¢

PLACES TO EAT

A long day of driving is sure to make you hungry. At the end of your journey, take a table at one of the following restaurants.

★★★ **CAFÉ MADDALENA.** *5801 Sacramento Ave, Dunsmuir (96025). Phone 530/235-2725. www.cafemaddalena.com.* Mediterranean menu. Closed Mon. Dinner. Innovative menu featuring Spanish, Italian, and Provencal cuisine. $$

★★ **THE HIGHLAND HOUSE.** *1000 Siskiyou Lake Blvd, Mount Shasta (96067). Phone toll-free 800/958-3363. www.mountshastaresort.com.* American menu. Lunch, dinner. Upscale white-tablecloth dining room featuring modern American cuisine and outdoor seating with views of Mount Shasta. $$$

★★ **PIEMONT.** *1200 S Mt Shasta Blvd, Mount Shasta (96067). Phone 530/926-2402.* American, Italian menu. Closed Mon; Thanksgiving, Dec 24-25; also Tues in Jan and Feb. Dinner. Bar. Children's menu. Totally nonsmoking. $ D

★★ **SERGE'S RESTAURANT.** *531 Chestnut St, Mount Shasta (96067). Phone 530/926-1276.* French menu. Closed Mon, Tues. Dinner. Intimate country restaurant with outdoor seating available. $$

Cascade Lakes Scenic Byway
✹ OREGON

Quick Facts

LENGTH: 66 miles.

TIME TO ALLOW: 3 to 5 hours.

BEST TIME TO DRIVE: June through October.

BYWAY TRAVEL INFORMATION: Bend Visitor Center and Chamber of Commerce: toll-free 800/905-2362; Byway local Web sites: www.fs.fed.us/r6/deschutes; www.ctws.org/museum; www.covisitors.com.

SPECIAL CONSIDERATIONS: Winter snowfall closes a portion of the Byway from mid-November until late May each year.

RESTRICTIONS: The first 17 miles of the Byway from just outside Bend to Mount Bachelor are open year-round, as are the last 4 miles north of Highway 58. The remaining 48 miles from Mount Bachelor to the Cutoff are closed in the winter due to snow. When parking for more than a few hour near trailhead markers, expect to obtain a permit and pay parking fees. Purchase permits at most outdoor shops, the Bend Chamber of Commerce, and the National Forest Service.

BICYCLE/PEDESTRIAN FACILITIES: This Byway is popular with bicyclists. The section of Byway from Bend to Mount Bachelor is best suited to bicyclists; although narrower, the remaining portions of the Byway are also suited for bicycle travel. The Byway is not suitable for regular pedestrian travel, but the hiking oportunities off the Byway are excellent.

The towering Cascade Mountains provide the backdrop for this scenic drive. These mountains also offer fabulous hiking and challenging rock climbing. The Byway climbs into the Deschutes National Forest, where fishing, hiking, rafting, and other outdoor sports are plentiful. This area is also a winter playground; for example, Mount Bachelor's ski resort is filled with snow through June. This Byway also crosses paths with those of early explorers and trappers, such as Kit Carson, John C. Fremont, and Nathaniel J. Wyeth.

As you drive by many bodies of water along the route, it is easy to see why this route was named after the Cascade Lakes. Some of the lakes that you encounter include Todd Lake, Sparks Lake, Cultus Lake, and Crane Prairie Reservoir. As you can imagine, this is an angler's paradise. Anglers can spend hours at the banks of these lakes, fishing for Atlantic salmon and other freshwater fish. Waterfowl and many species of plants thrive here as well.

THE BYWAY STORY

The Cascade Lakes Scenic Byway tells archaeological, historical, natural, recreational, and scenic stories that make it a unique and treasured Byway.

Archaeological

The history of how this area was formed is preserved at The High Desert Museum, along with displays and artifacts of the area's Native Americans and original cowboys. Also on display are remakes of prehistoric dwellings.

Oregon

✻ Cascade Lakes Scenic Byway

Historical

This same scenic drive was once traveled by early mountain men explorers Kit Carson, John C. Fremont, and Nathaniel J. Wyeth. In the days of horse and buggy, this was a well-worn, 100-mile dirt road called the Century Drive. Also, along this Byway in the area of Benham Falls, the classic movies *The Indian Fighter, Rooster Cogburn,* and *Up the Creek* were filmed.

The Lava River Cave, Oregon's longest uncollapsed lava tube, tells the tale of the area's once-active volcanic past. It is closed during winter months, and warm clothing is advised when touring at other times of the year. The Lava Lands Visitor Center and Lava Butte are also available to observe volcanic cones and formations. There are also other displays and films available on the area's volcanic history.

Natural

The geology of the Cascade Lakes Scenic Byway is especially significant. The volcanic Cascade Mountains (unique to the Pacific Northwest) are part of the Ring-of-Fire volcanic mountain chain that borders the Pacific Ocean. Nowhere else in the country (and possibly in the world) is there ready access to such a great diversity of volcanic features.

You can see stratovolcanoes, shield volcanoes, cinder cones, sheets of pumice and ash, sheets of ashflow tuffs, maars, caves, and several kinds of lava flows and domes. Volcanism and glaciation formed more than 150 small and large lakes for which this region is well known.

This area is also featured in geology textbooks and was used as a training ground for the Apollo moon missions in the 1960s. In 1971, astronaut Jim Irwin (aboard *Apollo 15*) placed a rock from Devil's Lake (a lake along this Byway) on the lunar surface—the only Earth rock on the moon!

The route also traverses through the drier forests that include Lodgepole pine and older ponderosa pine. Also, 262 species of birds and animals reside here—including two endangered species: the bald eagle and the northern spotted owl.

Recreational

You'll find many recreational activities along the Cascade Lakes Scenic Byway. Due to elevation differences and compact geography, six months out of the year, you can ski in the morning and hike, fish, bicycle, or kayak in the afternoon.

Within the Deschutes National Forest and the Three Sisters Wilderness Area, you'll find snow-capped peaks, over 150 lakes, and a Wild & Scenic River. With its dependable, dry powder snow and 3,300-foot elevation drop, Mount Bachelor offers the best downhill skiing in the Northwest. The same snow conditions also provide excellent cross-country skiing, snowmobiling, and dog sledding.

Excellent camping, fishing, boating, bicycling, hiking, backpacking, mountain climbing, and horseback riding are also available. Boaters can motorboat, canoe, sail, or wind surf on the lakes. You can also whitewater raft on the Deschutes River.

Scenic

As you drive along the Cascade Lakes Scenic Byway, dramatic snow-capped peaks tower over you. These peaks are most often mirrored in crystal-clear alpine lakes.

The Summit Express lift can take you to the 9,065-foot peak of Mount Bachelor in the summer. The dramatic 360-degree view sweeps a volcanic mountain skyline. You can see for hundreds of miles—from Mount Adams in Washington to Mount Shasta in California.

The view from Dutchman Flat (a pumice-covered area at the 6,000-foot base of Mount Bachelor) may look familiar to you. The scenic panorama has been featured in the movies *Homeward Bound, Rooster Cogburn,* and *The Postman.*

The area of Sparks Lake and Meadow (with South Sister Mountain looming in the background) has been chosen as the site to commemorate Ray Atkeson, Oregon's photographer laureate.

HIGHLIGHTS

The following scenic tour gives you a chance to enjoy the highlights of this Byway:

- Starting from **Bend** and traveling the Cascade Lakes Scenic Byway, you come across **Drake Park,** at the Hwy 97 and Franklin Avenue intersection. Park in Mirror Pond Parking Lot (just west of the Franklin and Wall intersection) and explore the charming downtown area. The original site of Bend was selected around this area because it was an easy location for early travelers to cross the Deschutes River.

- Fifteen miles west of Bend on the Cascade Lakes Highway are hiking, mountain biking, and cross-country skiing opportunities at the **Swampy Lakes** area. From the trailhead at the north end of the parking lot, you can enjoy a variety of marked skiing and hiking trails from 2 to 10 miles in length. The area provides five shelters that are usually stocked with wood in the winter.

- **Mount Bachelor Ski and Summer Resort** is west of the Swampy Lakes, an area where you can spend a whole day to recreate and ski or fish. Just west of the entrance to Mount Bachelor, a whole new scenic landscape beckons to be enjoyed and appreciated. By some quirk of nature, the small pumic desert, called **Dutchman Flat,** has not accumulated enough soil nutrients to sustain the growth of many plants. Pusspaws with pink blooms and sulfur flowers with yellow blooms are a few of the hardy plants that grow in this unique area. Stop to take pictures and take note of it as you pass by; this was where the movie *How the West Was Won* was filmed.

- On the Byway, you pass **Todd Lake, Sparks Lake,** and **Green Lakes Trailhead,** all worthy stops. Continue on west of the Green Lakes Trailhead to a small but scenic area with several springs surfacing from the edge of a huge lava flow, creating a little meadow. Along with the lush meadow grass, you'll find moss, blue lupines, and Indian pictographs, painted on the face of a large dacite boulder, which indicate an ancient Indian trail. This place is **Devils Garden**—recount the legend of the area and explore a bit of the ancient Indian trail.

- Continue on the Byway to pass picturesque **Devils Lake, Elk Lake, Hosmer Lake, Lava Lake, Little Lava Lake, Cultus Lake,** and **Little Cultus Lake** until you come to the **Osprey Observation Point.** Constructed in 1929, it has become an outstanding fishing area and a breeding ground for the osprey (fish hawk), identified as a potentially endangered species in 1969. From the parking lot, a short walk takes you to an observation area on the west side of the reservoir. Here, you can view snags and artificial nesting poles inhabited by the birds. Many visitors are entertained as osprey dive for fish from more than a hundred feet above the water. Continue south to come to the end of the Byway.

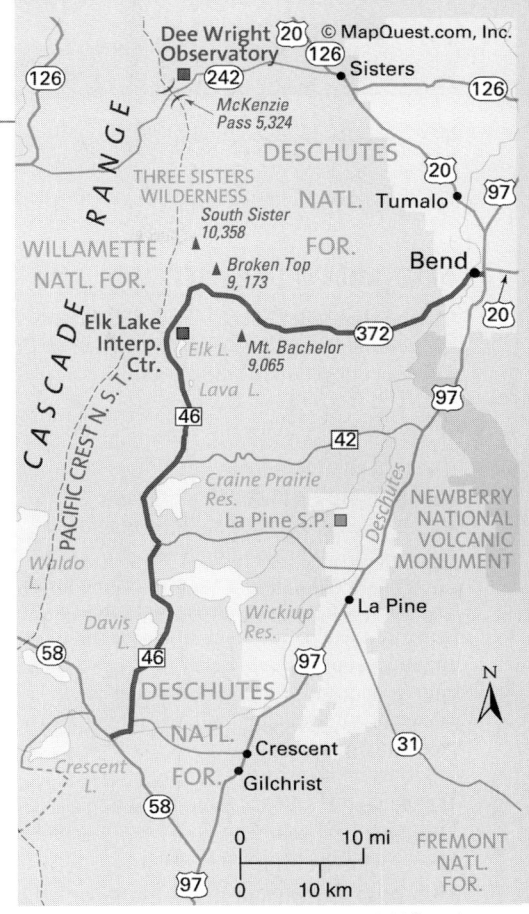

see page A14 for color map

Oregon

❋ *Cascade Lakes Scenic Byway*

THINGS TO SEE AND DO

Driving along the Cascade Lakes Scenic Byway will certainly keep your senses engaged, but if you yearn to get out of the car and stretch your legs, or if you'd like to make a mini-vacation out of your trip, check out these attractions along the route.

THE HIGH DESERT MUSEUM. *59800 S Hwy 97, Bend (97702). Phone 541/382-4754. www.highdesert.org.* Regional museum with indoor/outdoor exhibits featuring live animals and cultural history of Intermountain Northwest arid lands; hands-on activities; ongoing presentations. Galleries house wildlife, Western art, and Native American artifacts; landscape photography; walk-through dioramas depicting opening of American West. Desertarium showcases seldom-seen bats, burrowing owls, amphibians, and reptiles. Visitor center. Open daily 9 am-5 pm; closed Jan 1, Thanksgiving, Dec 25. **$$**

LAVA BUTTE AND LAVA RIVER CAVE. *58201 Hwy 97 S, Bend (97707). Phone 541/593-2421.* Lava Butte is an extinct cinder cone. Paved road to the top provides a view of Cascades; interpretive trails are available through pine forest and lava flow. One mile south, Lava River Cave offers a lava tube 1.2 miles long (fee); ramps and stairs make walking easier. **$$**

MOUNT BACHELOR SKI AREA. *PO Box 1031, Bend (97709). Phone 541/382-2442 or -2607. www.mtbachelor.com.* Panoramic, scenic view of forests, lakes, and the Cascade Range. Facilities at base of 6,000 feet; 6,000 acres. Ten chairlifts; patrol, school, rentals; cafeterias, concession areas, bars, lodges; day care. Longest run 1 1/2 miles; vertical drop 3,365 feet. Fifty-six miles of cross-country trails. Open mid-Nov-May, daily. **$$$$**

PILOT BUTTE. *2880 NE 27th St, Bend (97701). Phone 541/388-6055.* A 101-acre park noted for a lone cinder cone rising 511 feet above the city. The summit affords an excellent view of the Cascade Range. No water, no camping.

TUMALO FALLS. *Skyliner Rd and Tumalo Falls, Bend (97701). Phone 541/383-5300.* A 97-foot waterfall deep in a pine forest that was devastated by a 1979 fire.

WHITEWATER RAFTING. SUN COUNTRY TOURS. *531 SW 13th St, Bend (99701). Phone 541/382-6277. www.suncountrytours.com.* Choose from two-hour or all-day trips. Also canoeing and special programs. Open May-Sept. **$$$$**

PLACES TO STAY

If you choose to include an overnight stay in your trip along this Byway, Mobil Travel Guide recommends the following lodgings.

★ **BEST WESTERN ENTRADA LODGE.** *19221 Century Dr, Bend (97702). Phone 541/382-4080; toll-free 800/780-7234. www.bestwestern.com.* 79 rooms. Ski plans. Pet accepted; fee. Complimentary continental breakfast. Check-out noon. TV. In-room modem link. Health club privileges. Outdoor pool, whirlpool. Downhill, cross-country ski 17 miles. Whitewater rafting. On 31 acres. **¢**

★★★ **INN OF THE SEVENTH MOUNTAIN.**
18575 SW Century Dr, Bend (97702).
Phone 541/382-8711; toll-free 800/452-6810.
www.innofthe7thmountain.com. With breathtaking views both in summer and winter, this beautiful oasis is set in Deschutes National Forest. Whitewater rafting, horseback riding, golfing, and canoeing make it Oregon's premier resort destination. Guests can spread out in the condo-style accommodations. 300 rooms, 200 kitchen units, 3 story. No elevator. Package plans. Check-out noon. TV, VCR available (movies). Two pools, wading pool, whirlpools, poolside service, lifeguard (summer). Playgrounds. Supervised children's activities (June-Sept), ages 4-11. Dining rooms 7 am-10 pm. Box lunches. Bar 4 pm-1 am. Coin laundry. Meeting rooms. Business services available. Grocery. Sports director. Tennis, pro. Canoeing, rafting trips. Downhill, cross-country ski 14 miles. Outdoor ice skating/roller rink; horse-drawn sleigh rides. Snowmobile, bike tours. Bicycles. Lawn games. Sauna. Movies. Recreation room. Some refrigerators, microwaves, fireplaces. Private patios. Picnic tables, grills. ¢

★★ **ROCK SPRINGS GUEST RANCH.** *64201 Tyler Rd, Bend (97701). Phone 541/382-1957; toll-free 800/225-3833. www.rocksprings.com.* 26 cottages. Check-out 11 am, check-in 4:30 pm. TV in sitting room. Outdoor pool, whirlpool. Free supervised children's activities (late June-Aug), ages 3-16. Dining room (sittings). Box lunches. Picnics. Grocery 3 miles. Guest laundry. Business services available. Free airport transportation. Lighted tennis, pro. Downhill, cross-country ski 20 miles. In-house fitness room. Massage. Lawn games. Western trail rides. Game room. Fish pond. Refrigerators, fireplaces. Picnic tables. $$

★★ **RIVERHOUSE RESORT.** *3075 N Hwy 97, Bend (97701). Phone 541/389-3111; toll-free 866/453-4480. www.riverhouse.com.* 220 rooms, 2 story. Ski, golf plans. Pet accepted. Check-out noon. TV; cable (premium), VCR (movies). In-room modem link. Laundry services. Restaurant. Room service. In-house exercise facility. Two pools, one indoor; poolside service. Golf, greens fee $28-$42. On the Deschutes River. ¢

★★★ **SUNRIVER RESORT.** *1 Center Dr, Sunriver (97707). Phone 541/593-1000; toll-free 800/801-8765. www.sunriver-resort.com.* Experience the best of the Northwest at this resort. The rustic lodges are spacious and beautiful. With four restaurants and loads of activity year-round, the whole family will enjoy time spent here. 211 units (1-3 bedroom) in 2-story lodge units, 77 kitchen units, 230 houses (1-4 bedroom). Check-out 11 am, check-in 4 pm. TV; cable (premium), VCR available (movies). Three pools, three wading pools, outdoor whirlpools, lifeguard. Playground. Supervised children's activities (June-Sept), ages 3-14. Dining rooms. Coin laundry. Meeting rooms. Business center. Grocery. Barber, beauty shop. Airport transportation. Ski bus. Sports director. 28 tennis courts. Three 18-hole golf courses, six pros, putting greens, driving ranges, pro shops. Canoes; whitewater rafting. Cross-country ski on site. Skating rink, equipment (fee). Racquetball. Bicycles; 30 miles of bike trails. Nature center. Stables. Indoor, outdoor games. Game room (fee). Entertainment. Massage. Health club privileges. Fishing guide service. 5,500-foot airstrip. Marina. Houses with full amenities and private patios. Some microwaves. Balconies. Picnic tables. 3,300 acres on the Deschutes River. $

77

Oregon

❄ *Cascade Lakes Scenic Byway*

★★ **MOUNT BACHELOR VILLAGE RESORT.** *19717 Mt Bachelor Dr, Bend (97701). Phone 541/389-5900; toll-free 800/452-9846. www.mountbachelorvillage.com.* 130 condos, some A/C, 2 story. Ski, golf plans. Check-out noon. TV. Heated pool; whirlpools. Restaurant. Coin laundry. Business center. Downhill ski 18 miles, cross-country ski 14 miles. Tennis. Health club privileges. Refrigerators, fireplaces; some microwaves. Private patios, balconies. Picnic tables. Woodland setting along the Deschutes River. $-$$$

PLACES TO EAT

A long day of driving is sure to make you hungry. At the end of your journey, take a table at one of the following restaurants.

★★★ **ERNESTO'S ITALIAN RESTAURANT.** *1203 NE 3rd St, Bend (97701). Phone 541/389-7274.* A family restaurant housed in a converted church. Italian menu. Dinner. Bar. Children's menu. $$
SC

★★★ **MEADOWS.** *1 Center Dr, Sunriver (97707). Phone 541/593-1000. www.sunriver-resort.com.* Northwest High Desert menu. Dinner. Bar. Reservations accepted. Totally nonsmoking. $$
D

★★ **PINE TAVERN.** *967 NW Brooks St, Bend (97701). Phone 541/382-5581. www.pinetavern.com.* Steak, seafood menu. Lunch, dinner (dinner only Sun). Bar. Salad bar (lunch). Children's menu. Reservations accepted. Outdoor seating. 100-foot pine tree in dining room. $$
D

★ **ROSZAK'S FISH HOUSE.** *1230 NE 3rd St, Bend (97701). Phone 541/382-3173.* Seafood, steak menu. Closed Memorial Day, Labor Day. Lunch (weekdays only), dinner. Bar. Children's menu. Reservations accepted. Totally nonsmoking. $$
D

★ **TONY'S.** *415 NE 3rd St, Bend (97701). Phone 541/389-5858.* Italian, American menu. Closed Dec 25. Breakfast, lunch, dinner. Bar. Children's menu. Reservations accepted. Early American building; original paintings, fireplace. Family-owned. $$
D SC

★ **WESTSIDE BAKERY & CAFÉ.** *1005 NW Galveston Ave, Bend (97701). Phone 541/382-3426.* Closed Thanksgiving, Dec 25. Breakfast, lunch. Children's menu. $
D

Hells Canyon Scenic Byway

✸ OREGON   AN ALL-AMERICAN ROAD

Quick Facts

LENGTH: 218 miles.

TIME TO ALLOW: 8 hours.

BEST TIME TO DRIVE: Late May to October, when you see spectacular snow-capped mountains, lush green hills, and wildflowers in bloom. High season is in July and August.

BYWAY TRAVEL INFORMATION: Eastern Oregon Visitors Association: 541/856-3272; Byway travel and tourism Web site: www.eova.com.

SPECIAL CONSIDERATIONS: You won't find any services beyond Joseph, so make sure you have plenty of gas before leaving Baker City or La Grande. Before starting out, take notice of the travel times as well as mileage between stops and keep your fuel tank as full as possible. Be prepared for temperatures that vary as much as 50 degrees as the day wears on.

RESTRICTIONS: Wallowa Mountain Loop USFS Road 39, between Joseph and Halfway, is closed from November through February due to heavy snow.

BICYCLE/PEDESTRIAN FACILITIES: Distances between destinations make pedestrian activity impractical along much of the Byway, except along Highway 351 around Wallowa Lake. Most of the local pedestrian activity occurs in the communities along the Byway, where you find sidewalks and crosswalks.

Leave the fast pace and fenced-in views of Interstate 84 and follow the contours of the land into slower times and wilder places. Travel this 218-mile journey from river's edge to mountaintop and down to valley floor. Have lunch overlooking a Wild & Scenic River. Share a canyon road with a cattle drive. Pass through lush valleys rimmed by the snow-tipped Wallowa Mountains. Savor the scent of pine on the fresh mountain air. Enjoy panoramic views of rugged basalt cliffs and grassy open ridges. Stand next to the majestic Snake River as it begins its tumbling course through North America's deepest canyon. Place your hand in the weathered track of a wagon wheel. Hear the wind rushing through the forest. This is a journey you won't forget.

The route of the Hells Canyon Scenic Byway is a loop that encircles the Wallowa Mountains, intersecting with Interstate 84 at La Grande and Baker City. Small towns scattered along the drive offer visitor services. The entire route is on a paved highway, but plan ahead: you'll find stretches of more than 80 miles without gas stations and with few services. A segment of the Byway between Joseph and Halfway closes due to snow in winter but allows access to winter recreation areas, offering a different kind of northeast Oregon adventure.

THE BYWAY STORY

The Hells Canyon Scenic Byway tells archaeological, cultural, historical, natural, recreational, and scenic stories that make it a unique and treasured Byway.

Oregon

✵ *Hells Canyon Scenic Byway*

Archaeological
Extremes in the land have dictated the course of the area's natural and cultural history. Relatively mild winters and abundant wildlife drew people to the canyon over 7,000 years ago. Archeological evidence, ranging from rock art to winter "pithouse" villages, can be found in the Snake River corridor. Pictographs and petroglyphs are scattered along the river where Native Americans spent their winters. Please use care when viewing these sites; these national treasures have stood the test of time and will be enjoyed long into the future.

Cultural
On the map, northeastern Oregon looks far removed from metropolitan area amenities. However, you may be surprised by the availability of arts and culture. Musical events along the Byway range from old-time fiddling to blues to Beethoven. Plays, concerts, and living-history productions can be enjoyed daily in Baker City. The small town of Joseph has earned a national reputation for its bronze foundries and galleries. Some of the nation's most highly acclaimed artists cast their bronzes at one of the four area foundries or show their work in one of the many galleries that line the town's picturesque main street. Eastern Oregon University, located in La Grande, offers theatrical productions and concerts, including a full season of music from the Grande Ronde Symphony Orchestra. The Historic Elgin Opera House in Elgin is also a crowd pleaser for concerts, movies, and plays.

Historical
For many centuries, the Grande Ronde Valley was used seasonally by Native Americans. Covered largely by wetlands, the beautiful valley was lush with grass and alive with game. Herds of elk summered in the surrounding high country and wintered in the milder valley. Mule deer, pronghorn antelope, and big-horn sheep browsed the hills and meadows. This bountiful scene was a neutral meeting place for members of the Umatilla, Yakima, Shoshone, Cayuse, and Bannock nations, who came to enjoy the hot springs, hunt, graze their horses, and gather plants for food. The picturesque Wallowa Valley was the beloved home of the Nez Perce Indians. By winter of 1877, settlement conflicts drove young Chief Joseph to make a harrowing attempt to reach Canada with a group of 250 men, women, and children. They struggled to within 24 miles of safety before being captured at Montana and sent to reservations.

This area remains a significant religious and cultural center for the Nez Perce, Umatilla, and Cayuse Indians. Every fall, when leaving the valley to winter in the milder climate along the Columbia plateau, these early residents lit huge fires in the valleys, burning off old grass and allowing for healthy regrowth in the spring.

Natural
Millions of years ago, the Wallowa Mountains formed the coast of what would eventually be called Oregon. Uplifted layers of limestone on the peaks harbor fossilized shells that once sat at the bottom of the ocean. Eons of volcanic action and faulting pushed the masses of rock upward while new land formed to the west. The Coast Range, Cascade Mountains, and upland desert of central Oregon now separate the Wallowas from the ocean by hundreds of miles. Flows of plateau basalt, batholiths of granite, and layers of shale were buckled and folded to form the mountain range. Raging rivers and gigantic glaciers carved the peaks and canyons. In short, nature took a long time to sculpt the dramatic beauty you see along the Byway.

Recreational
Recreational opportunities along the Hells Canyon Scenic Byway are seemingly endless and range from tranquil to thrilling. Four distinct seasons alter the scenery and determine the activities.

In spring, warm sunshine carpets the hills with green grass and colorful wildflowers. The landscape becomes a patchwork quilt with fields of freshly plowed soil, sprouting crops, and blossoming fruit trees. It's a great time for sightseeing from a car or on a bike. Watch the meadows for frisky new calves and wobbly foals. Along the streams, willows, dogwood, and mock orange create a changing palette of yellows, pinks, and vibrant greens. Fish for steelhead or trout on the Grande Ronde, Minam, Wallowa, and Imnaha rivers. Take a thrilling raft or jet boat ride through the Class III and IV rapids on the Snake River or float the waters of the Grande Ronde and Minam rivers.

Summer bursts with energy. Warm, dry weather and lots of sunshine make the outdoors impossible to resist. Microclimates at different elevations and aspects mean you can always find a cooler or hotter spot within miles. The Wallowa-Whitman National Forest, along with county and state parks departments, operates numerous campgrounds, trail systems, viewpoints, and picnic facilities along or near the route. Hike or mountain bike into the high country. Cast a fishing line on several of the rivers and streams and at Wallowa Lake. Hire a private outfitter to experience horseback riding and pack trips, rafting, parasailing, or jet boat adventures. Cycle the back roads or mountain trails for the amazing views. Watch hang gliders and hot air balloonists catch the breeze high above the Wallowa and Grande Ronde valleys.

In autumn, cooler temperatures and shorter days turn tamarack (western larch) needles to gold and leaves to jewel tones of yellow, orange, and red. Canadian geese are on the move, filling the air with melancholy calls. Hunt for deer, elk, bear, cougar, and bighorn sheep or use them as photo opportunities.

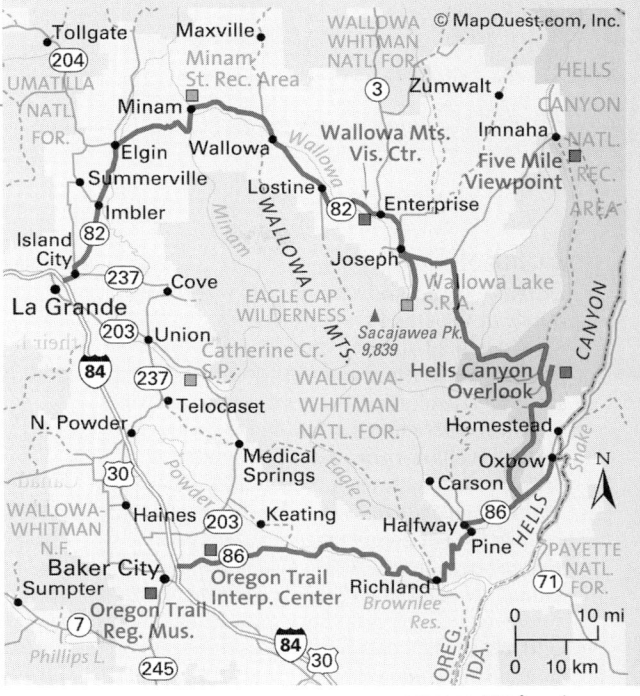

Fall is also the time for cattle drives, harvesting, and blue-sky days crisp with the smell of winter. Catch the small-town spirit by watching a high school football game in splendid, scenic surroundings—visitors are always welcome.

Winter's dry, powdery snow opens area ski resorts and turns backcountry side trips and hiking trails into a giant playground for adventurers on skis, snowmobiles, and snowshoes. The FS Road 39 section of the Byway between Joseph and Halfway is closed to auto and truck traffic in winter, when it becomes an especially popular route for snowmobilers. It connects into much larger networks providing access to hundreds of miles of groomed trails in the region. Enjoy winter raptor viewing in Minam and Hells canyons, a horse-drawn sleigh ride in Joseph, or ice fishing on Wallowa Lake. Near the Byway, ride a horse-drawn wagon through a herd of Rocky Mountain elk at the Elkhorn Elk Feeding Site and find out about the majestic animal's history in the area. By day, surround yourself with spectacular scenery topped with fresh white snow. By night, relax before a crackling fire in cozy lodgings.

see page A15 for color map

Oregon

Hells Canyon Scenic Byway

Scenic

Travel the Hells Canyon Scenic Byway and see much of the majesty and mystery of the West within a 218-mile corridor. The magnificent Snake River twists and churns over boulders and past towering cliffs. Pungent sagebrush and bunch grasses cover the flats and crouch at the feet of dramatic rock formations. Sparkling streams tumble through thick forests of pine and mixed conifers. Lush valleys lie at the feet of magnificent mountain ranges with peaks that tower to nearly 10,000 feet. Fields of hay, wheat, grass, mint, and canola color the valley floor. Cattle, sheep, and horses graze on a menu of sweet clover and timothy. Historic barns and houses bring human warmth and scale to the dramatic scenery.

HIGHLIGHTS

- Start your summer outdoors tour at midday so you can go to the **Wallowa Mountains Visitor Center** (about half a mile northwest of Enterprise) to get current and detailed information about camps and hikes in the area. Spend the night camping in the Wallowa Mountains or beside the Imnaha River.
- Visit **Wallowa Lake** (about 6 miles south of Joseph) and relax for a few hours of swimming, fishing, boating, or hiking. You can also take a tram from here to the peak of Mount Howard and enjoy wonderful views.
- Next, visit the **Hell's Canyon Overlook.** The overlook is about 30 miles along the Byway from the lake. This is a staggering view, 5,400 feet above the canyon floor.
- In Copperfield (about 15 miles south of the Overlook), secure a jetboat tour on the **Snake River.** You can also rent rafts and such here. After a few hours of enjoying the Snake, end your day at the **Hole-in-the-Wall Slide.** The geographically intriguing slide is about 30 miles west on the Byway from Copperfield.

THINGS TO SEE AND DO

Driving along the Hells Canyon Scenic Byway will certainly keep your senses engaged, but if you yearn to get out of the car and stretch your legs, or if you'd like to make a mini-vacation out of your trip, check out these attractions along the route.

ANTHONY LAKES SKI AREA. *47500 Anthony Lake Hwy North Powder, Baker City (97814). Phone 541/856-3277. www.anthonylakes.com.* Triple chairlift, Pomalift; patrol, school, rentals; nursery; day lodge, cafeteria, concession area, bar. Longest run 1 1/2 miles; vertical drop 900 feet. Fishing, hiking, cabin rentals, store (open summer). Cross-country trails. Open mid-Nov-mid-Apr, Thurs-Sun. $$$$

✷ **HELLS CANYON NATIONAL RECREATION AREA.** *612 SW 2nd St, Enterprise (97828). Phone 541/426-5546. www.fs.fed.us/hellscanyon/.* Created by the Snake River at the Idaho/Oregon border, Hells Canyon is the deepest river-carved gorge in North America—1 1/2 miles from Idaho's He Devil Mountain (elevation 9,393 feet) to the Snake River at Granite Creek (elevation 1,408 feet). An overlook at Hat Point, southeast of Imnaha, is a fire lookout. The recreation area includes parts of the Wallowa-Whitman National Forest. Activities include float trips, jet boat tours, boat trips into the canyon from the Hells Canyon Dam, backpacking, and horseback riding. Some developed campgrounds; much of the area is undeveloped, and some is designated wilderness. Be sure to inquire about road conditions before planning a trip; some roads are rough and open for a limited season.

NATIONAL HISTORIC OREGON TRAIL VISITOR CENTER. *Hwy 86, Baker City (97814). Phone toll-free 800/523-1235. www.nps.gov/oreg/oreg.htm.* Built and operated by the Bureau of Land Management, this center was built as a monument to emigrants who journeyed on the Oregon Trail. It is highly regarded for the quality of exhibits and the commanding view from its hilltop location. Exhibits, living-history presentations, and multimedia displays. Open Nov-Mar 9 am-4 pm, Apr-Oct 9 am-6 pm; closed Jan 1, Dec 25. $$$

OREGON TRAIL REGIONAL MUSEUM. *2490 Grove St, Baker City (97814). Phone toll-free 800/523-1235.* This museum houses one of the most outstanding collections of rocks, minerals, and semiprecious stones in the West. Also an elaborate sea-life display, wildlife display, period clothing, and artifacts of early Baker County. Open late Mar-Oct, daily. $

SUMPTER VALLEY RAILWAY. *OR 7, Baker City (97814). Phone toll-free 800/523-1235. www.srvy.com.* Restored gear-driven Heisler steam locomotive and two observation cars travel 7 miles on a narrow-gauge track through a wildlife game habitat area where beavers, muskrats, geese, waterfowl, herons, and other animals may be seen. Also passes through the Sumpter mining district, location of the Sumpter Dredge that brought up more than $10 million in gold between 1913 and 1954 from as far down as 20 feet. Open May-Sept, Sat, Sun, holidays. $$

VALLEY BRONZE OF OREGON. *307 W Alder St, Joseph (98746). Phone 541/432-7445. www.valleybronze.com.* This company produces finished castings of bronze, fine and sterling silver, and stainless steel. The showroom displays finished pieces. Tours of the foundry depart from the showroom (by reservation). Open May-Nov, daily; rest of year, by appointment.

WALLOWA LAKE STATE PARK. *72214 Marina Ln, Joseph (97846). Phone 541/432-4185; toll-free 800/452-5687. www.oregonstateparks.org/park_27.php.* The park has 201 forested acres in an alpine setting formed by a glacier at the base of the rugged Wallowa Mountains. Swimming, water sport equipment rentals, fishing, boating (dock, motor rentals); picnicking, concession, improved tent and trailer sites (dump station). Park at the edge of the Eagle Cap wilderness area; hiking and riding trails begin here. Horse stables are nearby.

WALLOWA-WHITMAN NATIONAL FOREST. *47794 Oregon Hwy 244, Baker City (97814). Phone 541/523-6391. www.fs.fed.us/r6/w-w/.* More than 2 million acres include the 14,000-acre North Fork John Day Wilderness, the 7,000-acre Monument Rock Wilderness, the 358,461-acre Eagle Cap Wilderness, and the 215,500-acre Hells Canyon Wilderness. Snowcapped peaks, Minam River; alpine meadows, rare wildflowers; Buckhorn Lookout; Anthony Lake and Phillips Lake. Stream and lake trout fishing; elk, deer, and bear hunting; float and jet boat trips; saddle and pack trips. Picnic area. Camping. $

PLACES TO STAY

If you choose to include an overnight stay in your trip along this All-American Road, Mobil Travel Guide recommends the following lodgings.

★★ **ELDORADO INN.** *695 Campbell St, Baker City (97814). Phone 541/523-6494; toll-free 800/537-5756.* 56 rooms, 2 story. Pet accepted; fee. Check-out noon. TV, VCR available. Indoor pool. Restaurant open 24 hours. Business services available. Refrigerators available. ¢

Oregon

Hells Canyon Scenic Byway

★ **RODEWAY INN.** *810 Campbell St, Baker City (97814). Phone 541/523-2242; toll-free 800/228-5151. www.rodewayinn.com.* 54 rooms, 2 story. Pet accepted; fee. Complimentary continental breakfast. Check-out noon. TV. Pool privileges. Restaurant nearby. Meeting rooms. Some refrigerators. ¢

★★ **CHANDLERS BED, BREAD, AND TRAIL INN.** *700 S Main St, Joseph (97846). Phone 541/432-9765; toll-free 800/452-3781. www.eoni.com/~chanbbti.* 5 rooms, 2 share bath, 2 story. No A/C. No room phones. Children over 11 years only. Complimentary full breakfast. Check-out 11 am, check-in 2 pm. Whirlpool. Downhill, cross-country ski 6 miles. Picnic tables. Cedar and log interiors with high vaulted ceilings. Outdoor gazebo. Totally nonsmoking. ¢

★ **INDIAN LODGE MOTEL.** *201 S Main, Joseph (97846). Phone 541/432-2651; toll-free 888/286-5484.* 16 rooms. Pet accepted; fee. Check-out 11 am. TV; cable (premium). Lake 1 mile. ¢

★ **HOWARD JOHNSON EXPRESS INN.** *2612 Island Ave, La Grande (97850). Phone 541/963-7195; toll-free 800/446-4656. www.hojo.com.* 146 rooms, 2 story. Pet accepted. Complimentary continental breakfast. Check-out noon. TV; cable (premium). Outdoor pool, whirlpool. Restaurant adjacent open 24 hours. Free laundry. Meeting rooms. Business services available. In-house fitness room; sauna. Refrigerators. Private patios, balconies. ¢

★ **ROYAL MOTOR INN.** *1510 Adams Ave, La Grande (97850). Phone 541/963-4154; toll-free 800/990-7575. www.royal-motor-inn.com.* 43 rooms, 2 story. Check-out 11 am. TV; cable (premium). Restaurant nearby. ¢

★★ **STANG MANOR BED & BREAKFAST.** *1612 Walnut St, La Grande (97850). Phone 541/963-2400; toll-free 888/2UNWIND. www.stangmanor.com.* 4 rooms, 2 story. No A/C. Children over 10 years only. Complimentary full breakfast. Check-out 11 am, check-in 3 pm. TV in some rooms, living room; VCR available. Totally nonsmoking. $

PLACES TO EAT

A long day of driving is sure to make you hungry. At the end of your journey, take a table at one of the following restaurants.

★★ **GEISER GRILL.** *1966 Main St, Baker City (97814). Phone toll-free 866/826-3850.* American menu. Breakfast, lunch, dinner. Located in the Geiser Grand Hotel, which has the largest stained-glass ceiling in the West. $$

★★ **THE PHONE COMPANY.** *1926 First St, Baker City (97814). Phone 541/523-7997.* American menu. Closed Mon. Lunch, dinner. Upscale restaurant housed in a classic 1910 building that once housed the local telephone company. Known for local originality. $$

★★ **FOLEY STATION.** *1011 Adams, La Grande (97850). Phone 541/963-7473.* American menu. Closed Mon. Breakfast, lunch, dinner. Chef-owned restaurant known for eclectic breakfasts. $$

★★ **TEN DEPOT STREET.** *10 Depot St, La Grande (97850). Phone 541/963-8766.* American menu. Closed Sun. Lunch, dinner. Innovative cuisine in a turn-of-the-century brick two-flat with antique furnishings. $$

★ **WILDFLOWER BAKERY.** *600 N Main St, Joseph (97846). Phone 541/432-7225.* American menu. Closed Thurs, Fri, Sat. Breakfast, lunch. Organic baked goods, breakfast items, and sandwiches in a small, out-of-the-way building. $

Historic Columbia River Highway

✵ OREGON   AN ALL-AMERICAN ROAD

Quick Facts

LENGTH: 70 miles.

TIME TO ALLOW: 3 to 5 hours.

BEST TIME TO DRIVE: Mid-week sees the fewest crowds along the Byway. Fall has the best weather; spring provides the best time to view the waterfalls. High season is April through September.

BYWAY TRAVEL INFORMATION: US Forest Service—Columbia River Gorge National Scenic Area: 541/386-2333; Byway local Web site: www.odot.state.or.us/hcrh.

SPECIAL CONSIDERATIONS: Some attractions are closed during the winter months. Also, the Byway is narrow and winding, so you may want to consider traveling in a car instead of an RV.

RESTRICTIONS: The Multnomah Falls Lodge is open daily throughout the year. The Vista House is open from April through September.

BICYCLE/PEDESTRIAN FACILITIES: You can bike fairly safely on this highway because of the relatively low volume of automobiles. You'll also find plenty of trails around the Byway on which you can bike. Most notably, portions of the Historic Columbia River Highway that were abandoned during the construction of I-84 are being restored as multi-use trails. Numerous other trailheads are located along the Byway, as well. These trails have a good range of length and difficulty, ranging from flat, paved trails to high mountain trails.

The Historic Columbia River Highway (HCRH) is exquisite: drive through the Columbia River Gorge for nearly 50 miles and sweep past majestic waterfalls, including Multnomah Falls, the most visited natural site in Oregon. This Byway also travels through a spectacular river canyon that you often view from the tops of cliffs over 900 feet above the river. During the spring, you experience magnificent wildflower displays, including many plants that exist only in this area.

This is the first scenic highway in the United States to gain the distinction of National Historic Landmark. (To give you an idea of what this means, less than 3 percent of the sites on the National Register of Historic Places become Landmarks.) The construction of this highway was considered one of the greatest engineering feats of the modern age. Its engineer, Samuel C. Lancaster, did "not [want] to mar what God had put there." It was designed in 1913-1914 to take advantage of the many waterfalls and other beautiful spots.

Make sure to travel both the well-known western section of the Byway from Troutdale to Dodson and the less-traveled eastern section from Mosier to The Dalles. The difference in vegetation zones and views between the two sections is amazing.

THE BYWAY STORY

The Historic Columbia River Highway tells historical, natural, recreational, and scenic stories that make it a unique and treasured Byway.

Oregon

Historic Columbia River Highway

Historical
The HCRH has many nationally significant historic features on the National Register of Historic Places—one of which is the highway itself. It is also a National Historic Civil Engineering Landmark that includes 23 unique bridges. The historic district includes not only the highway, but also the Portland Women's Forum State Scenic Viewpoint, Crown Point and Vista House, Multnomah Falls Lodge and Recreation Site, Eagle Creek Recreation Area, and several other waterfall areas.

Natural
The Columbia River Gorge is a spectacular river canyon, 80 miles long and up to 4,000 feet deep, cutting the only sea-level route through the Cascade Mountain Range. The Gorge includes 16 endemic plant species (those that exist only within the Gorge) and over 150 rare plant species. Bald eagles, peregrine falcons, Snake River salmon, and Larch Mountain salamanders also reside here. Wildflower tours of the Historic Columbia River Highway are common in the spring.

Recreational
Recreational facilities in the Columbia River Gorge National Scenic Area are also of national significance, including the three major highways (Historic Columbia River Highway, I-84, and Washington State Route 14) that are used extensively for pleasure driving. The highways provide access to many hiking trails, windsurfing sites, and the Mount Hood Railroad, a scenic and historic passenger and freight route up the Hood River Valley.

Scenic
The HCRH leaves the Sandy River and climbs to the top of the cliffs, offering spectacular views of the landscape. The Byway was designed in 1913-1914 to take advantage of the many waterfalls and other attractive sites along the route. The corridor contains some of the most dramatic views available anywhere in the country, including the Columbia River, with basalt cliffs and canyon walls; Multnomah Falls, a 620-foot, two-tiered waterfall that is the most visited natural attraction in the state of Oregon; the largest aggregation of high waterfalls outside of Yosemite, including Multnomah Falls, Horsetail Falls, Latourell Falls, Bridal Veil Falls, and Wahkeena Falls, plus numerous small falls; and giant basalt cliffs and monoliths, including Beacon Rock, Rooster Rock, Crown Point (a National Natural Landmark), Oneonta Bluff, and others.

HIGHLIGHTS

Start your must-see tour in Troutdale, the western entry point to the Historic Columbia River Highway. The attractive setting, unique shopping district, and convenient distance from the interstate make this small town a perfect start to your tour of the highway.

- Drive east. The first stop along the tour is **Sandy River.** An old iron bridge crosses the river at this point. Cross and enjoy. You can even take a side trip to the left to visit Lewis and Clark Park, but be sure to return to the Byway to continue your journey east.

- If you want a stunning scenic vista, you must stop at **Portland Women's Forum State Scenic Viewpoint.** It is located about 10 minutes from Troutdale (milepost 10.3).

- **Crown Point** and historic **Vista House** is next, about a mile farther east (milepost 11.5). Take a stroll around the point (carefully—the road curves around the building here) and enjoy yet another wonderful view of the river and the **Columbia River Gorge.**

- Scattered throughout the next few miles are many waterfalls, each with its own history and qualities. **Latourell Falls, Shepherd's Dell, Wahkeena Falls,** and **Bridal Veil Falls** each whet your appetite for the most visited waterfall on the Byway: **Multnomah Falls.** This beautiful double-cascade falls more than 650 feet. Stop and take the hike up to the bridge crossing the waterfall for an up-close view.

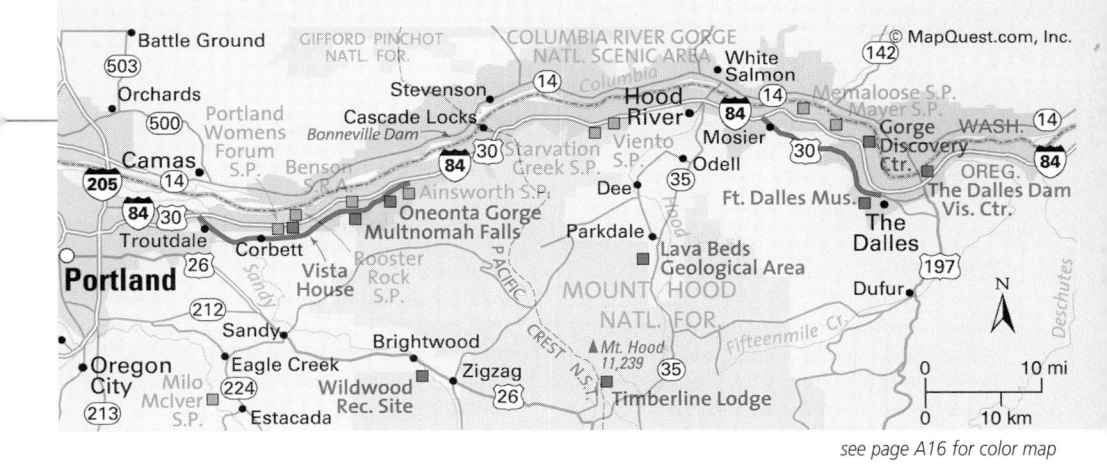

- Back on the highway, you shortly encounter **Oneonta Gorge.** This narrow canyon and its associated stream is a cool, dark, and shady hike. To enjoy it fully, follow the path to its river crossing, take off your shoes, and wade in the chilly stream.

- Continuing east, you rejoin the interstate for a while. The **Bridge of the Gods at Cascade Locks** connects Oregon to Washington.

- The city of **Hood River,** at the confluence of the Hood River and the Columbia River, is the windsurfing capital of the world. Stop and watch expert windsurfers from the riverside or from vantage points at hotels and viewpoints along the river. Or visit the **downtown historic district** and stop by the **Hood River County Museum.**

- Take time to leave your car and walk a portion of the Historic Columbia River Highway between Hood River and Mosier that has been converted to a **state trail.** Remnants of the original auto highway and railings may still be seen. Or, if you continue in your car along the main highway instead, look for tunnels and roadbed high above you—a visible clue to a tremendous engineering feat.

- As you leave the rain forest of the Gorge and enter the drier, wide rolling plains west of Rowena and The Dalles, stop a moment at the **Memaloose Overlook** near the **Tom McCall Preserve.** Below you, the highway twists in the hairpin turns of the **Rowena Loops.** This engineering achievement remains remarkable even by today's standards.

- After you navigate the switchbacks of the Rowena Loops, catch your breath with a stop at the **Gorge Discovery Center** and **Wasco County Museum.** Opened in 1997, this museum offers interpretive exhibits about the human and natural history of the Columbia River Gorge.

- End your trip on the Historic Columbia River Highway at **The Dalles.** You can view the nearby **Dalles Lock and Dam** or tour the **historic district** of this city.

THINGS TO SEE AND DO

Driving along the Historic Columbia River Highway will certainly keep your senses engaged, but if you yearn to get out of the car and stretch your legs, or if you'd like to make a mini-vacation out of your trip, check out these attractions along the route.

BONNEVILLE LOCK AND DAM. *Cascade Locks (97014). Phone 541/374-8820.* The dam consists of three parts: one spillway and two powerhouses. It has an overall length of 3,463 feet and extends across the Columbia River to Washington. It was a major hydroelectric project of the US Army Corps of Engineers. On the Oregon side is a five-story visitor center with underwater windows into the fish ladders and new navigation lock with viewing facilities. There are audiovisual presentations and tours of fish ladders and the original powerhouse. The state salmon hatchery is adjacent. Fishing (salmon and sturgeon ponds); picnicking. Open June-Sept, daily or by appointment; closed Jan 1, Thanksgiving, Dec 25. **FREE**

Oregon

✻ Historic Columbia River Highway

COLUMBIA GORGE. *Cascade Locks (97014). Phone 541/374-8427. www.sternwheeler.com.* This sternwheeler makes daytime excursions, sunset dinner and brunch cruises, harbor tours, and special holiday cruises. Reservations are required except for daily excursions mid-June-Sept. **$$$$**

■ **COLUMBIA GORGE DISCOVERY CENTER.** *5000 Discovery Dr, The Dalles (97058). Phone 541/296-8600. www.gorgediscovery.org.* This building, at over 26,000 square feet, is the official interpretive center for the Columbia River Gorge National Scenic Area. Hands-on and electronic exhibits detail the volcanic upheavals and raging floods that created the Gorge, describe the history and importance of the river, and look to the Gorge's future. There are also Early Explorers, Steamboats and Trains, and Industry and Stewardship exhibits. Guided tours, seminars, classes, and workshops (some fees). Library and collections (by appointment). Café. Open daily; closed Jan 1, Thanksgiving, Dec 25. **$$**

THE DALLES DAM AND RESERVOIR. *Exit 88, The Dalles (97058). Phone 541/296-1181.* Two-mile train tour with views of a historic navigation canal, visitor center, petroglyphs, and fish ladder facilities. Open daily Memorial Day-Labor Day; Apr-May and Oct-Mar, Wed-Sun. **FREE**

■ **MOUNT HOOD NATIONAL FOREST.** *65000 E Hwy 26, Welches (97067). Phone 503/622-4822; toll-free 888/622-4822. www.fs.fed.us/r6/mthood/.* Mount Hood (11,235 feet) is the natural focal point of this large forest of over 1 million acres. Its white-crowned top, the highest point in Oregon, can be seen for miles on a clear day. It is also popular with skiers, who know it has some of the best slopes in the Northwest. There are five winter sports areas. Throughout the year, however, you can take advantage of the surrounding forest facilities for camping (1,600 camp and picnic sites), hunting, fishing, swimming, mountain climbing, golfing, horseback riding, hiking, and tobogganing. The Columbia Gorge cuts through the Cascades here. You have your choice of nine routes to the summit, which has fumed and smoked several times since the volcanic peak was discovered. Only experienced climbers should try the ascent, and then only with a guide.

MOUNT HOOD RAILROAD. *110 Railroad Ave, Hood River (97031). Phone 541/386-3556; toll-free 800/872-4661 (reservations). www.mthoodrr.com.* This historic railroad (built in 1906) offers four-hour round-trip excursions through the Hood River Valley. Dinner and brunch excursions are also available. Open late Mar-mid-Dec; daily schedule varies. **$$$$**

PANORAMA POINT. *Hwy 35 S and E Side Rd, Hood River (97031). Phone toll-free 800/366-3530.* Observation point for Hood River Valley and Mount Hood.

PLACES TO STAY

If you choose to include an overnight stay in your trip along this All-American Road, Mobil Travel Guide recommends the following lodgings.

★★ **BEST WESTERN HOOD RIVER INN.** *1108 E Marina Way, Hood River (97031). Phone 541/386-2200; toll-free 800/828-7873. www.hoodriverinn.com.* 149 rooms, 2-3 story.

Pet accepted. Check-out noon. TV; cable (premium). Outdoor pool. Restaurant, bar; entertainment. Room service. Coin laundry. Business services available. In-room modem link. Private patios. Beach access; windsurfing. In the Columbia River Gorge. ¢

★★★ **COLUMBIA GORGE HOTEL.** *4000 Westcliff Dr, Hood River (97031). Phone 541/386-5566; toll-free 800/345-1921. www.columbiagorgehotel.com.* Nestled in the Columbia Gorge National Scenic Area, trees and mountain peaks adorn the scenery at this hotel, featuring a waterfall and beautiful gardens. For outdoor enthusiasts, there is windsurfing, skiing, and fishing. 40 rooms, 3 story. Pet accepted; fee. Complimentary full breakfast. Check-out noon. TV, VCR available. Restaurant (see COLUMBIA GORGE DINING ROOM). Bar. Business services available. Health club privileges. Restored building (1920s) with formal gardens. Jazz Age atmosphere. $$

★ **RIVERVIEW LODGE.** *1505 Oak St, Hood River (97031). Phone 541/386-8719; toll-free 800/789-9568. www.riverviewforyou.com.* 20 rooms, 2 story. Ski plans. Check-out 11 am. TV; cable (premium). Business services available. Indoor pool; whirlpool. Refrigerators, microwaves. Some balconies. ¢

★★★ **DOLCE SKAMANIA LODGE.** *1131 SW Skamania Lodge Way, Stevenson (98648). Phone 509/427-7700; toll-free 800/221-7117. www.dolce.com/skamania/.* With remarkable design, ultimate comfort, and a setting that will leave you breathless, this spectacular mountain resort is a must-see. Guests bask in the glory of the beautiful surroundings. 195 rooms, 4 story. Check-out noon. TV. Indoor pool; whirlpool. Playground. Restaurant, bar. Room service. Meeting rooms. Business center. In-room modem link. Sundries. Tennis. Mountain bike rentals. 18-hole golf, pro, greens fee $40, putting green, driving range. In-house fitness room; sauna. Massage. Game room. Lawn games. Refrigerators. Some balconies. $

★★ **BEST WESTERN RIVER CITY INN.** *112 W 2nd St, The Dalles (97058). Phone 541/296-9107; toll-free 800/935-2378. www.bestwestern.com.* 65 rooms, 2-4 story. Pet accepted; $5. Check-out 11 am. TV; cable (premium). Outdoor pool. Restaurant, bar. Room service. Meeting rooms. Business services available. In-room modem link. Health club privileges. Some refrigerators. ¢

★ **INN AT THE DALLES.** *3550 SE Frontage Rd, The Dalles (97058). Phone 541/296-1167.* 45 rooms, 4 kitchen units. Pet accepted. Check-out 11 am. TV. Indoor pool. Business services available. Free airport transportation. View of the Columbia River, Mount Hood, and The Dalles Dam. $

★★ **QUALITY INN COLUMBIA RIVER GORGE.** *2114 W 6th St, The Dalles (97058). Phone 541/298-5161; toll-free 800/848-9378. www.qualityinn.com.* 85 rooms, 16 kitchen units, 2 story. Pet accepted; $2. Check-out 11 am. TV. Outdoor pool, whirlpool. Restaurant. Coin laundry. Meeting rooms. Business services available. In-room modem link. Health club privileges. Some fireplaces. ¢

★★ **INN OF THE WHITE SALMON.** *172 W Jewett Blvd, White Salmon (98672). Phone 509/493-2335; toll-free 800/972-5226. www.innofthewhitesalmon.com.* 16 rooms, 5 suites, 2 story. Pet accepted. Complimentary full breakfast. Check-out noon, check-in 3 pm. TV. European-style inn built in 1937; antique décor, original art. $

Oregon

❅ *Historic Columbia River Highway*

PLACES TO EAT

A long day of driving is sure to make you hungry. At the end of your journey, take a table at one of the following restaurants.

★★ **MULTNOMAH FALLS LODGE.** 50000 Historic Columbia River Hwy, Bridal Veil (97010). Phone 503/695-2376. www.multnomahfallslodge.com. American menu. Breakfast, lunch, dinner. Elegant dining room with scenic views. $

★ **COUSIN'S.** 2115 W 6th St, The Dalles (97058). Phone 541/298-2771. American menu. Closed Dec 25. Breakfast, lunch, dinner. Bar. Children's menu. Frontier motif. $-$$ D

★ **WINDSEEKER.** 1535 Barge Way Rd, The Dalles (97058). Phone 541/298-7171. American menu. Breakfast, lunch, dinner. Small supper-club-style restaurant featuring contemporary American and pan-Asian cuisine. $

★ **WINDY RIVER RESTAURANT.** 315 E 3rd St, The Dalles (97058). Phone 541/296-2028. American menu. Closed Sunday. Lunch, dinner. Highly regarded locally, this restaurant focuses on pasta and seafood. $

★★★ **COLUMBIA GORGE DINING ROOM.** 4000 Westcliff Dr, Hood River (97031). Phone 541/386-5566. www.columbiagorgehotel.com. American menu. Breakfast, lunch, dinner. Restored 1920s hotel dining room with scenic views of the Columbia River Gorge. $$

★ **WILDFLOWER CAFÉ.** 904 2nd Ave, Mosier (97040). Phone 541/478-0111. American menu. Breakfast, lunch, dinner. Excellent pancakes; live music on weekends. $

★★ **BLACK RABBIT.** 2126 SW Halsey, Troutdale (97060). Phone 503/492-3086. Specializes in fresh Northwestern cuisine. Breakfast, lunch, dinner. Bar. Children's menu. Outdoor seating. Reservations accepted. Totally nonsmoking. $$ D

McKenzie Pass-Santiam Pass Scenic Byway
✹ OREGON

Quick Facts

LENGTH: 82 miles.

TIME TO ALLOW: 3 to 5 hours.

BEST TIME TO DRIVE: Spring to fall.

BYWAY TRAVEL INFORMATION: US Forest Service, McKenzie Ranger Station: 541/822-3381; Oregon Visitors Association: toll-free 800/800-8334; McKenzie River Chamber of Commerce: 541/896-3330.

SPECIAL CONSIDERATIONS: Services are available in the town of McKenzie Bridge.

RESTRICTIONS: Because of snow, Highway 242 is closed from mid-November to mid-June. Nearly the entire Byway is in a snow zone, so chains are sometimes required during the winter, especially over the Santiam Pass. Also, due to extremely sharp curves and narrow road width, Highway 242 over McKenzie Pass is closed to vehicles (either single or combined) longer than 35 feet. Trailers are discouraged. Parking passes can be purchased from the ranger station, allowing you to park and hike the trails along this Byway.

BICYCLE/PEDESTRIAN FACILITIES: This Byway is popular with bicyclists during the summer. While the Santiam Pass Highway (US 20) and Clear Lake Cutoff (Oregon 126) are well-traveled routes, they accommodate bicycles with paved shoulders and good sight distances. The McKenzie Pass Highway is narrow and winding, but it accommodates bicycles because no commercial traffic is allowed, recreational traffic is light, and vehicle speeds are low. One section of the Byway is accessible to pedestrians: the 26-mile McKenzie River National Recreational Trail. The remainder of the Byway is not suitable for pedestrian travel.

Experience dramatic, close-up views of the most beautiful of the snowcapped High Cascade Peaks. The panorama of lava fields and six Cascade peaks, as viewed from the summit of McKenzie Pass, is made even more striking by the contrast between the black lava and white snow. The mountains are mirrored in crystal-clear lakes, and the Byway passes spectacular waterfalls, including Sahalie and Koosah falls. Broken Top Mountain and the Three Sisters tower gloriously above the route.

THE BYWAY STORY

The McKenzie Pass-Santiam Pass Scenic Byway tells archaeological, cultural, historical, natural, recreational, and scenic stories that make it a unique and treasured Byway.

Archaeological

Sahalie Falls and Koosah Falls can be located on the old Clear Lake Cutoff on Highway 126. Sahalie (meaning "heaven") and Koosah (meaning "sky") are Chinook Jargon words—part of a rudimentary trade language that allowed people to exchange news and goods in the area. The Kalapuya, Molala, Sahaptain, and Chinook peoples traveled and traded here, perhaps on their way to obtain obsidian in the high Cascades for tools or to gather huckleberries. Connecting the two waterfalls is a loop trail that offers views of foaming white water, pouring over 3,000-year-old lava flows.

Cultural

Communities that reflect rural Western charm anchor the McKenzie Pass-Santiam Pass Scenic Byway and lead you to a variety of cultural events on both sides of the mountains.

Oregon

❋ McKenzie Pass-Santiam Pass Scenic Byway

The town of Sisters, especially, recalls the Old West with a sophisticated town center that features numerous antique shops, galleries, and Western boutiques. Sisters' annual events include a popular rodeo, an outdoor quilt show, and a Celebration of the Arts.

The town of McKenzie Bridge, known as Strawberry Flat back in 1902, is a small river settlement located on Highway 126 on the east end of the loop. One of several communities spanning the McKenzie River corridor, McKenzie Bridge offers tired travelers a place to hang their hats for the night in much the same tradition as a hundred years ago. Rustic riverside log cabins, natural hot spring pools, and deep forest campgrounds continue to welcome today's visitors.

The Santiam Wagon Road, which once served as a dominant access route over the Cascade Mountains to the Willamette Valley, operated from 1865 until 1939, when US 20 and State Highway 22 and 126 developments combined to make it obsolete. A segment of this road traverses the Fish Lake Historic Remount Depot on Highway 126, an early roadhouse for wagon road travelers, where lodging, food, and hay were purchased for less than $1 in 1890. Today, vintage pre-1940 vehicles and horse-drawn wagons can travel from here to Tombstone Pass by permit.

The annual John Craig Memorial Race commemorates mail carrier John Craig's journeys across the McKenzie Pass. Craig (1821-1877) died carrying the Christmas mail over this route. Today, Nordic skiers endure winter rain, sleet, hail, and snow to race over Historic Highway 242, which is closed in the winter. This event has been ongoing since the late 1800s and continues to be enjoyed—and endured—today.

Historical
Travel through the passes was arduous, and development was challenging. The Santiam Pass, one of the major highways crossing the Cascade Range, was discovered in 1859 by Andrew Wiley and was named for the Santiam Indians, a Kalapooian tribe living near the Santiam River. The Byway crosses the route of the Willamette Valley Cascade Mountain Wagon Road, later known as the Santiam Wagon Road. This road is still used today as a secondary road for public access. A portion of the original railroad grade of the Hogg Railroad, constructed as early as 1888, is visible from Santiam Pass near Hogg Rock.

The Fish Lake Work Center, also known as the Fish Lake Remount Station, is a Forest Service administrative site still in use on the northeastern shore of Fish Lake on Highway 126. Serving as the official Forest Service work center in the early 1900s, structures have been renovated to preserve the history of early horse-packing operations and summer headquarters for patrol and lookout employees.

In Oregon during the 1930s, the Civilian Conservation Corp (CCC) enhanced numerous recreational opportunities along the McKenzie Pass-Santiam Pass National Scenic Byway, including building the lava rock structure at the top of McKenzie Pass and naming it after the group's foreman, Dee Wright. Since its completion in 1935, the observatory has been a favorite attraction for thousands of visitors. Evidence of the CCC's work remains at Clear Lake, located on Highway 126, where a rough-hewn timber shelter is used today by groups that picnic in the area. This shelter stands as a reminder that while journeys through these passes have changed over time, elements of past experiences remain.

Natural
The natural qualities of the McKenzie Pass-Santiam Pass Scenic Byway are of national significance. You can find outstanding examples of both ancient and recent volcanoes, cinder cones, lava flows, and deep, glaciated canyons. Forests along the Byway contain rare old-growth fir and ponderosa pine and are home to a great variety of fish and wildlife, including

several endangered species, such as the bald eagle, the northern spotted owl, the chinook salmon, the steelhead, and the bull trout.

The geology along the route is especially significant. The McKenzie Pass-Santiam Pass area is the best place in the Pacific Northwest to see how the great bulk of the volcanic Cascade Range has been built. Here, basaltic shield volcanoes are produced on a regular basis. Some have grown into large, steep-sided volcanic cones, such as North Sister and Mount Washington. Glaciers have deeply eroded most of these cones, but a new group of shields, unaffected by glaciers, erupted between 1,500 and 400 years ago. Easily seen from McKenzie Pass, the best example of a new Cascade shield volcano is Belknap Crater, which has long, barren, gentle slopes of lava.

Recreational

The McKenzie Pass-Santiam Pass Scenic Byway area offers three wilderness areas, two national trails, several lakes, many snow-capped volcanoes, two Wild & Scenic Rivers, and a major resort. Recreational opportunities include hiking, horseback riding, camping, boating, fishing, swimming, bicycle touring, mountain biking, skiing, golf, and tennis. The Pacific Crest National Scenic Trail provides an opportunity that is unique in the country to hike the crest of a major volcanic mountain range. If you're a boater, you can choose lakes or whitewater rafting and kayaking on the McKenzie River.

The fishing is nationally famous. Anglers come from all over the United States to fly-fish for wild trout on the upper Metolius and to fish for trout, salmon, and steelhead on the upper McKenzie. During the winter, you can downhill ski at the Hoodoo ski area and snowmobile and cross-country ski on miles of marked trails. Because the Byway includes the drier east side of the Cascade Mountains, during several months of the year, you can ski in the morning at higher elevations and then hike, fly-fish, bicycle, or play tennis in the afternoon at lower elevations on the Byway.

Scenic

Along the McKenzie Pass-Santiam Pass Scenic Byway, you see dramatic, close-up views of the most beautiful snow-capped High Cascade Peaks, two Wild & Scenic rivers, and several waterfalls. The view of the Three Sisters and Broken Top Mountains (found at the start of the Byway on Highway 242 just outside the town of Sisters) represents the greatest concentration of snow-capped volcanoes with glaciers in the lower 48 states. In addition, the panoramic view of lava fields and six Cascade peaks from the summit of McKenzie Pass is made even more striking by the contrast between the black lava and white snow. The mountains are mirrored in crystal-clear lakes.

see page A17 for color map

Oregon

McKenzie Pass-Santiam Pass Scenic Byway

HIGHLIGHTS

Travelers generally access this Byway from two primary points. If you're heading west from Eugene/Springfield, begin the Byway at the junction of historic Highway 242 and Highway 126, about 5 miles west of the full-service community of McKenzie Bridge. If you're arriving from the east, access the Byway from Sisters, a lively town chock-full of arts and crafts offerings and special events, such as the annual quilt show and jazz festival, following an early Western theme set back in time to the 1800s.

The following list of stops along the Byway indicates milepost numbers, so you can use it regardless of your direction of travel on the Byway.

- **Milepost 2.1—Junction Highway 126 and 242:** Turn right to travel up 242, the McKenzie Pass Route. The forest along the Byway on this portion is dark green, characterized by water-loving species such as hemlocks, cedars, and firs. The climb eastward up Highway 242 is through a thickly vegetated, narrow corridor. Here the road meanders, and travel is slow.

- **Milepost 8.8—Proxy Falls Trailhead:** To take in the beauty of both falls, plan to spend about an hour to hike the 1 1/4-mile loop trail into the Three Sisters Wilderness.

- **Milepost 7.0—Scott Road Historical Marker/Pulloff:** Take a few moments to get off the highway after your slow wind up Dead Horse Grade. Open views of the Three Sisters Mountains, part of the Cascade Range and originally named Faith, Hope, and Charity in the 1840s, lie to the east. The Scott Road, was really an old settler trail named after Felix Scott, Jr. (1829-1879), who pioneered a wagon trail/road over the Cascades northeast of McKenzie Bridge. This route, part of which is maintained trail into the Three Sisters Wilderness, proved to be almost impossible for wagon travel.

- **Milepost 2.7—Belknap Crater Viewpoint:** A great photo opportunity awaits you here. You can view Big Belknap Crater and the smaller cone of Little Belknap Crater. Don't let its size fool you—Little Belknap was the origin of the immense lava fields in the foreground. Use caution when walking out onto the lava.

- **Milepost 3.5—Dee Wright Observatory:** Plan on an hour to tour the observatory and walk the 1/2-mile Lava River Trail.

- **Milepost 3.2—Windy Point Viewpoint:** At an elevation of 4,909 feet, Windy Point offers a picturesque view of the lava flows and volcanic peaks. Although little vegetation grows on the lava fields, as you make your descent down from the summit of the McKenzie Pass, a mixed conifer forest returns, eventually giving way to ponderosa pines at the lower elevation. It is the dramatic transition between these diverse natural environments that defines the uniqueness of this Byway. Geologic interpretive information is available at the viewpoint.

- **Milepost 11.5—East Portal, Sisters:** The Santiam Pass Route begins at the Sisters Portal, heading north at the junction of Highway 126/20 and 242.

- **Milepost 6.5—Black Butte:** Black Butte is the prominent composite cone north of the highway. In spite of its youthful profile, Black Butte is older than many of the dissected High Cascade peaks. The US Forest Service still operates a lookout on the top.

- **Milepost 9.3—Mount Washington Viewpoint:** Geologic and forest interpretive information is available here. For a quick stop, this roadside pull-off offers a spectacular view of the volcanic peak and basin.

- **Milepost 19.5 (Sahalie Falls) and milepost 0.4 (Koosah Falls):** The McKenzie River surges over a 70-foot high basalt cliff called Koosah Falls. Plan to spend half an hour here to take pictures and view the interpretive panels featuring geologic history. Then hike for an hour on the Waterfalls Loop trail that connects this site with Sahalie Falls (or drive to the site).

THINGS TO SEE AND DO

Driving along the McKenzie Pass-Santiam Pass Scenic Byway will certainly keep your senses engaged, but if you yearn to get out of the car and stretch your legs, or if you'd like to make a mini-vacation out of your trip, check out these attractions along the route.

BLUE RIVER DAM AND LAKE. *51668 Blue River Dr, Vida (97488). Phone 541/822-3317.* Saddle Dam Boating Site offers a boat ramp. Mona Campground offers swimming, fishing, and picnicking. The dam is a US Army Corps of Engineers' project, while recreation areas are administered by the US Forest Service. Camping is available from mid-May to mid-Sept for a fee.

CARMEN-SMITH HYDROELECTRIC DEVELOPMENT. *McKenzie Bridge (97413). Phone 541/484-2411.* This salmon-spawning facility near Trail Bridge Dam includes three stocked reservoirs: Trail Bridge, Smith, and Carmen (open daily). Boat launching (free). Picnicking. Camping at Lake's End, north end of Smith Reservoir, at Ice Cap Creek on Carmen Reservoir, and at Trail Bridge (ten-day limit). $$$

COUGAR DAM AND LAKE. *51668 Blue River Dr, Vida (97488). Phone 541/822-3317 or 541/896-3614.* A 6-mile-long reservoir. Echo Park is a day-use area with boat ramp (free). Slide Creek campground offers swimming, water-skiing, fishing, and a boat ramp. Delta and French Pete campgrounds offer fishing and picnicking. The campgrounds are maintained and operated by US Forest Service, while the dam is a US Army Corps of Engineers' project. Open May-Sept; most areas are closed the rest of year. Picnicking is free; camping includes a fee.

✪ MOUNT HOOD NATIONAL FOREST. *65000 E US 26, Welches (97067). Phone 503/522-7674; toll-free 888/622-4822. www.fs.fed.us/r6/mthood/.* Mount Hood (11,235 feet) is the natural focal point of this forest of more than 1 million acres headquartered in Sandy. Its white-crowned top, the highest point in Oregon, can be seen for miles on a clear day. It is also popular with skiers, who know that it offers some of the best slopes in the Northwest. There are five winter sports areas. Throughout the year, you can take advantage of the surrounding forest facilities for camping (1,600 camp and picnic sites), hunting, fishing, swimming, mountain climbing, golfing, horseback riding, hiking, and tobogganing. The Columbia Gorge, which cuts through the Cascades here, has many spectacular waterfalls, including Multnomah Falls (620 feet). There are nine routes to the summit, which has fumed and smoked several times since the volcanic peak was discovered. Only experienced climbers should try the ascent, and then only with a guide.

PLACES TO STAY

If you choose to include an overnight stay in your trip along this Byway, Mobil Travel Guide recommends the following lodgings.

★★★ BLACK BUTTE RANCH. *13653 Hawks Beard Rd, Black Butte Ranch (97759). Phone 541/595-6211; toll-free 800/452-7455. www.blackbutteranch.com.* 162 rooms, 1 story. Offers a mix of luxury suites and private vacation homes in a full-service hotel environment. Check-out 11 am, check-in 4 pm. Restaurants. Pools. Golf. Tennis. $$

Oregon

❊ McKenzie Pass-Santiam Pass Scenic Byway

★★★ **BELKNAP LODGE & HOT SPRINGS.** 59296 N Belknap Springs Rd, Blue River (97413). Phone 541/822-3512. 24 rooms, 2 story. Extensive lawns and perennial gardens make this mountain retreat on the banks of the McKenzie River one of the state's most enjoyable. $$

★ **SLEEPY HOLLOW MOTEL.** 54791 McKenzie Hwy, Blue River (97413). Phone 541/822-3805. 19 rooms, 2 story. Apr-Oct; closed rest of year. Check-out 11 am. TV in some rooms. Restaurant nearby. Refrigerators. ¢

★★★ **METOLIUS RIVER RESORT.** 2551 SW F. S. Rd #1419, Camp Sherman (97730). Phone toll-free 800/818-7688. www.metolius-river-resort.com. 12 cabins, 2 story. Located on one of Oregon's premier fly-fishing rivers, this area offers fully furnished cabins with kitchens and private decks. All linens are provided. $$

★★ **BIG RED BARN BED & BREAKFAST.** 69482 Squaw Creek Dr, Sisters (97759). Phone 541/549-6425; toll-free 888/257-1275. www.bigredbarnbb.com. 3 rooms, 2 story. Located in a renovated turn-of-the-century barn and farmhouse with wraparound windows and comfortable rooms with 5 acres of open valley to explore. Complimentary breakfast. Check-out 11 am, check-in 3-6 pm. Pool. Tennis. Totally nonsmoking. $

★ **SUTTLE LAKE RESORT & MARINA.** Hwy 20, Sisters (97759). Phone 541/595-6662. 15 rooms, 1 story. Historic 1920s cabins and houseboats. Full-service marina with boat and bike rentals. ¢

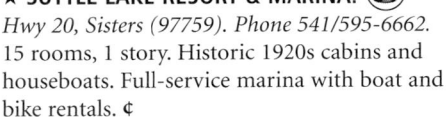

PLACES TO EAT

A long day of driving is sure to make you hungry. At the end of your journey, try the following restaurants.

★★ **LOG CABIN INN.** 56483 McKenzie Hwy, McKenzie Bridge (97413). Phone 541/822-3432. www.logcabininn.com. Lunch, dinner, Sun brunch. Bar. Children's menu. Outdoor seating. Built as a stagecoach stop in 1906. $$
D

★ **THE LAKESIDE BISTRO.** 13653 Hawks Beard Rd, Black Butte Ranch (97759). Phone 800/452-7455. www.blackbutteranch.com. American menu. Lunch, dinner. Serves country-style Western barbecue that features ingredients from the Northwest. $

★★ **THE LODGE RESTAURANT.** 13653 Hawks Beard Rd, Black Butte Ranch (97759). Phone 800/452-7455. www.blackbutteranch.com. French menu. Dinner. An elegant setting with incredible views of the surrounding mountains and lake and modern French cuisine that utilizes Northwest products. $

★★ **BRONCO BILLY'S RANCH GRILL.** 190 E Cascade, Sisters (97759). Phone 541/549-7427. www.broncobillysranchgrill.com. American menu. Lunch, dinner. Located in the historic Sisters Hotel, this establishment serves up modern interpretations of Old West cooking in a unique, period environment. $

★ **SEASON'S CAFÉ AND WINE BAR.** 411 E Hood, Sisters (97759). Phone 541/549-8911. American menu. Closed Mon. Freshly unique sandwiches and other light fare with a great wine selection by the glass. $

Outback Scenic Byway
✵ OREGON

Quick Facts

LENGTH: 171 miles.

TIME TO ALLOW: 3 to 4 hours.

BEST TIME TO DRIVE: Spring to fall.

BYWAY TRAVEL INFORMATION: Lake County Chamber of Commerce: 541/947-6040.

SPECIAL CONSIDERATIONS: Most supplies should be available in towns near the Byway.

RESTRICTIONS: Highway 31 and US Highway 395, along with Country Roads 5-10, 11, and 11A are maintained year-round. On rare occasions, winter snowstorms may slow traffic, but the roads are almost never closed.

BICYCLE/PEDESTRIAN FACILITIES: No special bike paths have been provided along the Byway, but the road has low traffic and a high percentage of straight stretches with good sight distances. Pedestrians are able to stretch their legs or take short hikes at Fort Rock National Landmark, Summer Lake Rest Area, Chandler Wayside, and Gooselake state parks. The town of Lakeview also has sidewalks along Highway 395. Along the rest of the Byway, pedestrians share the shoulder of the road with vehicles.

Outback means "isolated rural country," and this area of Oregon is indeed rugged and remote. This Byway takes you through Oregon's outback, where the agricultural and timber industries employ many of the residents, where the landscape ranges from lush green forests to arid desert, and where the people who live here seek independence yet know each other by first names. While you're here, you'll notice that community is paramount to the people who call this area home.

THE BYWAY STORY

The Outback Scenic Byway tells archaeological, cultural, natural, recreational, and scenic stories that make it a unique and treasured Byway.

Archaeological

The Outback Scenic Byway transects the Fort Rock Cave National Register Site, the Picture Rock Pass National Register Site, and the Lake Abert National Register District. All these sites contain significant historic and prehistoric cultural values. The districts have one of the highest cultural site densities in the Great Basin Region, and several archaeological papers and reports of regional and national significance have been published regarding the rock art and sagebrush sandals found here.

Cultural

Some of this Byway's cultural flavor can be seen in the buildings along the Byway, which reflect the influence of the Old West.

Natural

Among the many natural attributes, the Fort Rock State Natural Area is listed as a National

Oregon

❋ Outback Scenic Byway

Natural Landmark. Fort Rock is a volcanic marr formation that homesteading families of long ago appropriately named for its four-sided towering walls. This ideal natural fort is colored orange/brown.

Abert Rim, another natural attraction, is one of the nation's longest and most continuous fault escarpments. This rim rises more than 2,000 feet above the highway.

The Summer Lake State Wildlife Area is 18,000 acres in size and home to more than 250 species of birds. The marshlike area, located in the high desert, is strategically important for habitat and nesting. Regionally, it is one of the most important stops for migrating birds that use the Pacific Flyway. Many sensitive, threatened, or endangered species, such as bald eagles, American peregrine falcons, western snowy plovers, greater sand hill cranes, and trumpeter swans, can be seen using this habitat. More than 15,000 bird watchers flock here annually. Seasonal access by foot and vehicle is designated. This is truly a bird-watcher's paradise.

Recreational

The thermal updrafts that are created from the warming of the valley and the mountains make the Lakeview area ideal for hang gliding. In fact, Lakeview has been named the hang gliding capital of the West by many hang-gliding and sport magazines. An annual hang gliding festival around the Fourth of July attracts hundreds of pilots, making it one of the most unique recreational events in Oregon. The US Hang Gliding Association has held two national championships in the Lakeview area. Pilots from around the world come to catch the thermals.

The Byway brings visitors in close proximity to six national designations, including the Gearhart Mountain Wilderness, the Christmas Valley National Back Country Byway, the Lake Abert and the Warner Wetlands Areas of Critical Environmental Concern, the Hart Mountain National Wildlife Refuge, and the Lakeview to Steens Back Country Byway.

Scenic

The Outback Scenic Byway is one of the most scenic routes in the Great Basin Region. You pass through different environments as you drive the Byway, and the changes between environments are dramatic. The different environments include old-growth ponderosa and lodgepole pine stands found in the Eastern Cascades, the sage brush steppe, the wetlands, and the other high-desert ecosystems.

One of the most striking scenic features along this Byway is the sweeping view of Winter and Abert Rims. These rims are 2,000-foot fault escarpment blocks that tower above the Byway. Abert Rim is Oregon's longest, most dramatic, and most photographed fault escarpment. This rim is also considered one of the most continuous fault escarpments in the United States.

HIGHLIGHTS

Starting at the southern end of the Byway coming out of California on US 395, you'll see the following sites. If you start on the other end of the Byway, begin at the bottom of this list and make your way up.

- **Lakeview, Oregon,** is the hang-gliding capital of the West. One mile north of Lakeview is the only active geyser in the West, called **Old Perpetual.** Bring your camera to take a picture of the geyser, which erupts every 90 seconds.

- Continue north on the Byway and, if you have an extra 30 to 60 minutes, head east on Hwy 395 to the Abert Rim drive and **Lake Abert.** If you don't have that much time, continue north on State Route 31 to the town of **Paisley** and the annual Mosquito Festival that occurs there every July. Continue on past the **Summer Lake Lodge** and wilderness area; if you have a day to spend in the woods, the area is excellent for fishing and hiking.

- Just south of Silver Lake is **Picture Rock Pass,** an area named for the ancient Indian petroglyphs that decorate rock within walking distance of the highway.

- Continue your drive on Route 31 to Fort Rock. While there, visit the remnants of an ancient volcano at **Fort Rock State Park**, just 7 miles off the Byway. Nearby is the **Homestead Village Museum**, which takes from 30 to 60 minutes to explore. From Fort Rock, continue on Route 31, where the Byway ends as it meets US Highway 97.

- If you end up having extra time to see additional points of interest, from Fort Rock you can travel country road 5-12 past Cougar Mountain to many volcanic formations, such as **Hole-in-the-Ground**, **Devils Garden**, **The Blowouts**, and **Derrick Cave**. If you have even more time, from Country Road 5-12, head east to Country Road 5-12B and then south on BLM Road 6109C to **Four Craters Lava Flow** and **Crack in the Ground**. Keep heading south to Christmas Valley, head east on Country Road 5-14, and then go north on Country Road 5-14D to the **Sand Dunes** and the **Lost Forest**.

THINGS TO SEE AND DO

Driving along the Outback Scenic Byway will certainly keep your senses engaged, but if you yearn to get out of the car and stretch your legs, or if you'd like to make a mini-vacation out of your trip, check out these attractions along the route.

DREWS RESERVOIR. *Lakeview (97630). Phone 541/947-3334.* Fishing, boat launch, and camping are available here.

FORT ROCK VALLEY HISTORICAL HOMESTEAD MUSEUM. *PO Box 84, Fort Rock (97735). Phone 541/576-2468. www.fortrockmuseum.com.* The purpose of this village museum is to preserve some of the homestead era structures by moving them from original locations to the museum site, just west of the town of Fort Rock. The Webster cabin and Dr. Thom's office were the two buildings that were in place for the opening in 1988. Since that time, several homes and a church have been moved to the village, as well as pieces of equipment. As this is an ongoing project; more structures and other pieces will be moved in the future. The moving of the buildings has been accomplished by volunteers from the community, Lake County Road Department, and Midstate Electric Cooperative. Restoration has been done by a few local members. Open Memorial Day weekend-weekend after Labor Day Fri-Sun 9 am-dusk.

FREMONT NATIONAL FOREST. *1300 S G St, Lakeview (97630). Phone 541/947-2151. www.fs.fed.us/r6/fremont/.* This forest, more than 5 million acres, includes remnants of ice-age lava flows and Abert Rim, the largest and most defined exposed geologic fault in North America, on the east side of Lake Abert. Abert Rim is most spectacular at the east side of Crooked Creek Valley. Many of the lakes are remnants of post-glacial Lake Lahontan.

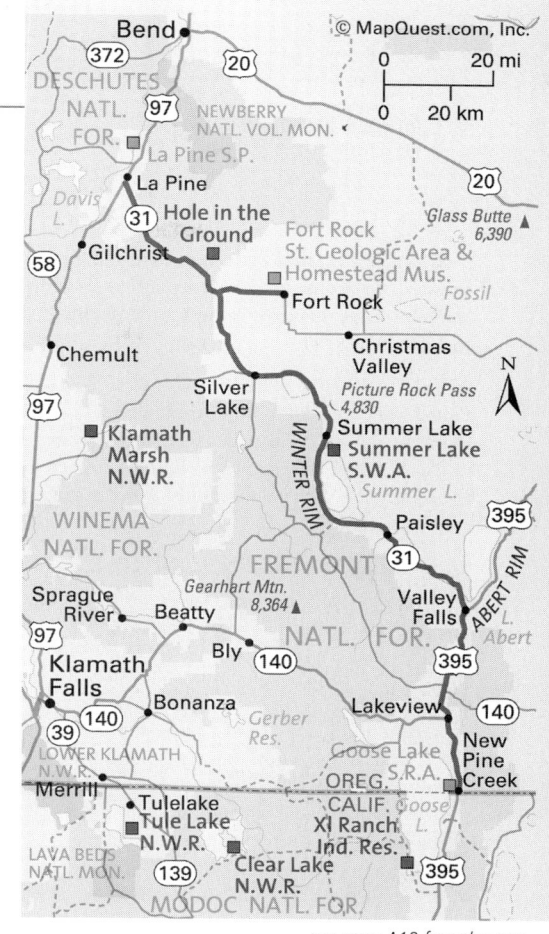

see page A18 for color map

Oregon

❈ Outback Scenic Byway

Gearhart Mountain Wilderness is rough and forested, with unusual rock formations, streams and Blue Lake. Fishing, hunting, picnicking, and camping.

GEYSER AND HOT SPRINGS. *Lakeview (97630). Phone 541/947-2817.* Old Perpetual is said to be the largest continuous hot-water geyser in the Northwest. It spouts as high as 70 feet approximately every 90 seconds. A hot springs area is nearby.

HART MOUNTAIN NATIONAL ANTELOPE REFUGE. *PO Box 21, Plush (97637). Phone 541/947-3315. pacific.fws.gov/refuges/field/OR-hartmn.htm.* The 275,000-acre Hart Mountain National Antelope Refuge was established in 1936 to provide spring, summer, and fall range for remnant antelope herds. These herds usually winter in Catlow Valley, to the east, and on the Sheldon National Wildlife Refuge about 35 miles southeast in Nevada. Since then, the purpose of the refuge has been expanded to include management of all wildlife species characteristic of this high-desert habitat and to preserve natural, native ecosystems for the enjoyment, education, and appreciation of the public.

SCHMINCK MEMORIAL MUSEUM. *128 S East St, Lakeview (97630). Phone 541/947-3134. www.lakecountyoregon/schminck.htm/.* This museum offers a range of fascinating exhibits: pressed-glass goblets, home furnishings, dolls, toys, books, clothing, quilts, guns, saddles, tools, and Native American artifacts. Open Feb-Nov, Tues-Sat; also by appointment; closed holidays. **FREE**

PLACES TO STAY

If you choose to include an overnight stay in your trip along this Byway, Mobil Travel Guide recommends the following lodgings.

★ **BEST WESTERN SKYLINE MOTOR LODGE.** *414 N G St, Lakeview (97630). Phone 541/947-2194; toll-free 800/780-7234. www.bestwestern.com.* 38 rooms, 2 story. Pet accepted, some restrictions; $10. Complimentary continental breakfast. Check-out 11 am. TV; cable (premium). In-room modem link. Laundry services. Indoor pool, whirlpool. Downhill, cross-country skiing within 10 miles. ¢

★★ **HERYFORD HOUSE INN.** *108 S F St, Lakeview (97630). Phone 541/947-4727; toll-free 888/295-3402.* 6 rooms, 3 story. Located in a 1911 brick Queen Anne Victorian mansion in downtown Lakeview. $

★ **LAKEVIEW LODGE MOTEL.** *301 N G St, Lakeview (97630). Phone 541/947-2181.* 40 rooms. Crib free. Pet accepted. Check-out 11 am. TV; cable (premium). Downhill, cross-country ski 8 miles. In-house fitness room; sauna. Whirlpool. Microwaves available. ¢

★★ **DIAMOND STONE GUEST LODGE.** *16693 Sprague Loop, LaPine (97739). Phone 541/536-6263; toll-free 800/600-6263. www.diamondstone.com.* 3 rooms, 2 story. Sits adjacent to Quail Run Golf Course at the gateway to Newberry National Volcanic Monument, with the Cascade

Mountains as a backdrop. Surrounded by open meadows and pines with plenty of trails for hiking and exploring. Complimentary breakfast. **$**

PLACES TO EAT

A long day of driving is sure to make you hungry. At the end of your journey, take a table at one of the following restaurants.

★★ **COWBOY DINNER TREE.** *4 miles S of Silver Lake on Hager Mountain Rd (97638). Phone 541/576-2426. www.cowboydinnertree. homestead.com/main.html.* American menu. Closed Mon, Tues, Thurs. Dinner. A traditional Old West restaurant with a limited menu and hours, but worthwhile for the great food and atmosphere. Located in a turn-of-the-century ranch. **$$**

★ **HOMESTEAD.** *Hwy 31 N, Paisley (97636). Phone 541/943-3187.* American menu. Breakfast, lunch, dinner. Classic American food in a historic location. **$**

Pacific Coast Scenic Byway
✻ OREGON   AN ALL-AMERICAN ROAD

Quick Facts

LENGTH: 363 miles.

TIME TO ALLOW: 10 to 12 hours.

BEST TIME TO DRIVE: Spring to fall.

BYWAY TRAVEL INFORMATION: Oregon Coast Visitor's Association Oregon Tourism Commission: 503/986-0000.

SPECIAL CONSIDERATIONS: Services may be several miles apart or closed at night. Slides and floods caused by extreme weather conditions sometimes temporarily disrupt access. With the ocean providing year-round air-conditioning, temperatures are comfortably in the 60s and 70s in the summer and rarely drop below freezing in the winter. Be prepared for fog, drizzle, or rain showers any time of year, but mainly in the winter and spring. Steady breezes are common most of the year. However, winter storms occasionally bring gusts above 50 mph. At the Oregon Dunes National Recreation Area, temperatures are at their highest and winds are at their lowest during the early fall. Be prepared for rapidly changing weather conditions.

BICYCLE/PEDESTRIAN FACILITIES: This Byway is designated by the Oregon Department of Transportation as a state bike route. Signage and stripes are provided for the bike route and pedestrian crossings. Bicycling on the Oregon Coast Bike Route is considered to be the most exciting way to explore the scenery along this Byway.

This Byway trots along the full length of the Oregon coast. The northern end starts in the shadow of the impressive Astoria-Megler Bridge, where the mouth of the Columbia River gapes wide (Astoria is the oldest US settlement west of the Rockies). Shining beaches and temperate rain forests govern the following dozens of miles. Parallelling the Lewis and Clark Trail, the route stops by attractive places, such as the resort town of Seaside, famous for its 2-mile beachfront promenade, and the busy Garibaldi fishing port on Tillamook Bay.

The southern portion of the Byway changes a little because it is dominated by rugged cliffs, farms, and sandy beaches. This segment maintains some of the most photographed areas in Oregon; photographers often capture Siletz and Depoe Bays, the colorful Oregon skies, lots of dairy land, and the city of Tillamook (the producer of the famous brand of cheese).

THE BYWAY STORY

The Pacific Coast Scenic Byway tells archaeological, cultural, historical, natural, recreational, and scenic stories that make it a unique and treasured Byway.

Archaeological

The relics and structures located in this area indicate that people have lived and prospered here for several millennia. This Byway's archaeological residue fits into two main categories: relics of a native people that reveal an Eden-like past (such as ancient campsites) and evidences of the activities of a more recent people. Of the ancient people, scientists have found remnants of spears, knives, and other hunting equipment.

103

Oregon

✱ *Pacific Coast Scenic Byway*

Discoveries of bones near campsites indicate the type of food these people ate: fish, large animals (elk and deer), and some birds. The people were largely industrious and thrived in this area for thousands of years.

The sites from a more recent people are mostly historic bridges and lighthouses such as Yaquina Head's 125-year-old lighthouse, the 125-foot Astoria Column in Astoria, and the occasional shipwreck, such as the one known as *Peter Iredale* at Fort Stevens State Park. Some of these impressive structures still stand as landmarks to help guide travelers, while others function as attractions for tourists.

Cultural

Appreciate this area more by taking part in everyday activities to familiarize yourself with the area's culture. For instance, go to Lincoln City to soar a colorful kite alongside the locals; after that, visit some of Lincoln City's many art galleries. Another popular destination is Bandon, a charming town famous for its lighthouse, its giant seastacks, its cheese factory, and the cranberry harvest.

You might stop in Tillamook and see Oregon's largest cheese factory for a taste-testing tour: something residents like to do every now and then. This impressive factory has been around for over 100 years. It boasts of continuing to use the time-tested recipe that has made its cheese famous. Other areas of note include North Bend and Coos Bay, cities that comprise the coast's largest urban area; here, you find cultural activities galore, such as fantastic symphonies, art galleries, and restaurants.

Historical

The gorgeous and rich Oregon coast has drawn and sustained native people for centuries, and it has done likewise for sightseers and settlers ever since Lewis and Clark highly acclaimed the area. Each new wave of people who came to live around the route added a new facet of culture and history to it and left their mark through historical and archaeological remains. These remains, shadows of the past, are waiting in places like Astoria. Other important historical sites on the Byway include Fort Clatsop National Memorial, a life-size replica of Lewis and Clark's 1805-1806 winter outpost; historic Battle Rock Park in Port Orford, one of Oregon's oldest incorporated towns; and Yaquina Head's lighthouse, a testament to the area's historical shipping industry. The area's history is also evidenced in the many Victorian homes that scale the hillside, the 1883 Flavel House, and the shipwreck of the *Peter Iredale* at Fort Stevens State Park.

Natural

The Byway runs along the coastline, bringing highway travelers to the sea and away again, winding by estuarine marshes, clinging to exposed seaside cliffs, passing through gentle agricultural valleys, and brushing against wind-sculpted dunes. Travelers encounter the scenic splendor of sea-stack rock formations that are eroding under constant surf, as well as a plethora of unusual plants and animals that provide natural wonder.

The highest waterfall in the Coast Range is an easy side trip from the Byway. To find this waterfall, go 7 miles south of Tillamook, and then watch for a small sign to Munson Creek Falls. Follow the narrow road 1 1/2 miles to the parking area. A short stroll takes you to the base of this 266-foot cataract.

Many travelers enjoy watching water wildlife along this Byway. Waysides and state parks along the coast make excellent vantage points for watching gray whales that migrate between December and May.

Recreational

Beaches along the Byway are open to public use. In addition, many state parks run the length of the Byway and provide public access and protection to beaches. An abundance of public campsites, motel rooms, beach houses, and eateries along the Byway corridor ensure a delightful extended stay along Oregon's Pacific Coast Scenic Byway.

Florence is the gateway to the Oregon Dunes National Recreation Area, a 47-mile sandbox with areas designated for bird-watching and dune riding. Honeyman State Park is a popular place to water-ski and camp. As you travel on through the dunes, take a side trip to the Dean Creek Elk Viewing Area at Reedsport. The Oregon Dunes National Recreation Area has more than 31,000 acres. Visitors can camp, arrange a tour, take an exhilarating off-highway vehicle ride, or just walk along tranquil lakes, forest trails, and beaches.

Tucked in among some of the highest coastal dunes in the world, you'll find plenty of fishing and boating opportunities in small communities like Winchester Bay and Lakeside. The dunes end near the cities of North Bend and Coos Bay, the coast's largest urban area. As Oregon's deepest natural harbor, Coos Bay has long been a major shipping port for the timber industry and a haven for sport-fishing enthusiasts.

Depoe Bay also offers fishing and whale-watching excursions from the world's smallest navigable harbor.

Flying large, beautiful kites is a common practice all along the coast, but is especially popular in Lincoln City, which was recognized by *KiteLines* magazine as the best place to fly a kite in North America. Annual spring and fall kite festivals draw kite enthusiasts from all over. Get out your kite and watch with the crowds as the delicate crafts are lofted up into the sky by the strong coastal winds.

Scenic

Keep your camera handy so that you can capture the coast's most photographed seascape, Cape Foulweather and the churning waves at Devil's Punch Bowl. The superb scenery continues through Waldport and Yachats to the Cape Perpetua Scenic Area. Here, you can watch the waves rush in and out of Devil's Churn, or you can hike on trails high above it. As the rugged cliffs give way to graceful sand dunes, you'll arrive in Florence, a city that explodes with wild rhododendrons in the spring. The drive into

see page A19 for color map

Brookings saves some of the best scenery for last. For example, Samuel Boardman State Park shows off 9 miles of rocky viewpoints and quiet beaches at the base of the Siskiyou Mountains. After crossing the crystal blue Chetco River, the Pacific Coast Scenic Byway ends in redwood country at the California border.

HIGHLIGHTS

Consider taking the Pacific Coast Highway's must-see tour:

- **Astoria:** You will pass through Long Beach and go on to the city of Astoria, the oldest American settlement west of the Rockies. Astoria offers more points of historical interest than any other place on the Oregon coast.
- **Fort Clatsop National Memorial:** For a glimpse into life on one of the most important expeditions in the nation's history, travel

Oregon
✣ Pacific Coast Scenic Byway

3 miles east on Alternate (Old) 101 to Fort Clatsop Road and follow signs to the memorial. It is operated by the National Park Service on the site where the Lewis and Clark Expedition spent the winter of 1805-1806.

- **Seaside:** You reach the city of Seaside, which was Oregon's first seashore resort. The Turnaround there is the location of the statue designating the end of the Lewis and Clark Trail. At the south end of the Promenade, you will find the Lewis and Clark Salt Cairn, where members of the expedition made salt from seawater.
- **Cannon Beach:** The site of the famous annual Sandcastle Building Contest in early June. The beach was named for a cannon washed ashore in 1846 after the wreck of the schooner *Shark*.
- **Lincoln County:** Lincoln County has miles of ocean beaches known for fine agates and other minerals, ocean cruises, and whale-watching trips out of Depoe Bay and Newport. Lincoln City also has Oregon's first factory outlet shopping center.
- **Yaquina Bay Lighthouse:** The lighthouse houses a museum and is open during scheduled hours.
- **Devil's Churn:** The basalt that forms the shore here is penetrated by a split in the rock that narrows to a few feet before finally disappearing into the cliff. Fascinating in summer, it is awe-inspiring during winter storms and is an excellent spot for photographers.
- **Cape Perpetua Viewpoint:** Just south of Devils Churn you'll find a road going inland. At the branch in the road, turn left and continue climbing sharply to the Cape Perpetua Viewpoint. There is a fine view of the coast both north and south.
- **Heceta Head Lighthouse State Scenic Viewpoint (formerly Devil's Elbow State Park):** This pretty little cove is the place to see Heceta Head Lighthouse up close. Just walk up the trail to the former assistant lighthouse keeper's home, Heceta House, and continue on to the lighthouse.
- **Sea Lion Caves:** These natural caves are home to Steller sea lions.
- **Florence:** There are many delightful shops, restaurants, and galleries near the Siuslaw River in this town.
- **Oregon Dunes National Recreation Area (NRA):** The Oregon Dunes NRA extends from Florence to North Bend with many access points off the Byway.
- **Umpqua River:** The Umpqua River Bridge is one of the historic coast bridges. The Umpqua is one of the major rivers in Oregon and is navigable by fairly large vessels upstream as far as Scottsburg.
- **Cape Blanco:** Five miles west of the Byway, Cape Blanco was discovered by the Spanish explorer Martin de Aguilar in 1603. The lighthouse is located at the westernmost point in Oregon.
- **Prehistoric Gardens:** In the rain forest atmosphere of the Oregon coast, the developers of Prehistoric Gardens have created life-sized replicas of dinosaurs.

THINGS TO SEE AND DO

Driving along the Pacific Coast Scenic Byway will certainly keep your senses engaged, but if you yearn to get out of the car and stretch your legs, or if you'd like to make a mini-vacation out of your trip, check out these attractions along the route.

ALDER HOUSE II. *611 Immonen Rd, Lincoln City (97367). Phone 541/996-2483. www.alderhouse.com.* Set in a grove of alder trees, this is the oldest glass-blowing studio in Oregon. Watch molten glass drawn from a furnace and shaped into pieces of traditional or modern design. Open mid-Mar-Nov; daily. **FREE**

AZALEA PARK. *Hwy 101 and North Bank Chetco River Rd, Brookings (97415). Phone 541/469-2021; toll-free 800/535-9469. www.brookingsor.com/playing/azaleapark.shtml.* A 36-acre city park with five varieties of large native azaleas, some blooming twice a year. Observation point. Hiking. Picnicking.

C&M STABLES. *90241 Hwy 101, Florence (97439). Phone 541/997-7540. www.oregonhorsebackriding.com.* Experience the spectacular scenery of Oregon's coast on horseback. Beach (1 1/2 to 2 hours), dune trail (1 to 1 1/2 hours), sunset (2 hours, with or without a meal), and coast range (half-day or all-day) rides. Must be 8 years or older. Open daily 10 am to dusk; closed Thanksgiving, Dec 25. **$$$$**

CAPE ARAGO. *Coos Bay (97420). Phone 541/888-8867. www.oregonstateparks.org/park_94.php.* This 134-acre promontory juts 1/2 mile into the ocean. Two beaches, fishing; hiking (on the Oregon Coast Trail), picnicking. Observation point (whale and seal watching).

CAPE BLANCO STATE PARK. *91814 Cape Blanco Rd, Port Orford (97465). Phone 541/332-6774. www.oregonstateparks.org/park_62.php.* A 1,880-acre park, once a ranch owned by the hard-working Hughes family, affords marvelous views of the Cape Blanco Lighthouse and boasts the historic Hughes house, hiking trails, beach access, and a campground. River access for boats. Picnicking. Horse camp, horse trails, rustic cabins. Improved campsites.

CAPE LOOKOUT STATE PARK. *13000 Whiskey Creek Rd, Tillamook (97141). Phone 503/842-4981. www.oregonstateparks.org/park_186.php.* A 1,974-acre park with a virgin spruce forest and observation point. One of the most primitive ocean shore areas in the state. Hiking trail to the end of the cape. Picnicking. Tent and trailer sites (dump station). Open daily. **$**

CAPE SEBASTIAN STATE PARK. *Gold Beach (97444). Phone 541/469-2021. www.oregonstateparks.org/park_73.php.* Approximately 1,143 acres of open and forested land. Cape Sebastian is a precipitous headland, rising more than 700 feet above the tide with a view of many miles of coastline. There is a 1.5-mile trail to the tip of the cape; beach access. A short roadside through the forest area is marked by wild azaleas, rhododendrons, and blue ceanothus in season. Trails; no rest rooms or water. Open daily. **FREE**

CARL G. WASHBURNE MEMORIAL. *93111 Hwy 101, Florence (97439). Phone 541/547-3416; toll-free 800/551-6949. www.oregonstateparks.org/park_123.php.* This 1,089-acre park is a good area for the study of botany. Two-mile-long beach, swimming, fishing, clamming, hiking, picnicking, tent and trailer campsites with access to the beach. Elk may be seen in campgrounds and nearby meadows. Open daily.

CHINOOK WINDS CASINO & CONVENTION CENTER. *1777 NW 44th St, Lincoln City (97367). Phone 541/996-5825; toll-free 888/CHINOOK. www.chinookwindscasino.com.* About 80 miles south of the Washington border on the scenic Oregon coast, Chinook Winds is the largest convention facility between Seattle and San Francisco. With more than 1,200 machines and tables, the modern casino has

Oregon

✽ *Pacific Coast Scenic Byway*

all the requisite games—slots, blackjack, keno, poker, roulette, craps, and even bingo—with a betting limit of $500. The cavernous showroom sees regular performances by classic rock bands, country artists, and comedians, many of them household names. There are also three restaurants (an upscale room, a buffet, and a deli), a lounge, and childcare services and an arcade for the kids, but no hotel rooms. (There are plenty of the latter in Lincoln City, however.) Best of all, the casino's beachfront location is serene. Hours vary.

COLUMBIA RIVER MARITIME MUSEUM. *1792 Marine Dr, Astoria (97213). Phone 503/325-2323. www.crmm.org.* Rare maritime artifacts and memorabilia of the Columbia River, its tributaries, and the Northwest coast. *Lightship Columbia 604* at moorage in Maritime Park. Fishing industry, discovery and exploration, steamship, shipwreck, navigation, and steamboat exhibits. Coast Guard and Navy exhibits. Open daily 9:30 am-5 pm; closed Thanksgiving, Dec 25. **$$**

DEAN CREEK ELK VIEWING AREA. *3 miles E on OR 38, Reedsport (97467). Phone 541/756-0100.* Area has 440 acres of pasture and bottomland where Roosevelt elk (Oregon's largest land mammal) and other wildlife can be viewed. Interpretive center. No hunting. Open daily. **FREE**

DEVIL'S ELBOW. *84505 Hwy 101, Florence (97439). Phone 541/997-3641.* A 545-acre park. Ocean beach, fishing; hiking, picnicking. Observation point. Open daily. **$**

DEVIL'S PUNCH BOWL. *Newport (97365). Phone 541/265-9278; toll-free 800/551-6949. www.oregonstateparks.org/park_217.php.* An 8-acre park noted for its bowl-shaped rock formation that fills at high tide; ocean-carved caves, marine gardens. Beach. Trails. Picnicking. Observation point. Open daily. **FREE**

ECOLA STATE PARK. *Ecola Rd, Cannon Beach (97110). Phone 503/436-2844; toll-free 800/551-6949. www.oregonstateparks.org/park_188.php.* The end of the trail for Lewis and Clark expedition. A 1,303-acre park with 6 miles of ocean frontage, sea lion and bird rookeries on rocks and offshore islands, and the Tillamook Lighthouse. Beaches, fishing; hiking (on the Oregon Coast Trail), picnicking at Ecola Point. Whale-watching at observation point. Open daily. **$**

FLAVEL HOUSE. *441 8th St, Astoria (97103). Phone 503/325-2203. www.oldoregon.com/Pages/Havel.htm.* Built by Captain George Flavel, pilot and shipping man; outstanding example of Queen Anne architecture (1883-1887). Restored Victorian home houses antique furnishings and fine art; collection of 19th- and 20th-century toys. Carriage house, museum store, orientation film. Open daily; closed holidays. **$$**

✪ **FORT CLATSOP NATIONAL MEMORIAL.** *Cannon Beach (97110). Phone 503/861-2471. www.nps.gov/focl/.* This site marks the western extremity of the territory explored by Meriwether Lewis and William Clark in their expedition of 1804-1806. The fort is a reconstruction of their 1805-1806 winter quarters. The original fort was built here because of its excellent elk hunting grounds, its easy access to ocean salt, its protection from the westerly coastal storms, and the availability of fresh water. The expedition set out on May 14, 1804, to seek "the most direct and practicable water communication across this continent" under orders from President Thomas Jefferson. The first winter was spent near Bismarck, North Dakota. In April 1805, the party, then numbering 33, resumed the journey. On November 15, they had their first view of the ocean from a point near McGowan, Washington. The company left Fort Clatsop on March 23, 1806, on their return trip and returned to St. Louis on September 23 of the same year. The Lewis and Clark Expedition was one of the greatest explorations in the history of the US, and its journals depict one of the most fascinating chapters in the annals of the American frontier. The visitor center has museum exhibits and provides audiovisual programs. The canoe landing has replicas of dugout canoes of that period. Ranger talks and living-history demonstrations are presented mid-June-Labor Day. Open daily; closed Dec 25. **$**

FORT STEVENS STATE PARK. *Off Hwy 101, 10 miles W of Astoria, in Hammond (97121). Phone 503/861-1671; toll-free 800/452-5687. www.oregonstateparks/park_179.php.* A 3,763-acre park adjacent to an old Civil War fort. Wreck of the *Peter Iredale* (1906) is on the ocean shore. Fort Stevens is the only military post in the lower 48 states to be fired upon by foreign forces since 1812. On June 21, 1942, a Japanese submarine fired several shells from its 5-inch gun; only one hit land. Visitor center and self-guided tour at the Old Fort Stevens Military Complex. Ocean beach, lake swimming, fishing, clamming on beach, boating (dock, ramp); bicycling, picnicking at Coffenbury Lake. Improved tent and trailer sites. Dump station. Open daily. **$**

HARRIS BEACH. *1655 Hwy 101, Brookings (97415). Phone 541/469-2021. www.oregonstateparks.org/park_79.php.* A 171-acre park with scenic rock cliffs along the ocean. Ocean beach, fishing; hiking trails, observation point, picnicking, improved tent and trailer campsites (dump station).

HATFIELD MARINE SCIENCE CENTER OF OREGON STATE UNIVERSITY. *2030 S Marine Science Dr, Newport (97365). Phone 541/867-0100. hmsc.oregonstate.edu.* Conducts research on oceanography, fisheries, water quality, marine science education, and marine biology; research vessel *Wecoma*; nature trail; aquarium-museum; films; special programs in summer. Winter and spring gray whale programs. Braille text and other aids for the hearing and visually impaired. Open Memorial Day weekend to late Sept, daily 10 am-5 pm; Oct-Memorial Day, Thurs-Mon 10 am-4 pm; closed Dec 25. **DONATION**

HECETA HEAD LIGHTHOUSE. *92072 Hwy 101 S, Yachats (97498). Phone 541/547-3696. www.hecetalighthouse.com.* A picturesque beacon set high on a rugged cliff. Heceta Head Lighthouse (1894) is one of the most photographed beacons in the United States. **$**

JERRY'S ROGUE RIVER JET BOAT TRIPS. *Hwy 101, Port of Gold Beach Boat Basin, Gold Beach (97444). Phone 541/247-4571; toll-free 800/451-3645. www.rougejets.com.* A six-hour (64-mile) round-trip into wilderness area; two-hour lunch or dinner stop at Agness. Also eight-hour (104-mile) and six-hour (80-mile) round-trip whitewater excursions. Rogue River Museum and Gift Shop (open all year). Open May-Oct, daily. **$$$$**

JESSIE M. HONEYMAN MEMORIAL. *84505 Hwy 101, Florence (97439). Phone 541/997-3641. www.oregonstateparks.org/park_134.php.* This park has 522 coastal acres with wooded lakes and sand dunes, an abundance of rhododendrons, and an excellent beach. Swimming, water-skiing, fishing, boat dock and ramps; hiking, picnicking, improved camping, tent and trailer sites (dump station). Open daily. **$**

MAIL BOAT WHITEWATER TRIPS. *94294 Rougeriver Rd, Gold Beach (97444) Phone 541/247-7033; toll-free 800/458-3511. www.mailboat.com.* A 104-mile round-trip by jet boat into the wilderness and whitewater of the upper Rogue River. Narrated 7 1/2-hour trip. Open mid-May-mid-Oct, daily. Also a 80-mile round-trip to the middle Rogue River. Narrated 6 3/4-hour trip departs twice daily. Reservations advised for all trips. Open mid-June-Sept. **$$$$**

MARINE DISCOVERY TOURS. *345 SW Bay Blvd, Newport (97365). Phone 541/265-6200; toll-free 800/903-2628. www.marinediscovery.com.* Whale-watching and river cruises. Hands-on activities. Hours vary seasonally; closed Dec 25. **$$$$**

Oregon

✼ *Pacific Coast Scenic Byway*

OFFICIAL ROGUE RIVER MAIL BOAT HYDRO-JET TRIPS. *94294 N Bank Rogue River Rd, Gold Beach (97444). Phone 541/247-7033; toll-free 800/458-3511. www.harborside.com~mailboat.* A 64-mile round-trip by jet boat up the Wild & Scenic Rogue River; two-hour lunch stop at Agness. Reservations advised. Open May-Oct, daily. $$$$

OREGON COAST AQUARIUM. *2820 SE Ferry Slip Rd, Newport (97365). Phone 541/867-3474. www.aquarium.org.* The aquarium houses 15,000 animals representing 500 species in unique habitats. Open daily, early Sept-Memorial Day weekend 10 am-5 pm; Memorial Day weekend-Labor Day weekend 9 am-6 pm; closed Dec 25. $$$

OREGON DUNES NATIONAL RECREATION AREA. *855 Hwy 101, Reedsport (97467). Phone 541/271-3611. www.fs.fed.us/r6/siuslaw/odnra.htm.* Large coastal sand dunes, forests, and wetlands comprise this 32,000-acre area in Siuslaw National Forest. Beachcombing; fishing; boating. Hiking, horseback riding, off-road vehicle areas. Picnicking. Camping (fee; some campgrounds closed Oct-May). Visitor center and headquarters in Reedsport at US 101 and OR 38. Open daily.

OSWALD WEST STATE PARK. *9500 Sandpiper Ln, Nehalem (97131). Phone 503/368-5943; toll-free 800/551-6949. www.oregonstateparks.org/park_195.php.* A 2,474-acre park with outstanding coastal headland; towering cliffs; low dunes; rain forest with massive spruce and cedar trees; road winds 700 feet above sea level and 1,000 feet below the peak of Neahkahnie Mountain. Surfing (at nearby Short Sands Beach), fishing; hiking trails (on the Oregon Coast Trail), picnicking, primitive campgrounds accessible only by a 1/4-mile foot trail.

SADDLE MOUNTAIN STATE PARK. *Off US 26, 8 miles NE of Necanicum Jct, Seaside (97138). Phone 503/368-5154 or 503/436-2844. www.oregonstateparks_197.php.* A 2,922-acre park with a trail to a 3,283-foot summit, one of the highest in the Coastal Range. Hiking. Picnicking. Primitive campsites. Open daily.

SALMON HARBOR. *100 Ork Rock Rd, Winchester Bay (97103). Phone 541/271-3407.* Excellent boat basin for charter boats and pleasure and fishing craft. Fishing for silver and chinook salmon in the ocean, a short run from the mouth of the Umpqua River. Open May-Sept, daily; rest of year, Mon-Fri.

SAND DUNES FRONTIER. *83960 Hwy 101 S, Florence (97439). Phone 541/997-3544. www.sanddunesfrontier.com.* Excursions aboard 20-passenger dune buggies or drive-yourself Odysseys; miniature golf; flower garden. Open daily. $$$$

★ **SEA LION CAVES.** *91560 Hwy 101 N, Florence (97439). Phone 541/547-3111. www.sealioncaves.com.* Descend 208 feet under a basaltic headland into a cavern (1,500 feet long) that is home to wild sea lions. These mammals (up to 12 feet long) are generally seen on rocky ledges outside the cave in spring and summer and inside the cave in fall and winter. Self-guided tours; light jacket and comfortable shoes suggested. Open daily at 9 am; closed Dec 25. $$

SEASIDE AQUARIUM. *200 N Prom, Seaside (97138). Phone 503/738-6211. www.seasideaquarium.com.* Deep-sea life and trained seals; seal feeding (fee). Open Mar-Nov, daily; rest of year, Wed-Sun; closed Thanksgiving, Dec 24-25. $$$

SHORE ACRES. *89814 Cape Arago Hwy, Coos Bay (97420) Phone 541/888-3732 or 541/888-8867. www.oregonstateparks.org/park_97.php.* Former grand estate of Coos Bay lumberman, noted for its unusual botanical and Japanese gardens and spectacular ocean views (743 acres). Ocean beach; hiking (on the Oregon Coast Trail), picnicking.

SIUSLAW PIONEER MUSEUM. *85294 US 101 S, Florence (97439). Phone 541/997-7884. www.florencechamber.com/RecAtt_PioneerM.html.* Exhibits preserve the history of the area; impressive display of artifacts and items from early settlers and Native Americans. Library room; extensive genealogy records; hundreds of old photographs. Open Jan-Nov, Tues-Sun; closed holidays. **$**

SUNSET BAY. *Coos Bay (97420). Phone 541/888-4902; toll-free 800/551-6789. www.oregonstateparks.org/park_100.php.* A 395-acre park with swimming beach on sheltered bay, fishing; hiking, picnicking, tent and trailer sites. Observation point.

TILLAMOOK COUNTY PIONEER MUSEUM. *2106 2nd St, Tillamook (97141). Phone 503/842-4553. www.tcpm.org.* Possessions of early settlers, a replica of a pioneer home and barn, a blacksmith shop, logging displays, war relics, relics from Tillamook Naval Air Station and Blimp Base, minerals, guns, books, vehicles, and natural history and wildlife exhibits that include nine dioramas; "great-grandma's kitchen." Open daily; closed Thanksgiving, Dec 25. **$$**

UMPQUA LIGHTHOUSE STATE PARK. *460 Lighthouse Rd, Reedsport (97467). Phone 541/271-4118. www.oregonstateparks.org/park_121.php.* This 450-acre park touches the mouth of the Umpqua River, borders the Umpqua Lighthouse Reservation, and skirts the ocean shore for more than 2 miles, with sand dunes rising 500 feet (the highest in the United States). Noted for its marvelous seasonal display of rhododendrons. Swimming; fishing. Hiking; trail to the beach and around Lake Marie. Picnicking. Tent and trailer sites. Whale-watching area.

YAQUINA HEAD. *Lighthouse Dr and Hwy 101, Newport (97365). Phone 541/574-3100. www.yaquinalights.org/yhead.html.* The lighthouse here is a popular spot for whale-watching and fully accessible tidal pool viewing. Also an interpretive center.

PLACES TO STAY

If you choose to include an overnight stay in your trip along this All-American Road, Mobil Travel Guide recommends the following lodgings.

★ **ASTORIA DUNES MOTEL.** *288 W Marine Dr, Astoria (97103). Phone 503/325-7111; toll-free 800/441-3319. astoriadunes.qwestdex.com.* 58 rooms, 18 A/C, 2-3 story. No elevator. Check-out 11 am. TV; cable (premium). Indoor pool; whirlpool. Restaurant nearby. Coin laundry. Business services available. Some refrigerators. Opposite the river. **¢**

★ **SPRINDRIFT MOTOR INN.** *1215 Chetco Ave, Brookings (97415). Phone 541/469-5345; toll-free 800/292-1171.* 35 rooms, 2 story. Check-out 11 am. TV; cable (premium). Restaurant opposite. Business services available. Refrigerators. **¢**

★ **BEST WESTERN HOLIDAY MOTEL.** *411 N Bayshore Dr, Coos Bay (97420). Phone 541/269-5111; toll-free 800/780-7234. www.bestwestern.com.* 77 rooms, 2 story. Check-out noon. TV; cable (premium). Laundry services. In-house fitness room. Indoor pool, whirlpool. **¢**

★★ **RED LION HOTEL COOS BAY.** *1313 N Bayshore Dr, Coos Bay (97420). Phone 541/267-4141; toll-free 800/359-4827. www.redlion.com.* 143 rooms, 1-2 story. Pet accepted, some restrictions. Check-out noon. TV; cable (premium). Pool. Restaurant, bar; entertainment Fri, Sat. Room service. Guest laundry. Meeting rooms. Business services available. In-room modem link. Free airport transportation. In-house fitness room. Refrigerators, microwaves available. On Coos Bay. **¢**

★ **BEST WESTERN PIER POINT INN.** *85625 Hwy 101, Florence (97439). 541/997-7191; toll-free 800/780-7243. www.bestwestern.com.* 55 rooms, 3 story. Complimentary continental breakfast. Check-out 11 am. TV; cable (premium). Sauna. Whirlpool. Overlooks the Siuslaw River. **$**

Oregon

❋ *Pacific Coast Scenic Byway*

★★★ **THE WESTIN SALISHAN LODGE AND GOLF RESORT.** *7760 Hwy 101 N, Gleneden Beach (97388). Phone 541/764-2371; toll-free 800/452-2300. www.salishan.com.* 205 rooms, 2-3 story. Pet accepted, some restrictions; $25. Check-out noon. TV; cable (premium), VCR available. Indoor pool; whirlpool, hydrotherapy pool. Restaurants, bar; entertainment weekends. Room service. Meeting rooms. Business services available. Shopping mall. Indoor/outdoor lighted tennis, pro. 18-hole golf, greens fee $35-$50, pro, putting greens, covered driving range. Self-guided nature trail. In-house fitness room; sauna. Massage. Game room. Refrigerators. Art gallery. Library. $

★★★ **TU TU' TUN LODGE.** *96550 N Bank Rogue, Gold Beach (97444). Phone 541/247-6664; toll-free 800/864-6357. www.tututun.com.* Enjoy the stone fireplace, the library, or the intimate bar in the main lodge of this rustic hideaway. Guests are welcomed with fresh flowers in each room. Don't miss a boat ride on the Rogue River, which can be arranged through the lodge. 16 rooms, 2 suites, 1 garden house. Check-out 11 am, check-in 3 pm. Outdoor pool. Complimentary hors d'oeuvres. Dining room open May-Oct (public by reservation): breakfast 7:30-9:30 am, lunch sitting (registered guests only) 1 pm; dinner sitting 7 pm. Bar. Business center. In-room modem link. Free airport transportation. Dock; guides, whitewater boat trips. Private patios, balconies. $

★ **COHO INN.** *1635 NW Harbor Ave, Lincoln City (97367). Phone 541/994-3684; toll-free 800/848-7006. www.thecohoinn.com.* 50 rooms, 31 kitchen units, 3 story. No A/C. No elevator. Pet accepted, some restrictions; $6. Check-out 11 am. TV; cable (premium). Some fireplaces. Sauna. Whirlpool. $

★★ **SHILO INN OCEANFRONT RESORT.** *1501 NW 40th Pl, Lincoln City (97367). Phone 541/994-3655; toll-free 800/222-2244. www.shiloinns.com.* 247 rooms, 3-4 story. Pet accepted, some restrictions; $10/day. Check-out noon. TV; cable (premium), VCR available. Indoor pool; whirlpool. Restaurant adjacent. Bar. Room service. Coin laundry. Meeting rooms. Business center. In-house fitness room, sauna. Health club privileges. Refrigerators, microwaves; some bathroom phones. Picnic tables. On the beach. Free airport transportation. $

★ **WHALER MOTEL.** *155 SW Elizabeth St, Newport (97365). Phone 541/265-9261; toll-free 800/433-9444. www.whalernewport.com.* 73 rooms, 3 story. No elevator. Complimentary continental breakfast. Check-out noon. TV; cable (premium). Indoor pool, whirlpool. Restaurant nearby. Coin laundry. In-house fitness room. Some refrigerators, microwaves, wet bars. Balconies. Ocean view. Free airport transportation. $

★ **BAY BRIDGE MOTEL.** *33 Coast Hwy, North Bend (97459). Phone 541/756-3151; toll-free 800/557-3156.* 16 rooms, 3 kitchen units. Pet accepted, some restrictions; fee. Check-out 11 am. TV. Some refrigerators. On Pacific Bay. ¢

★ **ANCHOR BAY INN.** *1821 Hwy 101, Reedsport (97467). Phone 541/271-2149; toll-free 800/767-1821.* 21 rooms, 4 kitchen units, 2 story. Pet accepted, some restrictions; fee. Complimentary continental breakfast. Check-out 10 am. TV; cable (premium), VCR available. Outdoor pool. Coin laundry. Business services available. Some refrigerators, microwaves. ¢

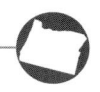

★ **EBB TIDE MOTEL.** *300 N Prom, Seaside (97138). Phone 503/738-8371; toll-free 800/468-6232. www.ebbtide.citysearch.com.* 99 rooms, 48 kitchen units, 3-4 story. No A/C. Check-out noon. TV; cable (premium), VCR available. In-room modem link. In-house fitness room, sauna. Indoor pool, whirlpool. On beach. ¢

★★★ **GILBERT INN BED & BREAKFAST.** *341 Beach Dr, Seaside (97138). Phone 503/738-9770; toll-free 800/410-9770. www.gilbertinn.com.* This Queen Anne Victorian home was built in 1892 and features a large fireplace in the parlor and a rich and warm atmosphere. It is located near shops, restaurants, beaches, and other attractions. 10 rooms, 1 suite, 3 story. No A/C. Closed Jan. Complimentary breakfast. Check-out 11 am, check-in 3-11 pm. TV. Free airport transportation. Totally nonsmoking. $

★★ **MARCLAIR INN.** *11 Main Ave, Tillamook (97141). Phone 503/842-7571; toll-free 800/331-6857.* 47 rooms, 6 kitchen units, 1-2 story. No A/C. Check-out 11 am. TV. Restaurant. Sauna. Heated pool, whirlpool. Sun deck. ¢

★★ **SHILO INN SUITES.** *1609 E Harbor Dr, Warrenton (97146). Phone 503/861-2181; toll-free 800/221-2244. www.shiloinns.com.* 63 rooms, 11 kitchen units, 4 story. Pet accepted; $10. Check-out noon. TV; cable (premium), VCR (movies). Indoor pool; whirlpool. Restaurant, bar. Room service. Coin laundry. Meeting rooms. Business services available. Sundries. Free airport transportation. In-house fitness room, sauna. Refrigerators, microwaves, wet bars. ¢

PLACES TO EAT

A long day of driving is sure to make you hungry. At the end of your journey, take a table at one of the following restaurants.

★★ **PIER 11 FEED STORE.** *77 11th St, Astoria (97103). Phone 503/325-0279.* Seafood, steak menu. Closed Thanksgiving, Dec 25. Breakfast, lunch, dinner. Bar. Reservations accepted. An old feed store on the pier (late 1800s); natural wood-beamed ceilings. $$

★★ **SHIP INN.** *1 2nd St, Astoria (97103). Phone 503/325-0033.* Seafood menu. Closed major holidays. Lunch, dinner. Bar. $$

★★ **SILVER SALMON GRILLE.** *1105 Commercial St, Astoria (97103). Phone 503/338-6640. www.silversalmongrille.com.* American, seafood menu. Lunch, dinner. Located on the beautiful Oregon coast in a 1924 commercial building; renovated interior featuring an abundance of regional specialties. $$

★★ **T. PAUL'S URBAN CAFÉ.** *1119 Commercial St, Astoria (97103). Phone 503/338-5133. www.tpaulsurbancafe.com.* American menu. Closed Sun. Lunch, dinner. Located on the north coast in the heart of Astoria, featuring eclectic local cuisine, regional wines, and microbrew beers. $

★★ **LORD BENNETT'S.** *1695 Beach Loop Dr, Bandon (97411). Phone 541/347-3663.* Come relish this restaurant's spectacular Pacific Ocean view and fresh, straightforward preparations of pasta, beef, pork, veal, chicken, and seafood. The atmosphere is refined but casual, with a slightly nautical feel, and the adjacent lounge offers great cocktails and live entertainment. Steak, seafood menu. Closed Dec 25, Jan. Lunch, dinner, Sun brunch. Bar. Children's menu. Casual attire. $$

Oregon

✳ *Pacific Coast Scenic Byway*

★★ **PORTSIDE.** *8001 Kingfisher Rd, Charleston (97420). Phone 541/888-5544.* Seafood menu. Lunch, dinner. Bar; entertainment Fri-Sun. Children's menu. Outdoor seating. $$
D

★★ **CLAWSON WINDWARD INN.** *3757 Hwy 101 N, Florence (97439). Phone 541/997-8243.* American menu. Closed Dec 25. Breakfast, lunch, dinner. Bar. Children's menu. $$
D SC

★★ **THE DINING ROOM AT SALISHAN.** *7760 Hwy 101 N, Gleneden Beach (97388). Phone 541/764-2371. www.salishan.com.* Regional American, seafood menu. Breakfast, lunch, dinner, Sun brunch. Bar. Children's menu. Reservations accepted. Valet parking. $$$
D

★★ **NOR'WESTER SEAFOOD.** *10 Harbor Way, Gold Beach (97444). Phone 541/247-2333.* Seafood, steak menu. Closed Dec, Jan. Dinner. Bar. Children's menu. Casual attire. $$
D

★★★ **BAY HOUSE.** *5911 SW Hwy 101, Lincoln City (97367). Phone 541/996-3222. www.bayhouserestaurant.com.* American menu. Dinner. Romantic dining room at the south end of the city, overlooking Siletz Bay. $$$

★ **DORY COVE.** *5819 Logan Rd, Lincoln City (97367). Phone 541/994-5180.* Seafood menu. Lunch, dinner. Children's menu. $$
D SC

★ **WHALE'S TALE.** *452 SW Bay Blvd, Newport (97365). Phone 541/265-8660.* Seafood menu. Closed Dec 24-25; Jan 2-Feb 14; Wed in spring, fall, winter. Breakfast, lunch, dinner. Children's menu. $$

★★ **HILLTOP HOUSE.** *166 N Bay Dr, North Bend (97459). Phone 541/756-4160.* Continental menu. Lunch, dinner. $$
D

★ **CAMP 18.** *42362 Hwy 26, Seaside (97138). Phone 503/755-1818.* American menu. Closed Dec 25. Breakfast, lunch, dinner, Sun brunch. Bar. Children's menu. $$
D

★★ **DOOGER'S SEAFOOD & GRILL.** *505 Broadway, Seaside (97138). Phone 503/738-3773.* Seafood, steak menu. Lunch, dinner. Children's menu. Totally nonsmoking. $$
D

Rogue-Umpqua Scenic Byway
❈ OREGON

Quick Facts

LENGTH: 172 miles.

TIME TO ALLOW: 7 to 8 hours.

BEST TIME TO DRIVE: Summer and fall; fall colors are particularly spectacular along this Byway.

BYWAY TRAVEL INFORMATION: Medford Visitors and Convention Bureau: 541/779-4847; Upper Rogue Regional Tourism Alliance: 541/878-3626; Roseburg Visitors and Convention Bureau: 541/672-9731; Byway local Web sites: www.visitroseburg.com; www.upperrogue.org; www.visitmedford.org.

SPECIAL CONSIDERATIONS: Check your car's fuel level often. Gas stations are few and far between. Also, during the winter months, the roads may be dangerous.

BICYCLE/PEDESTRIAN FACILITIES: Many trails are available along this Byway, and they vary in levels of difficulty. One of the highlights is a paved 11-mile bike path around Diamond Lake.

More commonly known as the "highway of waterfalls," the Rogue-Umpqua Scenic Byway ascends deep into the Cascades. About 18 miles east of Roseburg, the North Umpqua River meets head-on with the Little River at Colliding Rivers, one of the few places in the world where this head-on phenomenon occurs. The North Umpqua provides whitewater thrills and superb steelhead runs as it tumbles through the Umpqua National Forest.

After passing more than a half dozen waterfalls, the Byway reaches sparkling Diamond Lake, a year-round playground at the base of Mount Thielsen. The paved 11-mile path around the lake is one of the nicest family bike rides anywhere. From here, you're only moments away from Crater Lake's north entrance, which is usually open from June through October, and has attracted people from around the world to view its unusual beauty. Scientists from many places even come here to study the environment. In winter, you can swing through Highway 230 and Highway 62 to the south entrance, which is open year-round.

Whether you're learning about the rich history of the Native Americans, stretching in front of a tranquil lake, or experiencing the rush of whitewater rafting on the river known as an "emerald jewel" of Oregon, this Byway shares one of the state's best-loved areas with you.

THE BYWAY STORY

The Rogue-Umpqua Scenic Byway tells archaeological, historical, natural, recreational, and scenic stories that make it a unique and treasured Byway.

Oregon

Rogue-Umpqua Scenic Byway

Archaeological

The North Umpqua and Rogue Wild & Scenic rivers flow through this valley that was inhabited by prehistoric people for more than 8,000 years. Many dating techniques, such as radiocarbon and stratigraphic dating, indicate prehistoric occupations prior to the eruption of the volcano Mount Mazama, approximately 6,800 years ago. The presence of time-sensitive artifacts indicates that occupation may go as far back as 12,500 years.

The route encompasses lands once occupied by the ancestors of the Upland Takelma, Southern Molalla, Klamath, and Cow Creek Bands of the Umpqua and Upper Umpqua rivers. Along the route, interpretative panels are offered at the Colliding Rivers site at Glide, representing an Upper Umpqua village site. There is also a recorded prehistoric fishing locality that is located at the Narrows near Idleyld Park. The Susan Creek archaeological site contains cairns, representing vision questing. A trail provides access to the site, and an interpretive panel provides information on this site.

The nature and habitation of the valley changed with the eruption of Mount Mazama. When the volcano erupted, the Upper North Umpqua and Rogue River drainages were covered with a layer of airborne ash as far downstream as Dry Creek on the Umpqua and Elk Creek on the Rogue. A cloud of superheated gas and ash flowed across Diamond Lake and down the North Umpqua River to the Toketee Falls area and down the Rogue River towards Prospect, denuding the forest and destroying whatever plant and animal life happened to be in the way. Subsequent flood events carried ash and pumice farther downstream, blanketing terraces. Drainages were choked with ash, and their gravel beds became silted over, altering fish habitat. This cataclysmic event forced early inhabitants to adapt to their new surroundings, and archaeological sites within the Rogue and Umpqua corridors preserve a record of these adaptations, including alterations in clothing, food, and hunting techniques.

Historical

Early settlers to the Rogue-Umpqua Scenic Byway laid a foundation for life in this rugged landscape. The Fort Klamath military wagon road made its way over the formidable Cascades to the settlement of Union Creek. The city doesn't remain today, but the wagon trail was an important trail to get settlers and supplies over the mountains. In the 1850s, the Siskiyou Mountains in the Rogue River National Forest became home to many prospectors who were searching for gold. In the early days of the Byway, Indians, trappers, traders, explorers, and settlers all made their way into the surrounding area and worked or settled there.

The Civilian Conservation Corps (CCC) further developed the area surrounding the Byway during the 1930s. This organization provided work for thousands of people during a time of low employment. The CCC was responsible for a variety of projects, including reforestation, fire prevention, soil conservation, and development of recreational areas. Many structures that stand today along the Byway are a legacy to the CCC.

Stretching across the river near Steamboat is the historic Mott Bridge, a recognized Oregon Historic Civil Engineering Landmark. Constructed by the CCC in 1935-1936, the Mott Bridge is the only surviving example of three such structures built at that time in the Pacific Northwest. The CCC also built Diamond Lake's Visitor Center and guard station, as well as the ranger house at Colliding Rivers. Both of the historic structures at Diamond Lake and Colliding Rivers serve as visitor centers today.

Natural

Fisheries play an important role in the ecosystem. The spring-fed rivers flow high amounts of freshwater and support nationally significant fisheries of steelhead and salmon. The Upper Rogue and North Umpqua National Wild &

Scenic Rivers sustain critical habitats for a variety of resident and anadromous fish species, including summer and winter steelhead, fall and spring chinook, coho, and sea-run cutthroat. These rivers and others provide large and consistent numbers of native (non-hatchery) fish in the run. In 1997, following the listing of the Umpqua River cutthroat trout as an endangered species, fishing for trout in the mainstream Umpqua and tributaries was prohibited. Additionally, all wild steelhead and coho salmon caught in the North Umpqua River must be released.

Two fish hatcheries are also associated with the Rogue-Umpqua Scenic Byway. Located at the base of Lost Creek Dam on the Rogue River, the Cole M. Rivers Hatchery is the largest hatchery on the West Coast, built in 1973 to mitigate for a lost spawning area when three dams were constructed in the Rogue Valley. The Rock Creek Fish Hatchery, built in lower Rock Creek and 1/2 mile from SH 138, was constructed in the late 1800s. It still operates to supplement the summer steelhead, spring chinook, and coho fisheries of the Umpqua, the North Umpqua, and South Umpqua rivers.

Recreational

Many come to fish, hike, camp, bike, and soak in the sites. However, the recreational opportunity that's most popular here is whitewater boating, an exhilarating experience that brings people back each year because of its world-class fun. The 33.8-mile Wild & Scenic North Umpqua River offers an array of whitewater thrills, including rapids of intermediate to advanced experience levels. Averaging a vertical drop of 26 feet per river mile, deep emerald-green pools tail out into whitewater rapids ranging from Class II through Class V (Narrows and Deadline Falls). The Wild & Scenic section has been divided into five segments, each offering put-in and take-out areas that allow you to choose the length and difficulty of your trip. The most frequently used segments are from Boulder Flat Put-in to Gravel Bin Take-Out and Bogus Launch Site to Susan Creek Take-out; each offers a two- to four-hour float trip, depending on water flow.

For the days not spent braving the rapids, Joseph H. Stewart State Park on Lost Creek Reservoir is a water paradise, providing 151 campsites with electrical hook-ups; 50 tent sites with water; two group tent camping areas with the amenities of flush toilets, showers, volleyball and horseshoe pits; and day-use picnic areas. The boating facilities include a marina with a store and café, moorage facility, boat launch, boat rentals, and fish-cleaning facilities. You also find several other recreation sites on the 30 miles of shoreline created by Lost Creek Reservoir, including McGregor Park, a visitor center called "Spirit of the Rogue Nature Center," Takelma Recreation Area, and the Cole M. Rivers Fish Hatchery.

Scenic

The tremendous diversity of geologic and volcanic formations, coupled with 15 waterfalls, make the Rogue-Umpqua a photographer's paradise. Famous artists and photographers have come from all over the world to capture

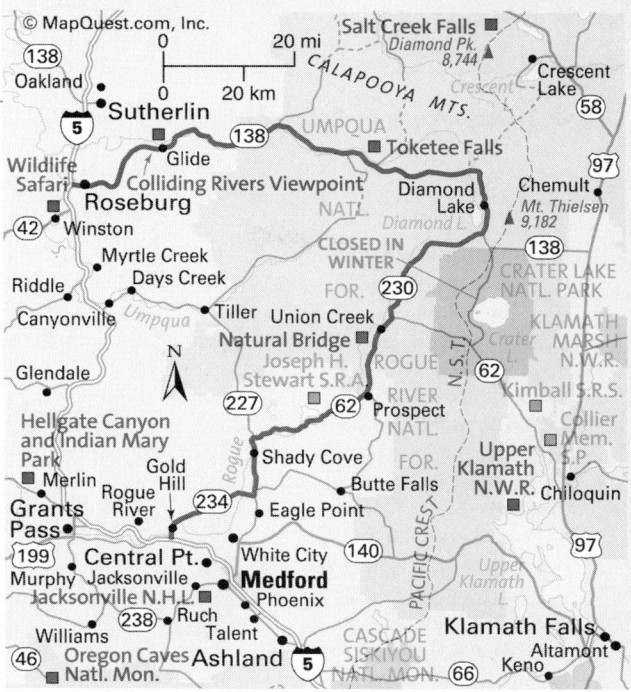

see page A20 for color map

Oregon

❋ Rogue-Umpqua Scenic Byway

awe-inspiring images. Nearly every stretch of the route provides serene places to enjoy the beauty of nature.

Volcanic activity ravaged this area, creating many distinctive and stunning landscapes. In the Diamond Lake area, the route is characterized by unique High Cascades volcanic remnants. Some of these include Crater Lake Rim and impressive peaks, such as Mount Thielsen (elevation 9,182 feet), Mount McLoughlin (elevation 9,495 feet), Mount Bailey (elevation 8,363 feet), and others.

The Umpqua Rocks Geologic Area parallels State Highway 138 from Marsters Bridge to Soda Springs. Along the Upper Rogue River, the highway is built on pumice and ash flows, which were part of the cataclysmic Mount Mazama eruption. The ash flows overlay 1.25 million-year-old lava flows. The river flows through lava tubes above and below the surface at the Rogue Gorge and Natural Bridge interpretive sites. Sedimentary and marine deposits are evident as the highway enters the Rogue Valley, with the exception of the notable Upper and Lower Table Rocks, which are remnants of High Cascades Province lava flows.

You'll find 15 notable waterfalls along this Byway, ranging in size and accessibility. One of the most popular is the Watson Falls, the third highest in Oregon. The water tumbles down 272 feet, which causes a cool mist to refresh you on a searing day.

THINGS TO SEE AND DO

Driving along the Rogue-Umpqua Scenic Byway will certainly keep your senses engaged, but if you yearn to get out of the car and stretch your legs, or if you'd like to make a mini-vacation out of your trip, check out these attractions along the route.

CALLAHAN RIDGE WINERY. *340 Busenbark Ln, Roseburg (97470). Phone 541/673-7901; toll-free 888/946-3487. www.callahanridge.com.* Tasting room. Open Apr-Oct, daily; other times call for appointment. **FREE**

✪ **CRATER LAKE NATIONAL PARK.** *Klamath Falls (97601). Phone 541/594-2211. www.nps.gov/crla/.* One of Crater Lake's former names, Lake Majesty, probably comes closest to describing the feeling visitors get from the deep blue waters in the caldera of dormant Mount Mazama. More than 7,700 years ago, following climactic eruptions, this volcano collapsed and formed a deep basin. Rain and snow accumulated in the empty caldera, forming the deepest lake in the United States (1,932 feet). Surrounded by 25 miles of jagged rim rock, the 21-square-mile lake is broken only by Wizard and Phantom Ship islands. Entering by road from any direction brings you to the 33-mile Rim Drive (July-mid-Oct or the first snow), leading to all observation points, park headquarters, and a visitor center at Rim Village (open June-September, daily). The Sinnott Memorial Overlook with a broad terrace permits a beautiful view of the area. On summer evenings, rangers give campfire talks at Mazama Campground (open late June-Sept). The Steel Center located at Park Headquarters (open daily) has exhibits about the natural history of the park and shows a movie daily.

The 286-square-mile park can be explored on foot or by car following spurs and trails extending from Rim Drive. Going clockwise from Rim Village to the west, The Watchman Peak is reached by a trail almost 1 mile long that takes hikers 1,800 feet above the lake with a full view in all directions; Mount Shasta in California, 105 miles away, is visible on clear days. The road to the north entrance passes through the Pumice Desert, once a flood of frothy debris from the erupting volcano. On the northeast side, Cleetwood Trail descends 1 mile to the shore and a boat landing, where two-hour launch trips depart hourly each day in summer (fee). From the boats, Wizard Island, a small volcano, and Phantom Ship, a craggy mass of lava, can be seen up close. Six miles farther on Rim Drive, going clockwise, is the start of a 2 1/2-mile hiking trail, 1,230 feet to Mount Scott, soaring 8,926 feet, the highest point in the park. Just to the west of the beginning of this trail is a 1-mile drive to the top of Cloudcap, 8,070 feet high and 1,600 feet above the lake. Four miles beyond this point, a road leads 7 miles from Rim Drive to The Pinnacles, pumice spires rising like stone needles from the canyon of Wheeler Creek.

Back at Rim Village, two trails lead in opposite directions. Counterclockwise, a 1 1/2-mile trek mounts the top of Garfield Peak. The other trail goes to Discovery Point, where in 1853, a young prospector, John Hillman, became the first settler to see the lake.

In winter, the south and west entrance roads are kept clear in spite of the annual 45-foot snowfall; the north entrance road and Rim Drive are closed from mid-October-June, depending on snow conditions. A cafeteria is open daily at Rim Village for refreshments and souvenirs. Depending on snow, the campground (fee) is open late June-mid-Oct. Mazama, at the junction of the south and west entrance drives, has a camp store, fireplaces, showers, laundry facilities, toilets, water, and tables; no reservations. You'll find six picnic areas on Rim Drive. Wildlife in the park includes black bears—keep your distance and never feed them. You may also see deer, golden-mantled ground squirrels, marmots, and coyotes. **$$$**

DOUGLAS COUNTY MUSEUM OF HISTORY AND NATURAL HISTORY. *1020 Lighthouse Rd, Roseburg (97467). Phone 541/440-4507. www.co.douglas.or.us/museum/.* Exhibits include early history and natural history displays of the region, a photographic collection, and a research library. Regional tourist information is also available. Open Mon-Fri 9 am-5 pm, Sat 10 am-5 pm, Sun noon-5 pm. **$**

HENRY ESTATE WINERY. *687 Hubbard Creek Rd, Umpqua (97486). Phone 541/459-5120 or -3614; toll-free 800/782-2686. www.henryestate.com.* Tours, tasting room, picnic area. Open daily; closed major holidays. **FREE**

HILLCREST VINEYARD. *240 Vineyard Ln, Roseburg (97470). Phone 541/673-3709; toll-free 800/736-3709.* Wine tastings, tours. Open daily 11 am-5 pm; closed holidays. **FREE**

⭐ ROGUE RIVER NATIONAL FOREST. *333 W 8th St, Medford (97501). Phone 541/776-3600. www.fs.fed.us/r6/rogue/.* This national forest has 632,045 acres, with extensive stands of Douglas fir, ponderosa pine, and sugar pine. The forest is in two sections, located in the Siskiyou Mountains (west of I-5) and Cascade Range (east of I-5). For anglers, the upper reaches of the Rogue River and other streams and lakes yield rainbow, cutthroat, and brook trout. Swimming, hiking, backpacking, downhill and cross-country skiing, picnic areas, and camping. Some fees.

Oregon

❋ *Rogue-Umpqua Scenic Byway*

UMPQUA NATIONAL FOREST. *2900 NW Stewart Pkwy, Roseburg (97470). Phone 541/672-6601. www.fs.fed.us/r6/umpqua/.* The Byway takes visitors through magnificent scenery to Diamond Lake, which offers fishing (rainbow, steelhead trout) and forest camps. The Colliding Rivers Visitor Information Center (open daily) is located along OR 138 in Glide; the Diamond Lake Visitor Center (open summer only) is located opposite the entrance to Diamond Lake Campground. The forest (nearly 1 million acres), named for Native Americans who once fished in the rivers, includes three wilderness areas: Boulder Creek, 19,100 acres; Mount Thielsen, 22,700 acres; and Roque-Umpqua Divide, 29,000 acres. Also in the forest is the Oregon Cascades Recreation Area, at 35,500 acres. Picnicking, lodging, hiking, camping (fee).

WILDLIFE SAFARI. *1790 Safari Rd, Winston (97496). Phone 541/679-6761; toll-free 800/355-4848. www.wildlifesafari.org.* This 600-acre drive-through animal park features 600 exotic specimens of African, Asian, and North American wildlife in natural habitats. Petting zoo, elephant, and train rides (seasonal). Guided and walk-through tours by reservation; restaurant. Open daily. $$$$

PLACES TO STAY

If you choose to include an overnight stay in your trip along this Byway, Mobil Travel Guide recommends the following lodgings.

★★★ **CRATER LAKE LODGE.** *565 Rim Village Dr, Crater Lake (97604). Phone 541/594-2255. www.crater-lake.com.* Situated in Crater Lake National Park, this lodge features spectacular views and beautiful furnishings. Guests can relax on the patio after a full day of adventures and watch the sunset with a nightcap before retiring to a restful night's sleep. 71 rooms, 4 story. No A/C. No room phones. Closed mid-Oct-mid-May. Check-out 11 am. Restaurant. Picnic tables, grills. On lake. Totally nonsmoking. $

★★ **STEELHEAD RUN BED & BREAKFAST.** *23049 N Umpqua Hwy, Glide (97443). Phone 541/496-0563; toll-free 800/348-0563. www.steelheadrun.com.* 6 rooms, 2 story. Located on a bluff overlooking the North Umpqua River with private beach and picnic area, trails, and fishing. $

★★ **DIAMOND STONE GUEST LODGE.** *16693 Sprague Loop, LaPine (97739). Phone 541/536-6263; toll-free 800/600-6263. www.diamondstone.com.* 3 rooms, 2 story. Sits adjacent to Quail Run Golf Course at the gateway to Newberry National Volcanic Monument with the Cascade Mountains as a backdrop. Surrounded by open meadows and pines with plenty of trails for hiking and exploring. $

★ **BEST WESTERN DOUGLAS INN.** *511 SE Stephens St, Roseburg (97470). Phone 541/673-6625; toll-free 877/368-4466. www.bestwestern.com.* 52 rooms, 2 story. Check-out noon. TV; cable (premium). In-room modem link. In-house fitness room, sauna. Whirlpool. ¢

★ **BEST WESTERN GARDEN VILLA INN.** *760 NW Garden Valley Blvd, Roseburg (97470). Phone 541/672-1601; toll-free 800/547-3446. www.bestwestern.com.* 122 rooms, 2 story. Pet accepted, some restrictions. Complimentary continental breakfast. Check-out noon. TV; cable (premium), VCR available. Room service. In-house fitness room. ¢

★ **TRAVELODGE.** *315 W Harvard Ave, Roseburg (97470). Phone 541/672-4836; toll-free 800/578-7878. www.travelodge.com.* 40 rooms, 1-2 story. Check-out 11 am. TV; cable (premium). Balconies. Valet services. Restaurant adjacent. Outdoor pool. Picnic tables. On the river. ¢

★★ **WINDMILL INN.** 🛎 *1450 NW Mulholland Dr, Roseburg (97470). Phone 541/673-0901; toll-free 800/547-4747. www.windmillinns.com.* 128 rooms, 2 story. Pet accepted, some restrictions. Complimentary continental breakfast. Check-out 11 am. TV; cable (premium). Outdoor pool, whirlpool. Restaurants, bar. Guest laundry. Meeting rooms. Business services available. In-room modem link. Valet service. Sundries. In-house fitness room, sauna. Microwaves available. Some balconies. Free airport transportation. ¢
✈ 🕴 ⌘ D 🐾 SC ≈

★★ **STEAMBOAT INN.** 🛎 *42705 N Umpqua Hwy, Steamboat (97447). Phone 541/498-2230; toll-free 800/840-8825. www.thesteamboatinn.com.* 3 rooms, 2 story. Located inside the Umpqua National Forest along the banks of the North Umpqua River. Offers spectacular views. $$

PLACES TO EAT

A long day of driving is sure to make you hungry. At the end of your journey, take a table at one of the following restaurants.

★★ **MON DESIR DINING INN.** *4615 Hanrick Rd, Central Point (97502). Phone 541/664-7558.* Continental menu. Closed Sun, Mon. Lunch, dinner. Bar. Outdoor seating. Converted mansion; fireplace, antiques; garden. Reservations accepted. Totally nonsmoking. $$

★ **SATIN SLIPPER.** *6463 Table Rock Rd, Central Point (97502). Phone 541/826-6000.* American menu. Breakfast, lunch, dinner. Home-style cooking in a fun, family-oriented environment. $

★★ **JIN GAI INTERNATIONAL RESTAURANT.** *805 SE Stephens, Roseburg (97638). Phone 541/673-8373.* Japanese, sushi menu. Lunch, dinner. Modern and traditional Japanese specialties in an unlikely location. $$

★★ **McMENAMINS ROSEBURG STATION.** 🛎 *700 SE Sheridan St, Roseburg (97470). Phone 541/672-1934. www.mcmenamins.com.* American menu. Lunch, dinner. Situated in an 87-year-old railway station in historic Roseburg, with a fine selection of local specialties and microbrews. $

Volcanic Legacy Scenic Byway

❋ OREGON   AN ALL-AMERICAN ROAD
Part of a multistate Byway; see also CA.

Quick Facts

LENGTH: 140 miles.

TIME TO ALLOW: 5 to 7 hours.

BEST TIME TO DRIVE: Spring to fall; summer is the high season.

BYWAY TRAVEL INFORMATION: Klamath County Department of Tourism: 800/445-6728; Byway local Web sites: www.sova.org/volcanic and www.volcaniclegacy.net.

SPECIAL CONSIDERATIONS: The portion of the route from the south rim of Crater Lake to the North Park Entrance, including Rim Drive, is closed from mid-October to mid-June each year due to snow. The opening of Rim Drive each year is a locally celebrated event that signals the beginning of summer. Views of Crater Lake are available year-round at the south rim near the visitor facilities. The route generally provides safe winter access.

RESTRICTIONS: The Byway from the Oregon/California border to Crater Lake National Park is open year-round. In Crater Lake National Park, the Byway from the south rim of Crater Lake to the North Park Entrance (including Rim Drive) is closed from mid-October to mid-June.

BICYCLE/PEDESTRIAN FACILITIES: Portions of this Byway are well suited for bicycle travel and pedestrian use (to some extent). The Highway 97 segment has paved shoulders, but it is less desirable for biking due to heavy truck traffic. The northern portion of Oregon Highway 140 over Doak Mountain to the Westside Road needs reconstruction to add bikeway shoulders to safely accommodate bike travel.

This diverse Byway follows the brims of lakes, diverse wetlands, scenic ranches, thriving croplands, and forests full of bald eagles. It passes brilliant Crater Lake National Park and historic Crater Lake Lodge. It also threads its way through volcanic landscapes, craggy mountain reaches, and high-desert wetlands.

As the Byway passes the 90,000 surface-acre Upper Klamath Lake, you can see over 1 million birds during peak migrations in the fall. The Klamath Basin is the largest freshwater ecosystem west of the Great Lakes. Six national wildlife refuges in these wetlands were favorite fishing spots of President Roosevelt.

You can also visit the same Pelican Bay where John Muir (naturalist, writer, conservationist, and founder of the Sierra Club) wrote *The Story of My Boyhood and Youth* in 1908.

THE BYWAY STORY

The Volcanic Legacy Scenic Byway tells archaeological, cultural, historical, natural, recreational, and scenic stories that make it a unique and treasured Byway.

Archaeological

This Byway was (and still is) littered with ancient Native American artifacts. Most of the artifacts that have been discovered along this route and are displayed among the 100,000 artifacts in the Byway's own Favell Museum of Western Art and Indian Artifacts. This museum focuses on the area's Native American tribes but also spotlights tribes across the country. It covers 12,000 years of history in its collections of basketry, beadwork, stone tools, and pottery.

Oregon

✻ *Volcanic Legacy Scenic Byway*

Cultural

The Klamath tribes (more specifically, the Klamaths, Modocs, and Yahooskin) are an integral part of the communities along the Byway because they lived here before anyone can remember. Also, the determination and grit they have demonstrated to survive the changes of years, famine, and new settlers have affected positively the attitudes of other groups who have lived in the area, including the groups who caused their setbacks.

The Klamath tribes have worked hard to maintain their own culture in spite of circumstances. When the Klamath tribes were forced to reservations in the 1860s, they turned to cattle ranching and made a profitable living. And even though the tribes were not federally recognized for about 30 years and had to work without supplemental human services or their reservation land, they have sustained the economy of Klamath County for decades; they contribute $12 million per year to the Klamath County economy. They have also instituted training schools to make their enterprises more competitive.

Historical

This Byway's past dwells in some of its historic buildings. By visiting these buildings, you can learn about the significant historical forces and events that shaped the area. For instance, logging was a major part of the early 20th century, and you can get a feel for the area's logging history at Collier State Park and Logging Museum. Through displays featuring actual equipment and other related items, the incredibly difficult life of a lumberjack is told.

Fort Klamath also tells an important story of early settlement. The fort was built in 1863 to protect Oregon Trail pioneers and southern emigrant trains from the nearby Modoc and Klamath tribes who were inclined to attack on occasion. Two notable events happened at this fort: one was when Captain Jack, a Modoc leader who figured centrally in the war of 1872-1873, was executed at the fort along with three other Modoc warriors in late 1873 (their graves are at the fort); the second was when the fort played an important part in the working out of the 1864 Council Grove peace treaty.

Crater Lake Lodge's historical guest register shows what a popular vacation spot Crater Lake has always been: it has hosted important visitors, such as First Lady Eleanor Roosevelt and author Jack London. It is listed on the National Register of Historic Places.

Natural

This Byway sustains masses of wildlife in its several wildlife refuge areas, bulky mountains, and unique geological formations. Six national wildlife refuges have been established in the area: Lower Klamath, Tule Lake, Clear Lake, Bear Valley, Upper Klamath, and Klamath Marsh. These refuges are diverse; they include freshwater marshes, open waters, grassy meadows, coniferous forests, sagebrush, juniper grasslands, agricultural lands, rock cliffs, and slopes. Over 400 different species have been identified in the refuges. In the spring, more than 1 million birds retreat here. This number is added to in the summer, as ducks and Canadian geese join the throng. In the fall, the birds (ducks, geese, swans, and green-winged teal) number in the millions. In addition, the Klamath Basin is home to the largest concentration of wintering bald eagles in the lower 48 states.

Crater Lake, Oregon's only national park, is not only a place for wildlife to refuge, but also is one of the nation's favorite places to retreat. The deepest lake in the United States, it was formed inside the collapsed peak of an ancient volcano, Mount Mazama, that erupted 8,000 years ago. The eruptions were 42 times greater than those of Mount St. Helens in 1980, and the ash spewed over eight states and three Canadian provinces. One of the finest and most accessible examples of a young caldera (a certain kind of volcanic crater) in the world, Crater Lake is recognized worldwide as a scenic wonder.

Recreational

You can do just about anything outdoorsy on the Volcanic Legacy Scenic Byway. In the summer, you can fish, camp, visit a horse and cattle ranch, whitewater raft, or hike. You can also tour the scenic shores of the Upper Klamath Canoe Trail by canoe. Crater Lake National Park is especially good for camping, hiking, and RV camping. Lake of the Woods is popular for any kind of summer activity and is also great for winter activities, such as cross-country skiing (although cross-country skiing is exceptional in many other areas along the Byway as well). Willamette Ski Lodge and Diamond Lake Resort are particularly good for downhill skiing.

Scenic

The Volcanic Legacy Scenic Byway is visually diverse: it starts out as 140 miles of craggy volcanic landscape, switches to the high desert, and then transforms to the wetland habitats of the Klamath Basin. Even though these scenes are varied, you'll feel the same surge of grandeur and affection as you experience the croplands' expanse, birds in flight at Upper Klamath Lake, the Wild & Scenic Klamath River, views of the majestic Mount Shasta, and wetlands and rising forests.

HIGHLIGHTS

When traveling the Byway from north to south, consider following this scenic-viewpoints tour. If you're starting from the south, simply read this list from the bottom up:

- **Crater Lake National Park:** Located 65 miles north of Klamath Falls on Highways 97 and 62. Here are the world-renowned views you've seen on postcards and in magazines. Many viewpoints are accessible by wheelchair; some are found at the ends of hiking trails.
- **Ouxkanee overlook:** A short drive off Highway 97 leads to a picnic area with a stunning overlook of the Williamson River valley and the surrounding landscape. Scan the horizon as far as Mount Shasta in northern California.

see page A13 for color map

- **Pelican Butte:** The summit offers breathtaking views of Upper Klamath Lake and Sky Lakes Wilderness. Old-growth timber lines the narrow, rough road to the top, which takes about an hour and is accessible only by high-clearance vehicle and by foot.
- **Calimus Butte:** This historic, cupola-style lookout was built by the Bureau of Indian Affairs in 1920 and overlooks the scene of the 48-square-mile Lone Pine fire in 1992, as well as Klamath Marsh and Sprague River Valley. Accessible by high-clearance vehicle only.
- **Herd Peak:** A gravel road off Highway 97 leads to Herd Peak, where a fire lookout is staffed during the summer months and is open to the public. The summit offers breathtaking views of Mount Shasta and the surrounding area.
- **Walker Mountain:** On a clear day, the view from the fire lookout extends from Mount Jefferson in central Oregon to Mount Shasta in northern California. There, you're surrounded by a sea of forest land. The mountain is accessible by high-clearance vehicle only.

THINGS TO SEE AND DO

Driving along the Volcanic Legacy Scenic Byway will certainly keep your senses engaged, but if you yearn to get out of the car and stretch your legs, or if you'd like to make a mini-vacation out of your trip, check out these attractions along the route.

Oregon

❈ *Volcanic Legacy Scenic Byway*

COLLIER MEMORIAL STATE PARK AND LOGGING MUSEUM. *46000 Hwy 97, Klamath Falls (97601). Phone 541/783-2471. www.collierloggingmuseum.org.* A 655-acre park located at the confluence of Spring Creek and Williamson River, Collier offers an open-air historic logging museum with displays of tools, machines, and engines; various types of furnished 1800s-era pioneer cabins; and a gift shop. Fishing; hiking, picnicking. Tent and trailer campsites (hookups, dump station). Open daily.

✪ CRATER LAKE NATIONAL PARK. *Klamath Falls (97601). Phone 541/594-2211. www.nps.gov/crla/.* One of Crater Lake's former names, Lake Majesty, probably comes closest to describing the feeling visitors get from the deep blue waters in the caldera of dormant Mount Mazama. More than 7,700 years ago, following climactic eruptions, this volcano collapsed and formed a deep basin. Rain and snow accumulated in the empty caldera, forming the deepest lake in the United States (1,932 feet). Surrounded by 25 miles of jagged rim rock, the 21-square-mile lake is broken only by Wizard and Phantom Ship islands. Entering by road from any direction brings you to 33-mile Rim Drive (open July to mid-October or until the first snow), leading to all observation points, park headquarters, and a visitor center at Rim Village (open June-September, daily). The park can be explored on foot or by car following spurs and trails extending from Rim Drive; the Watchman Peak is reached by a trail almost 1 mile long that takes hikers 1,800 feet above the lake with a full view in all directions; Mount Shasta in California, 105 miles away, is visible on clear days. Six miles farther on Rim Drive, going clockwise, is the start of a 2 1/2-mile hiking trail, 1,230 feet to Mount Scott, soaring 8,926 feet, the highest point in the park. In winter, the south and west entrance roads are kept clear in spite of the annual 45-foot snowfall; the north entrance road and Rim Drive are closed from mid-October to June, depending on snow conditions. Depending on snow, the campground (fee) is open from late June-mid-October. Mazama, at the junction of the south and west entrance drives, has a camp store, fireplaces, showers, laundry facilities, toilets, water, and tables; no reservations. The wildlife includes black bears—keep your distance. You may also see deer, golden-mantled ground squirrels, marmots, and coyotes. Do not feed any wildlife in park. **$$$**

FAVELL MUSEUM OF WESTERN ART AND NATIVE AMERICAN ARTIFACTS. *125 W Main, Klamath Falls (97601). Phone 541/882-9996; toll-free 800/762-9096. www.favellmuseum.com.* Contemporary Western art; working miniature gun collection; extensive display of Native American artifacts. Also art and print sales galleries. Gift shop. Open Tues-Sat. **$$**

KLAMATH COUNTY MUSEUM. *1451 Main St, Klamath Falls (97601). Phone 541/883-4208.* Local geology, history, wildlife, and Native American displays; research library has books on history, natural history, and anthropology of the Pacific Northwest. Open Tues-Sat; closed holidays. **$**

MIGRATORY BIRD REFUGE. *4009 Hill Rd, Tule Lake, CA (96134). Phone 530/667-2231.* Located in both California and Oregon, the six national wildlife refuges in the Kalmath Basin are a major stopover on the Pacific Flyway. Upper Klamath and Klamath Marsh refuges lie to the north, and Lower Klamath, Bear Valley, Tule Lake, and Clear Lake lie to the south of the city. A visitor center with exhibits stands at refuge headquarters in Tule Lake, California. Open daily. Waterfowl (Mar-Apr, Oct-Nov); bald eagles (Dec-Mar); migratory birds (Mar-Apr); waterfowl and colonial bird nesting (summer). **FREE**

WINEMA NATIONAL FOREST. *2819 Dahlia, Klamath Falls (97601). Phone 541/883-6714. www.fs.fed.us/r6/winema/.* This forest (more than 1 million acres) includes former reservation lands of the Klamath Tribe, high country of Sky Lakes, portions of Pacific Crest National Scenic Trail, and several recreation areas (Lake of the Woods, Recreation Creek, Mountain Lakes Wilderness, and Mount Theilson Wilderness). Swimming, boating; picnicking, camping (some areas free). $$

PLACES TO STAY

If you choose to include an overnight stay in your trip along this All-American Road, Mobil Travel Guide recommends the following lodgings.

★ **BEST WESTERN OLYMPIC INN.** *2627 S 6th St, Klamath Falls (97603). 541/882-9665; toll-free 800/600-9665. www.bestwestern.com.* 71 rooms, 3 story. Complimentary continental breakfast. Check-out 11 am. TV; cable (premium). In-room modem link. In-house fitness room. Outdoor pool, whirlpool. ¢

★ **CIMARRON MOTOR INN.** *3060 S 6th St, Klamath Falls (97603). Phone 541/882-4601; toll-free 800/742-2648.* 163 rooms, 2 story. Pet accepted; fee. Complimentary continental breakfast. Check-out noon. TV; cable (premium). Outdoor pool. Restaurant adjacent open 24 hours. Meeting room. Business services available. ¢

★★ **QUALITY INN.** *100 Main St, Klamath Falls (97601). Phone 541/882-4666; toll-free 800/732-2025. www.qualityinn.com.* 80 rooms, 4 suites, 2 story. Pet accepted, some restrictions. Complimentary continental breakfast. Check-out noon. TV; cable (premium). Outdoor pool. Restaurant adjacent. Coin laundry. Meeting rooms. Business services available. In-room modem link. Some in-room whirlpools, microwaves. ¢

★★ **SHILO INN SUITES HOTEL.** *2500 Almond St, Klamath Falls (97601). Phone 541/885-7980; toll-free 800/222-2244. www.shiloinns.com.* 143 suites, 4 story. Golf plans. Pet accepted, some restrictions; fee. Complimentary continental breakfast. Check-out noon. TV; cable (premium), VCR (movies). Restaurant, bar. Room service. Meeting rooms. Business center. In-room modem link. Valet service. Sundries. Coin laundry. In-house fitness room, sauna. Health club privileges. Indoor pool; whirlpool. Refrigerators, microwaves, wet bars. Free airport transportation. $

PLACES TO EAT

A long day of driving is sure to make you hungry. At the end of your journey, try the following restaurant.

★★ **FIORELLA'S.** *6139 Simmer Ave, Klamath Falls (97603). Phone 541/882-1878.* Northern Italian menu. Closed Sun, Mon; Dec 25. Dinner. Bar. Children's menu. Reservations accepted. $$

West Cascades Scenic Byway
✹ OREGON

Quick Facts

LENGTH: 220 miles.

TIME TO ALLOW: 7 to 8 hours.

BEST TIME TO DRIVE: Late spring through early fall. Late spring offers lush green forests and wildflowers. Summer is the busiest season, but also the best season to visit both high alpine areas adjacent to the Byway and recreation lakes. After Labor Day, the Byway is quieter and less crowded.

BYWAY TRAVEL INFORMATION: Willamette National Forest: 541/225-6300; Mount Hood National Forest: 503/630-6861.

SPECIAL CONSIDERATIONS: Even though Forest Roads 19 and 46 are closed in the winter due to snow, the rest of the route is open during winter months and provides access to cross-country skiing, snowmobiling, snowshoeing, and winter-only cabin rentals at Fish Lake Remount Depot.

RESTRICTIONS: Forest Road 46 and Forest Road 19 are generally closed from approximately November 15 to April 30 due to snowfall. You need to buy a $5 day pass to access some of the park.

BICYCLE/PEDESTRIAN FACILITIES: Hundreds of miles of hiking trails are accessible from this Byway, most of which are located on National Forest Service lands. Several trails are also accessible to bicyclists, including the McKenzie River National Recreation Trail and the Breitenbush National Recreation Trail.

The West Cascades Scenic Byway isn't the shortest route between Portland and Eugene, but this 220-mile scenic alternative offers some of the best views of thundering waterfalls, lush ancient forests, rushing whitewater, and placid lakes. The Byway frequently intersects major routes that can reconnect you to I-5 or Highway 97, giving you the option of taking shorter loops. The Byway ends near the timber towns of Westfir and Oakridge.

The northernmost access to the Byway begins in the historic logging and hydropower city of Estacada, located only 40 minutes from Portland. From the very start, you're immersed in old-growth forest, skimming the edge of the breathtaking Clackamas River. From here, the Byway winds through the Western Cascades and its breathtaking, snowcapped volcanic peaks.

Although two segments of the Byway—Forest Roads 46 and 19—are closed in the winter due to snow, the rest of the Byway offers access to a range of winter sports. These winter sport facilities range from the most rustic, primitive facilities to highly developed, full-service facilities.

THE BYWAY STORY

The West Cascades Scenic Byway tells archaeological, historical, natural, recreational, and scenic stories that make it a unique and treasured Byway.

Archaeological

Archaeological remains confirm human use of these lands as early as 10,000 years ago. Previous native inhabitants include the Molalla, Kalapuya, Tenino, and Northern Paiute peoples. Even though the Byway has only a relative few archaeological remains, the story of early

Oregon
West Cascades Scenic Byway

inhabitants is told well through the Byway's more soft archaeology: rich written and oral histories intertwined with scattered discoveries of tool caches.

For example, a famous oral history is tied with an old trail that formed a natural pass up the Santiam River. The legend says that a fierce battle between the Molalla (of the west hills) and the Paiutes (from the east side) took place on this trail. After the battle was over, the souls of the dead warriors waited to make war on old enemies along both sides of the trail. When white men began to use the pass, they noticed that the Native Americans bypassed gorges along this trail where these souls were believed to be waiting.

Harder archaeological evidence shows that Native Americans hunted, fished, and gathered huckleberries and wild plants in the Santiam Basin at least 10,000 years ago. Gathering obsidian for their tools from the local Obsidian Cliffs, the tools they made (spear points and scraping tools) have been discovered in caches throughout the three major river basins.

Historical

Early industrial companies and the Civilian Conservation Corps (CCC) both helped shape the Byway as it is today. One such early industrial company that built structures along the route was the Portland General Electric Company (PGEC); the PGEC built a train bed in the 1920s that now serves as a portion of Highway 224. Also, the logging and power companies practically built the city of Estacada, and they specifically left what is now Estacada's Timber Park, featuring a dam that boasts the longest fish tunnel in the Pacific Northwest. Another company built the Hogg Railroad (now listed in the National Register of Historic Places) in the early 1900s, in an effort to connect the Willamette Valley with Eastern Oregon over the Santiam Pass.

In the 1930s, the CCC built many of the structures that are still used for recreation, education, and administration. Some specific places they developed are Camp Belknap (where the CCC workers actually stayed), Clear Lake Cutoff, Clear Lake Shelter, Paradise Campground, and the McKenzie Campgrounds. They also worked to develop the Willamette Valley Cascade Mountain Wagon Road (known today as the Santiam Wagon Road), which now serves as part of Highway 126.

Natural

This Byway's interdependent systems of mountains, vegetation, rivers, and wildlife support one another vitally. Wildlife thrives in the volcanic peaks and unique geologic formations of the High Cascades; they also flourish in the Western Cascades' jagged lava flows and smooth glacial valleys. These ranges' old-growth forests of Douglas fir and western red cedar are excellent habitat for the northern spotted owl and the bald eagle (both endangered) and also for the pine marten, pileated woodpecker, Roosevelt elk, black-tailed deer, and mule deer.

The mountains' heavy snow and rain percolates through porous volcanic rocks and reappears as hundreds of springs that feed the Byway's many rivers and lakes, many of which are designated as Wild & Scenic rivers. These rivers support a number of rare and threatened species of fish, including spring chinook, winter and summer steelhead, bull trout, and a rare species of cutthroat trout. This abundant moisture has allowed the development of dense, lush, old-growth forests: some trees measure over 6 feet in diameter and are more than 180 feet tall.

Recreational

A broad range of recreational activities are available along this Byway. Summer brings horseback riding, picnicking, primitive and rustic camping, and fishing. You can also enjoy any water and watercraft activity: drift and motor boating, canoeing, jet skiing, sailing, water-skiing, kayaking, rafting, and swimming. The hiking here is especially good because the US Forest Service maintains the Byway's three national recreation trails to the highest standard. Hundreds of miles of other trails are also accessed from the Byway. In the winter, you can snowmobile, sled, snowshoe, and downhill and cross-country ski.

Scenic

As you travel this "scenic alternative to I-5," you absorb immaculate mountainscapes, peer into plush forests, watch the mesmerizing flow of pure waters, and scrutinize each shade of autumn's slow-motion explosion. Spectacular views of snowcapped mountains (Jefferson, Washington, Three Fingered Jack, and the Three Sisters) are omnipresent as you skirt the Cascade Mountain Range and travel through the Mount Hood and Willamette National Forests.

Three Wild & Scenic rivers thread along sections of the Byway. These rivers are associated with other enchanting accumulations of water: glossy lakes, silken pools, rushing whitewater, coarse waterfalls, one-of-a-kind geologic formations, and glacier-carved canyons. One of the most striking and popular of these waters is 120-foot-deep Clear Lake, which is nationally known for its startling clarity.

HIGHLIGHTS

This tour shares the highlights of the West Cascades Scenic Byway. If you're starting at the other end, read this section from the bottom up.

- Start your tour at Westfir, which is the southern end of the Byway. In Westfir, take in the **Westfir Covered Bridge.** At 180 feet long, this unique bridge is the longest covered bridge in the state.

- Just a few miles north of the Bridge is the **Cougar Reservoir,** a good place to get out and stretch your legs. The dam at the north end of the reservoir is the tallest rock-filled dam in Oregon.

- Right near the Reservoir is the **Delta Campground and Nature Trail.** Ancient western red cedar and Douglas fir stretch up to 180 feet here. Walk under them along the nature trail.

- End your tour with a picnic lunch at **Box Canyon,** which is adjacent (to the North) of the **Delta Camp and Trail,** right along the McKenzie River.

THINGS TO SEE AND DO

Driving along the West Cascades Scenic Byway will certainly keep your senses engaged, but if you yearn to get out of the car and stretch your legs, or if you'd like to make a mini-vacation out of your trip, check out these attractions along the route.

BREITENBUSH HOT SPRINGS RETREAT AND CONFERENCE CENTER. *PO Box 578, Detroit (97342). Phone 503/854-3314. www.breitenbush.com.* Breitenbush Center is a privately owned resort in a sylvan old-growth forest setting. Open year-round, this unique resort offers hot springs, a sweat lodge, and a variety of workshops. $

see page A21 for color map

131

Oregon

❋ *West Cascades Scenic Byway*

SOUTH BREITENBUSH GORGE NATIONAL RECREATION TRAIL. *From Detroit Ranger Station, travel E on Hwy 22 for approximately 1 mile, turn left onto Breitenbush Rd 46, travel about 14 miles, turn right on Forest Rd 4685. Access #1 is 1/2 mile up Rd 4685. Access #2 is 2 miles on Rd 4685 at Roaring Creek, and access #3 is 1/4 mile past access #2. Phone 541/225-6301.* Meandering through giant trees in an old-growth grove, this popular trail follows the Wild & Scenic-eligible South Breitenbush River. A small Forest Service-operated campground is near the trailhead.

WILLAMETTE NATIONAL FOREST. *211 E 7th Ave, Eugene (97401). Phone 541/225-6300. www.fs.fed.us/r6/willamette/.* At more than 1.5 million acres, the Willamette National Forest is home to more than 300 species of wildlife. The forest includes the Cascade Mountain Range summit; the Pacific Crest National Scenic Trail with views of snowcapped Mount Jefferson, Mount Washington, Three Fingered Jack, Three Sisters, and Diamond Peak; Koosah and Sahalie Falls on the Upper McKenzie River; Clear Lake; the lava beds at summit of McKenzie Pass; and Waldo Lake near summit of Willamette Pass. Fishing; hunting, hiking, skiing, snowmobiling, camping (fee at some sites).

PLACES TO STAY

If you choose to include an overnight stay in your trip along this Byway, Mobil Travel Guide recommends the following lodgings.

★★ **HOLIDAY FARM RESORT.** *54455 McKenzie River Dr, Blue River (97413). Phone 541/822-3715; toll-free 800/823-3715. www.holidayfarmresort.com.* 15 cabins, 2 story. Located on 90 acres of woods and streams with guides for fishing and rafting available. $$

★ **ALL SEASONS MOTEL.** *130 Breitenbush Rd, Detroit (97342). Phone 503/854-3421.* 10 rooms, 1 story. Situated on 2.5 acres of wooded land in the foothills of central Oregon. An ideal location for hiking, boating, and recreation. ¢

★★ **BREITENBUSH HOT SPRINGS RETREAT.** *Mile 10 N, Rte 46, Detroit (97342). Phone 503/854-3320. www.breitenbush.com.* 3 cabins, 1 story. Unique hot springs resort with natural pools, steam sauna, and conference center in a 70-year-old lodge. $

★★ **CADDISFLY RESORT.** *56404 McKenzie Hwy, McKenzie Bridge (97413). Phone 541/822-3556. www.caddisflyresort.com.* 3 cabins, 2 story. Located at the entrance to the Willamette National Forest with fishing, hiking, rafting, hunting, and more available almost year-round. ¢

★★ **McKENZIE RIVER TROUT HOUSE BED & BREAKFAST.** *41496 McKenzie Hwy, Springfield (97478). Phone 541/896-9819. www.mckenzierivertrouthouse.com.* 5 rooms, 2 story. Located on the McKenzie River, this gated 3.5-acre estate offers beautifully landscaped grounds and in-room fireplaces. $$

★★★ **McKENZIE RIVER INN.** *49164 McKenzie River Hwy, Vida (97488). Phone 541/822-6260. www.mckenzieriverinn.com.* 3 rooms, 3 cabins, 2 story. Built in 1929, this is one of the oldest bed-and-breakfasts on the river. $

★★ **WAYFARER RESORT.** 46725 Goodpasture Rd, Vida (97488). Phone 541/896-3613; toll-free 800/627-3613. www.wayfarerresort.com. 13 cabins, 2 story. Located on the banks of the McKenzie River, with fully appointed cabins, open-beamed ceilings, spacious decks, and fireplaces. $$

★★★ **THE RESORT AT THE MOUNTAIN.** 68010 E Fairway Ave, Welches (97067). Phone 503/622-3101; toll-free 800/669-7666. www.theresort.com. 160 rooms, 60 kitchen units, 2 story. Ski, golf plans. Check-out noon, check-in 4 pm. TV; VCR (movies). Heated pool; whirlpool. Restaurant. Room service. Box lunches. Picnics. Bar; entertainment Sat, Sun. Business services available. In-room modem link. Grocery 1 mile. Coin laundry. Concierge. Valet service. Sports director. Social director. Lighted tennis. 27-hole golf, greens fee $40, pro, putting green. Downhill, cross-country ski 18 miles. Hiking trails. Bicycle rentals. In-house fitness room. Massage. Lawn games. Recreation room. Balconies. Picnic tables. 300 acres of forest at the Salmon River. Scottish amenities are reminiscent of the Highlands. $

PLACES TO EAT

A long day of driving is sure to make you hungry. At the end of your journey, take a table at one of the following restaurants.

★ **THE CEDARS RESTAURANT & LOUNGE.** 200 Detroit Ave, Detroit (97432). Phone 503/854-3636. American menu. Breakfast, lunch, dinner. Serving authentic local cuisine for more than 50 years. $

★ **KORNER POST RESTAURANT.** 100 S Detroit Ave, Detroit (97342). Phone 503/854-3735. www.kornerpost.com. American menu. Located in a former post office, this restaurant and gift shop serves classic American cuisine in a kitschy atmosphere. $

★ **MARION FORKS RESTAURANT.** Mile 66, Hwy 22, Marion Forks (97350). Phone 503/854-3669. American menu. Lunch, dinner. Offering classic American road food in a family-oriented environment. $

★★ **LOG CABIN INN RESTAURANT.** 56483 McKenzie Hwy, McKenzie Bridge (97413). Phone 541/822-3432. www.logcabininn.com. American menu. Lunch, dinner. Situated in the deep woods in an 1886 river house; features an extensive menu of Northwestern specialties. $$

★★★ **HIGHLANDS DINING ROOM.** 68010 E Fairway Ave, Welches (97067). Phone 503/622-2214. Breakfast, lunch, dinner, Sun brunch. Bar. Children's menu. Reservations accepted. Outdoor seating. Totally nonsmoking. $$

Chinook Scenic Byway

✳ WASHINGTON   AN ALL-AMERICAN ROAD

Quick Facts

LENGTH: 85 miles.

TIME TO ALLOW: 1.5 to 2 hours.

BEST TIME TO DRIVE: Late May to late October, when the entire route is open.

BYWAY TRAVEL INFORMATION: Enumclaw Chamber of Commerce: 360/825-7666; Yakima Valley Visitor and Convention Center: 800/221-0751; Mount Rainier Visitor Information: 360/569-2211; Washington State Tourism Division: 800/544-1800, extension 036; Byway local Web site: www.chinookscenicbyway.org.

SPECIAL CONSIDERATIONS: The park segment of the road is typically closed during the winter. However, the road is open on the northwest side of Mount Rainier National Park (milepost 57.6) and on the east side of Morse Creek (milepost 74.97). Mount Rainier National Park is open year-round, but only the Nisqually to Paradise road stays open. The east and west road segments outside of the park are open in the winter for recreational use. Also, tour buses are accommodated along the parkway under a permit system.

RESTRICTIONS: Autumn and spring access along the Byway is weather dependent. The typical opening dates for Cayuse and Chinook passes are May 2 and May 26, respectively. Closing dates for these same areas are normally December 6 and December 14.

BICYCLE/PEDESTRIAN FACILITIES: This Byway is popular for bicycling. In addition, the number of mountain bike routes off the Byway has increased yearly. Each year brings the annual Ride Around Mount Rainier in One Day (RAMROD) bicycle event, which is limited to 750 people.

The Chinook Scenic Byway (also known as the Mather Memorial Parkway) is possibly the most scenic route crossing the Cascade Mountain Range, and it is the most accessible road for viewing Mount Rainier. Mount Rainier National Park (which the Byway travels through) was established in 1890, and the Mather Parkway was established in 1931. Because of its national park status, all features of the park are protected.

The route has a uniquely varied landscape. Traveling east, the route climbs through a closed canopy of Douglas fir. At Chinook Pass, the roadway descends dramatically through the Wenatchee National Forest and along the American River. The road also passes the unique basalt flows of the Columbia Plateau. The Byway ends near the fertile agricultural valleys of Yakima County.

THE BYWAY STORY

The Chinook Scenic Byway tells archaeological, historical, natural, recreational, and scenic stories that make it a unique and treasured Byway.

Archaeological

Even though only about 2 percent of the park has been systematically surveyed for archaeological remains, it has 79 known sites in the park, of which 62 have been fully documented and recorded.

One prehistoric site dates to between 2,300 and 4,500 years ago. Sites just outside of the park hint at much earlier occupation, perhaps as much as 8,000 years, but most prehistoric archaeological sites are about 1,000 years old.

Later, the area was used on a seasonal basis by lowland tribes for hunting and gathering and for

Washington

❋ *Chinook Scenic Byway*

spiritual and ceremonial events. A few sites were hunting camps (killing and butchering sites), where cedar bark was stripped from trees, rock shelters created, and stone for tools procured.

In more modern centuries, five principal Native American tribes (specifically the Nisqually, Puyallup, Muckleshoot, Yakama, and Taidnapam) came to the park in the summer and early fall to hunt and to collect resources. These tribes continued to come even after the park was officially designated in 1899. Sites that were used by these tribes are littered with broken weapon points.

Sites from European settlements in the late 19th and early 20th centuries confirm mining, recreation, and early park development. Specifically, sites reveal old campsites, trash dumps, collapsed structures, mineshafts, and other debris.

Historical
Part of this Byway has a unique historic designation: that of a National Historic Landmark District. This district, called the Mount Rainier National Historic Landmark District, was designated so because it is one of the nation's finest collections of "national park rustic" architecture, both in the park's road system and in its historically developed areas.

In the 1920s, the park developed a plan—the Mount Rainier National Park's Master Plan—that was unusual at the time and is historically significant because it was the first and most complete national park plan developed by the National Park Service Landscape Division.

Natural
This Byway's wide range of plants and animals live relatively undisturbed and can, therefore, exist in greater abundance (some 50 species of mammals and 130 species of birds live here) and can attain greater longevity. For example, some high-elevation coniferous stands are more than 500 years old. Some of the highest alpine stands are up to 1,000 years old.

In addition, extraordinary geological processes have created this magnificent and unique landscape: Rainier's 25 glaciers form the largest single-peak glacier system in the United States outside of Alaska; the glacier-carved canyon of the Rainier fork of the American River is geologically rare; and mountain parks (lush subalpine meadows encircling the mountain between 5,000 and 7,000 feet) are without parallel in the Cascades or Pacific volcano system.

Mount Rainier has four main glaciers: Nisqually Glacier, Cowlitz-Ingraham Glacier, Emmons Glacier, and Carbon Glacier. Nisqually Glacier is one of the most accessible glaciers on Mount Rainier. It can easily be seen from Nisqually and Glacier Vistas, located less than 1 mile from the Paradise Visitor Center. Emmons Glacier has a surface area of 4.3 square miles, the largest area of any glacier in the contiguous United States. Carbon Glacier is best viewed from a 4-mile trail from Ipsut Creek Campground on the north side of Mount Rainier. This glacier has the greatest measured thickness (700 feet) and volume (0.2 cubic miles) of any glacier in the contiguous United States. Because of the weather patterns in recent years, all of these glaciers are slowly retreating.

Along the Byway and in your forays into Mount Rainier National Park, you can see four distinct life, or vegetation, zones. They are the lowland forest, montane zone, subalpine zone, and alpine zone. Each zone is filled with varied and splendid wildlife and flora.

In the lowland forest zone, a canopy of stately giants allow little sunlight to filter down to the forest floor. Deer browse in the shadows of western hemlock and western red cedar, among others. Hawks and owls perch in the trees waiting for prey to scurry across the shady floor. Bald eagles also thrive in these forests, diving down to grab fish from the water with their talons.

The montane zone is a bit farther up the mountainside and a little wetter and colder. The delicate and elusive calypso orchid blooms here in the spring, and patches of huckleberry

see page A22 for color map

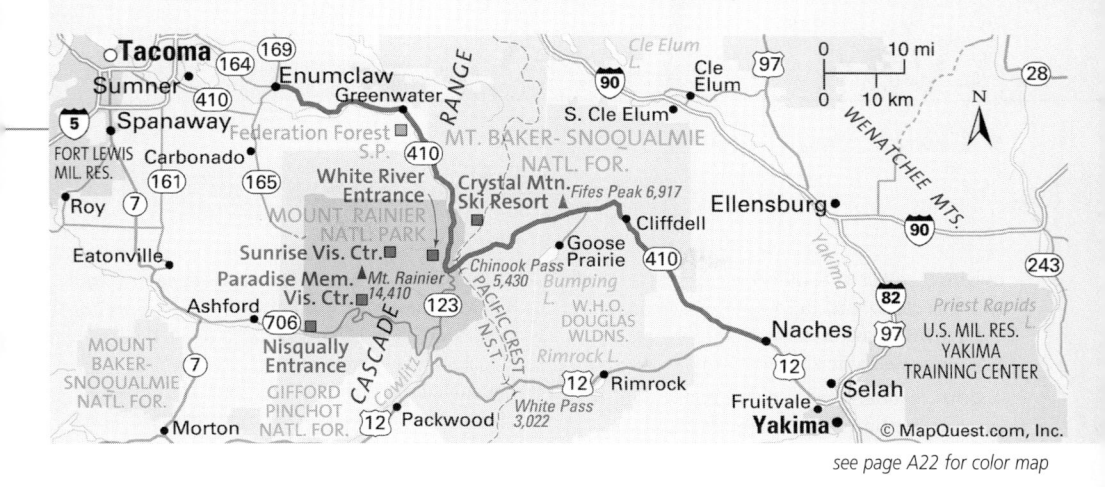

bushes abound. Black bears, which really like huckleberries, are one of this area's large predators, although you'll probably never encounter a black bear.

The subalpine zone is typified by tree "islands" mixed with open meadows. The snow lasts longer among the sheltering trees of this zone. By late July, a rainbow of wildflowers carpets the meadow. These flowers include white avalanche lilies, yellow marsh marigolds, purple lupine, magenta paintbrush, and plumed bear grass. Glacier lilies and snowbed buttercups bloom at the treeline. A special feature in the subalpine zone are the krummholzes, trees that are strikingly twisted and stunted due to the severe winds and snow. Trees only 3 feet in height may be centuries old.

The last and highest zone is the alpine zone. It is found above the timberline and is a world of extremes. On a summer day, the sun can shine warm and bright, but in just moments clouds can bring a sudden snow or lightning storm. During storms, the wind knifes across the tundra because there are no trees to break up the wind. Consequently, most alpine plants grow to be only a few inches tall.

Recreational

The area surrounding the Chinook Scenic Byway is rife with recreational activities. Any time of year affords a combination of beautiful scenery and fun things to do. A visit in summer offers great opportunities for fishing, hunting, hiking, biking, and rafting. Summer is not the only time to experience the beauty, however. Mount Rainier and its surrounding area is one of the snowiest places on Earth. In 1972, Paradise received 94 feet of snow, a world record. Naturally, snow sports also abound. Skiing and snowshoeing are the most popular, and plenty of snow-laden slopes and meadows provide remarkable experiences. Although people come here throughout the year, solitude is only a moment away. With more than 200 hiking and horse trails, 20 mountain biking trails, 50 Nordic ski trails, six designated wildlife/bird viewing areas, and 24 campgrounds with over 500 campsites, you can still find quiet among nature's majesty.

Spectacular scenery meets the eye with every turn of the Byway, and every stop along the way offers an interesting trail to try out. The grade and length of the trails vary, offering the perfect hike for every person. Many visitors love to hike trails in Mount Rainier National Park. Biking provides a great way to bring you into direct contact with more of the serene area of the Byway a little more quickly than hiking. The Byway itself is equipped to handle bicyclers. The shoulders along the road are paved varying from 2 to 8 feet in width.

Scenic

The Chinook Scenic Byway takes you through picturesque mountain towns and historical sites and guides you past Mount Rainier, "the shining jewel of the Northwest." The Byway's scenic properties are manifested largely in one of the world's greatest mountains, 14,411-foot Mount Rainier. Rainier is the tallest volcano in the 48 contiguous states and is the largest mountain in the Cascade chain of volcanoes extending from California to the Canadian border. At the numerous developed viewpoints along the roadside, you can enjoy the deep, shadowy forests, misty waterfalls, sparkling streams,

137

Washington

✻ *Chinook Scenic Byway*

towering peaks, and snowy rocky ridges that are all a part of Mount Rainier's wonder. Stands of old-growth Douglas fir found in few other places are available at every turn.

A short distance from SR 410 is the road to Sunrise, the highest point in the park accessible by car. The road to Sunrise winds through forests of cedar, fir, and hemlock, offering glimpses of the four dormant volcanoes, including Mount Baker and Mount Adams. Mount Rainier rises above alpine meadows profuse with delicate wildflowers to the rocky summit of Little Tahoma Peak visible to the left. Snap a few photographs: Mount Rainier's mountain meadows with their clear, icy lakes are among the most visited and photographed areas of the national park. From Sunrise, the views of Emmons Glacier, the largest on Mount Rainier, are breathtaking.

HIGHLIGHTS

Beginning near Naches and traveling northwest on the Byway, you enter Mount Rainier National Forest a few miles outside of the town of Cliffdell. This national park is known for its scenic, recreational, and natural resources.

After passing through Cliffdell, the road continues for a short space to the Builder Cave National Recreation Trail and Norse Peak, both known for their scenic beauty and recreational value. Here, the road changes to a southwesterly course, enters Mount Rainier National Park, and passes through old-growth environments that surround Fife Peak. Union Creek Waterfall is also located in this area. Edgar Rock Chinook Pass Historic CCC Work Camp is located at Chinook Pass, where the parkway resumes its northwestern direction. Tipsoo Lake is on the eastern side of the parkway shortly after the pass, followed by the Chinook Pass Overlook and Crystal Mountain Ski Resort.

Leaving Mount Rainier National Park, the parkway continues through the national forest to the Skookum Flats National Recreation Trail found at the edge of the forest. A popular viewpoint for Mount Rainier is also located here. The parkway travels through the town of Greenwater and the Federation Forest State Park before continuing on to Enumclaw, where the parkway ends.

THINGS TO SEE AND DO

Driving along the Chinook Scenic Byway will certainly keep your senses engaged, but if you yearn to get out of the car and stretch your legs, or if you'd like to make a mini-vacation out of your trip, check out these attractions along the route.

FEDERATION FOREST STATE PARK. *49201 Hwy 410 E, Enumclaw (98022). Phone 360/663-2207. www.parks.wa.gov/parks/.* Approximately 620 acres of old-growth timber make up the Federation Forest State Park. The Catherine Montgomery Interpretive Center displays exhibits on the state's seven life zones. Three interpretive trails, hiking trails, and part of the Naches Trail, one of the first pioneer trails between eastern Washington and Puget Sound. Fishing; hiking; picnicking. **FREE**

FLAMING GEYSER STATE PARK. *23700 SE Flaming Geyser Rd, Auburn (98002). Phone 253/931-3930. www.parks.wa.gov/parks/.* Two geysers (actually old test holes for coal) are in the park, one burning about 6 inches high and the other bubbling methane gas through a spring. Fishing, boating, rafting; hiking, picnicking, playground. Abundant wildlife, wildflowers. No camping. Open daily.

GREEN RIVER GORGE CONSERVATION AREA. *29500 SE Green River Gorge, Enumclaw (98022).* This conservation area protects a unique 12-mile corridor of the Green River, which cuts through unusual rock areas, many with fossils. Views of present-day forces of stream erosion through caves and smooth canyon walls. **FREE**

★ **MOUNT RAINIER NATIONAL PARK.** *Tahoma Woods, Star Rte, Ashford (98304). Phone 360/569-2211. www.nps.gov/mora/.* Majestic Mount Rainier, towering 14,411 feet above sea level and 8,000 feet above the Cascade Range of western Washington, is one of America's outstanding tourist attractions. More than 2 million people visit this 378-square-mile park each year to picnic, hike, camp, climb mountains, or simply admire the spectacular scenery along the many miles of roadways. The park's various "life zones," which change at different elevations, support a wide array of plant and animal life. Douglas fir, red cedar, and western hemlock, some rising 200 feet into the air, thrive in the old-growth forests. In the summer, the subalpine meadows come alive with brilliant, multicolored wildflowers. Mountain goats, chipmunks, and marmots are favorites among visitors, but deer, elk, bears, mountain lions, and other animals can also be seen here.

Mount Rainier is the largest volcano in the Cascade Range, which extends from Mount Garibaldi in southwestern British Columbia to Lassen Peak in northern California. The eruption of Mount St. Helens in 1980 gives a clue to the violent history of these volcanoes. Eruptions occurred at Mount Rainier as recently as the mid-1800s. Even today, steam emissions often form caves in the summit ice cap and usually melt the snow along the rims of the twin craters. A young volcano by geologic standards, Mount Rainier was once a fairly symmetrical mountain rising about 16,000 feet above sea level. But glaciers and further volcanic activity shaped the mountain into an irregular mass of rock. The sculpting action of the ice gave each face of the mountain its own distinctive profile. The glaciation continues today, as Mount Rainier supports the largest glacier system in the contiguous United States, with 35 square miles of ice and 26 named glaciers. The glaciers are the source of the many streams in the park, as well as several rivers in the Pacific Northwest. The meltwaters also nourish the various plants and animals throughout the region.

Winters at Mount Rainier are legendary. Moist air masses moving eastward across the Pacific Ocean are intercepted by the mountain. As a result, some areas on the mountain commonly receive 50 or more feet of snow each winter. Yet the park's transformation from winter wonderland to summer playground is almost magical. Beginning in June or July, the weather becomes warm and clear, although the mountain is occasionally shrouded in clouds. The snow at the lower elevations then disappears, meltwaters fill stream valleys and cascade over cliffs, wildflowers blanket the meadows, and visitors descend on the park for its many recreational activities.

You are offered several entrances to the park. The roads from the Nisqually entrance to Paradise and from the southeast boundary to Ohanapecosh are usually open year-round but may be closed temporarily during the winter. Following the first heavy snow, around November 1, all other roads are closed until May or June. Per vehicle **$$**

MUD MOUNTAIN DAM. *WA 410, Enumclaw (98022). Phone 360/825-3211.* One of the world's highest earth core and rock-fill dams.

Washington

✽ *Chinook Scenic Byway*

PLACES TO STAY

If you choose to include an overnight stay in your trip along this All-American Road, Mobil Travel Guide recommends the following lodgings.

★★ **ALEXANDER'S COUNTRY INN.** *37515 WA 706 E, Ashford (98304). Phone 360/569-2300; toll-free 800/654-7615. www.alexanderscountryinn.com.* 12 rooms, 7 with shower only, 2 guest houses, 3 story. No A/C. No room phones. Complimentary full breakfast, evening refreshments. Check-out 11 am, check-in 3 pm. Restaurant. Built in 1912. Totally nonsmoking. ¢

★ **THE NISQUALLY LODGE.** *31609 WA 706, Ashford (98304). Phone 360/569-8804; toll-free 888/674-3554. www.escapetothemountains.com.* 24 rooms, 2 story. Complimentary continental breakfast. Check-out 11 am. TV; VCR available. Restaurant. Whirlpool. Totally nonsmoking. ¢

★★ **PARADISE INN.** *Located in Mount Rainier National Park, Ashford (98304). Phone 360/569-2275. www.guestservices.com/rainier.* 117 rooms, 95 with bath, 2-4 story. No A/C. No elevator. No room phones. Closed early Oct-late May. Check-out 11 am. Restaurant, bar. Business services available. Sundries. Naturalist programs nightly. Shake-shingle mountain lodge built with on-site timber in 1916. Totally nonsmoking. $-$$

★★ **BEST WESTERN PARK CENTER HOTEL.** *1000 Griffin Ave, Enumclaw (98022). Phone 360/825-4490; toll-free 800/780-7234. www.bestwestern.com.* 40 rooms, 2 story. Pet accepted; $10. Check-out 11 am. TV. Restaurant, bar. Room service. Meeting rooms. Business services available. In-room modem link. In-house fitness room. Whirlpool. Some refrigerators, microwaves. Picnic tables. ¢

★ **APPLE COUNTRY BED & BREAKFAST.** *524 Okanogan Ave, Wenatchee (98801). Phone 509/664-0400. www.applecountryinn.com.* 5 rooms, 2 story. One of the first homes built in 1920 in the "Okanogan Heights" addition in Wenatchee. $

PLACES TO EAT

A long day of driving is sure to make you hungry. At the end of your journey, try the following restaurant.

★★ **ALEXANDER'S COUNTRY INN.** *37515 WA 706 E, Ashford (98304). Phone 360/569-2300; toll-free 800/654-7615. www.alexanderscountryinn.com.* Closed Mon-Thurs Nov-mid-Apr. Northwestern menu. Breakfast, lunch, dinner. Children's menu. Reservations accepted. $$

Mountains to Sound Greenway
I-90 ❋ WASHINGTON

Quick Facts

LENGTH: 100 miles.

TIME TO ALLOW: 1.5 to 2 hours.

BEST TIME TO DRIVE: Summer and fall. High season includes both summer and winter, when recreational sports are popular.

BYWAY TRAVEL INFORMATION: Washington State Tourism Division: 800/544-1800, extension 036; Washington State Deptartment of Trade and Economic Development: 360/753-5601; Byway local Web site: www.mtsgreenway.org.

SPECIAL CONSIDERATIONS: Interstate 90 provides a minimum of four lanes of high-speed, limited-access highway for the entire length of the greenway corridor. Road conditions vary during the winter season, lengthening the trip to as long as four hours for the entire route. The greenway is plowed throughout the winter, however, and pull-offs allow you to place chains on your tires. Electronic signs at every highway interchange provide drivers with up-to-the-minute road safety information.

RESTRICTIONS: Winter snow conditions on the I-90 Snoqualmie Pass regularly require the use of chains or other traction devices.

BICYCLE/PEDESTRIAN FACILITIES: The I-90 right-of-way is travelable by bicycle for the entire length of the greenway, including separated and landscaped trails along urban portions of the highway. Many recreational trails exist along the corridor in lands managed by the US Forest Service, the State Department of Natural Resources, state parks, and private lands.

Interstate 90 is the primary east/west highway in Washington. It begins at the historic Seattle waterfront and travels east over the Cascade Mountains to the dry plateaus of eastern Washington. As you travel east along this 100-mile Byway, you experience lush green forests, the marine beauty of Puget Sound, pastoral valleys, and a dramatic mountain landscape. You also pass through a complete change in climate, geology, and hometown style.

Each year, more than 20 million vehicles travel this route, making I-90 a popular gateway between Washington's largest city and its diverse and striking landscapes.

THE BYWAY STORY

The Mountains to Sound Greenway tells historical, natural, recreational, and scenic stories that make it a unique and treasured Byway.

Historical

The Byway's historic sites demonstrate different eras of modern history. Some sites possess the soul of the Old West, some seem to still embrace the spirit of early industry, and some retain the more obvious past of the last few decades.

The soul of the Old West is possessed in locations such as Fort Tilton, the site of an 1850s fort (also a wildlife wetland), and Meadowbrook Farm, a preserved historic landscape in the dramatic shadow of towering Mount Si. Meadowbrook Farm was the site of a Native American village that became the world's largest hop ranch at the turn of the century. The Klondike Gold Rush

Washington

I-90 ❈ Mountains to Sound Greenway

Museum, located in the historic Pioneer Square district, houses photos and memorabilia from Seattle's turn-of-the-century boom days. And what would the Old West be without a few mining operations? Catch a glimpse of a 19th-century coal-mining town at Roslyn. The town hasn't changed much in all these years, except for sprucing up the main street for the 1990s TV series *Northern Exposure*. Roslyn also has a museum that houses photos, mining tools, and historical information; the historic graveyard is divided into ethnic zones reflecting the many nations that sent miners here.

The spirit of early industry is still embraced in places like Preston, a turn-of-the-century Scandinavian mill town. Presently, Preston consists of the remnants of a small, northwoods logging town along the Raging River, including a number of historic homes and the church. The Thorp Grist Mill, built in 1883, is the oldest industrial artifact in Kittias County. The mill houses a remarkable collection of hand-made wooden mill machinery and is open to the public. In addition, Fall City Waterfront was the final upstream landing for early steamboats on the Snoqualmie River, Reinig Road Sycamore Corridor was the tree-lined main street of a former company town, and Mill Pond was the Snoqualmie Mill's former log-holding pond (and is now home to a variety of fish and wildlife).

Natural

The western flanks of the Cascade Mountains, through which the greenway passes, are some of the best conifer tree-growing lands in the world. The combination of temperate climate and ample rainfall produces record growth of Douglas fir, western red cedar, and western hemlock. Lumbering was Washington state's first industry, and trees from this region helped build San Francisco and many other 19th-century cities. You can still find remnants of the massive trees that once grew here: spend an hour in a beautiful old-growth forest just a mile from the interstate at exit 47 on the Asahel Curtis Nature Trail. Named for a founder of the Mountaineers, naturalist, photographer, and conservation leader, the Asahel Curtis Nature Trail provides an excellent glimpse of the ancient forest that once existed. You are surrounded by towering old-growth cedar, pine, and fir trees, as well as underbrush that ranges from devil's club to Canadian dogwood. The atmosphere is completed by rustling streams crossed by log bridges.

Recreational

Thousands of miles of recreational trails head from the Byway. Most of these trails support hiking, but some of the trails are also great for biking and horseback riding. These trails range in length and difficulty. Some are great for day trips, and others take you deep into the backcountry. Walkers and bicyclists can begin a journey into the mountains from the heart of Seattle on the separated I-90 trail that has its own tunnel and crosses the scenic lake Washington floating bridge. A series of regional trails lead to the John Wayne Pioneer Trail just south of North Bend (38 miles from Seattle). This converted rail/trail crosses the mountains on a wide and gentle slope and includes a 2.3-mile tunnel under the Snoqualmie Summit on its way to the Columbia River. Another of the more frequented hiking areas is the Burke Gilman Trail, which begins in Seattle and goes to Bothell, Woodinville, and Redmond, passing through suburban towns and pastoral farmland before arriving at Marymoore Park in the shadow of the Microsoft campus. At the Snoqualmie Summit, exit 52, you can gain access to the Pacific Crest Trail that runs from Mexico to Canada. By taking the trail northward from this exit, you enter the Alpine Lakes Wilderness Area and spectacular high alpine country, dotted with hundreds of small lakes and profuse displays of wildflowers.

Another popular hiking area is in the Cougar Mountain Regional Wildland Park, the largest wild park in an urban area in America at 4,000 acres. This network through wetland and forest passes 19th-century coal-mining shafts and concrete foundations. Another park, the Squak Mountain State Park, offers excellent hiking, because its 2,000 wooded acres are a first-rate wildlife habitat. The Tiger Mountain State Forest has the state's most heavily used trails. This web of trails for hikers, mountain bikers, and equestrians winds through 13,000 acres of working forest and conservation area. The two access points are just minutes from Seattle suburbs.

At 4,190 feet, Mount Si towers over the town of North Bend and is a favorite hiking destination with its strenuous 8-mile round-trip trail to the summit or its 5-mile round-trip trail to Little Si. Also, the Rattlesnake Ledge Trail climbs steeply (1,175 feet in 1 mile) from Rattlesnake Lake through classic western Washington forests to rock outcrops that provide sweeping views of the Central Cascades and Snoqualmie Valley. The Middle Fork Snoqualmie River Valley, on the edge of the Alpine Lakes Wilderness, has a variety of trails that wind among more than 100,000 acres of both ancient and recently harvested forests. The valley is minutes from North Bend but is lightly visited. An unpaved, 12-mile road leads to a footbridge, the access to many miles of backcountry trails. Other great places to hike around this Byway are Twin Falls State Park, the Asahel Curtis/Annette Lake Trail, the trail to Denny Creek and Franklin Falls, Snoqualmie Pass Summit, the John Wayne/Iron Horse Trail and Snoqualmie Tunnel, and the Coal Mines Trail.

Scenic

In 100 miles, the Mountains to Sound Greenway starts in the bustle of a major port city, passes through a suburban town where the interstate highway itself won a national award for highway design, and quickly enters dense forests. The front range of the Cascade Mountains looms over the flat, pastoral Snoqualmie Valley at North Bend and from there, looking eastward, dramatic mountain peaks are continuously visible. From the Snoqualmie Summit eastward, Interstate 90 passes two large lakes, which provide both recreational opportunities and irrigation water for the dryer lands of central Washington. At the end of the 100-mile greenway, you can leave the interstate, drive north a few miles through the historic town of Thorp, and circle back westward on old Highway 10, a dramatic geologic landscape carved and eroded by the Yakima River. Highway 10 rejoins I-90 just east of Cle Elum, where you can head east or west.

All the views along the drive are splendid; however, only a handful of travelers know about an especially magnificent viewpoint. Just west of Snoqualmie Pass, a spot exists where the corridor's diverse richness is most visible. The view extends from the rocky mountaintops of the Cascades to the flourishing green valleys of the Puget Sound lowlands. A little farther west, the view from Snoqualmie Point, a promontory just south of I-90, becomes panoramic—take exit 27, go right up the hill, and park at a gate. A short walk leads to a view that encompasses Mount Si towering nearby; Mount Baker is visible in the far distance on a clear day. The view follows

143

Washington

I-90 ✱ Mountains to Sound Greenway

the curve of the corridor past North Bend and on into alpine zones sheathed in silvery snow.

The term "greenway" is particularly applicable to this particular scenic Byway. A sizable portion of this Byway passes through national forests, enabling you to experience the grandeur of many varieties of trees. A blanket of thick forests of Douglas fir, true fir, hemlock, and cedar make this road truly a greenway. Two kinds of trees that can reach enormous proportions are cedars and Sitka spruce. Many of the old cedars were logged, and you can see their disintegrating stumps dotting the landscape around the forests that have since grown in. With a bit of looking and luck, you may find patches of the old trees, which had diameters of more than 15 feet.

THINGS TO SEE AND DO

Driving along the Mountains to Sound Greenway will certainly keep your senses engaged, but if you yearn to get out of the car and stretch your legs, or if you'd like to make a mini-vacation out of your trip, check out these attractions along the route.

ALKI BEACH. *1100 Alki Ave SW, Seattle (98116). Phone 206/684-4075.* Skirting the northwestern waterfront of the South Seattle neighborhood, the 2.5-mile Alki Beach is a mecca for outdoor enthusiasts—joggers, divers, bicyclists, beach volleyball players, sunbathers, and in-line skaters. The beach, administered by the Seattle Parks Department, runs from Duwamish Head to Alki Point on Elliot Bay and offers stunning views of Puget Sound and the city skyline. Facilities are a notch above the norm, with scads of picnic tables, a playground, small boat access, and a multi-use path. At Alki Point (the southern end of the beach), you'll find a bathhouse/art studio and a plaque commemorating the landing of the first settlers here in 1851. At Duwamish Head (the northern tip of the beach) are the sea-walled site of a former amusement park and a miniature version of the Statue of Liberty.

BOEHM'S CHOCOLATE FACTORY. *255 NE Gilman Blvd, Issaquah (98027). Phone 425/392-6652.* The home of Boehm's Candies was built here in 1956 by Julius Boehm. The candy-making process and the Edelweiss Chalet, filled with artifacts, paintings, and statues, can be toured. The Luis Trenker Kirch'l, a replica of a 12th-century Swiss chapel, was also built by Boehm. Tours by appointment, July and Aug. **FREE**

BOEING FIELD—KING COUNTY INTERNATIONAL AIRPORT. *8285 Perimeter Rd S, Seattle (98108). Phone 206/296-7380. www.metrokc.gov/airport.* The Observation Park has airplane viewing and picnicking facilities.

DISCOVERY PARK. *3801 W Government Way, Seattle (98119). Phone 206/386-4236.* An in-city wildlife sanctuary and nature preserve, the 534-acre Discovery Park, located on the western shores of the swanky Magnolia neighborhood, is the largest park in Seattle. Centered on a tall bluff that formerly served as a post for the US Army, the park offers great views of the Olympic Mountains to the west and the Cascades to the east, with waterfront access to the north and west. An extensive trail system lures joggers, bikers, and other fitness buffs from all over the city, but the educational program is at the heart of the park's mission, hence the "Discovery" tag. School buses and day campers frequent the park year-round, but the events calendar has something for every age and interest. A diverse population of flora and fauna—including wildflowers, owls, hummingbirds, and crustaceans—calls the park's dunes, thickets, forests, and tide pools home. **FREE**

FERRY TRIPS. *Colman Dock (foot of Madison St), Seattle (98104). Phone 206/464-6400.* Access to the Olympic Peninsula; a number of interesting ferry trips. **$$$$**

KLONDIKE GOLD RUSH NATIONAL HISTORICAL PARK. *117 S Main St, Seattle (98104). Phone 206/553-7220. www.nps.gov/klgo/.* This park details the gold rush stampede of 1897-1898 with displays, photomurals, artifacts, slide and film programs; gold-panning demonstrations. Visitor center in the historic Pioneer Square District. Open daily; closed Jan 1, Thanksgiving, Dec 25. **FREE**

LAKE SAMMAMISH STATE PARK. *20606 SE 56th St, Issaquah (98027). Phone 425/455-7010. www.parks.wa.gov/parks/.* At approximately 430 acres, this park offers swimming, fishing, boating (launch); hiking and picnicking.

MEADOWBROOK FARM. *From eastbound I-90, take exit 27, turn left, turn left again onto Meadowbrook Ave, and turn right onto Meadowbrook-North Bend Rd. From westbound I-90, take exit 31, turn north, follow the curve onto State Rte 202, and turn right onto Boalch Ave. The farm lies on 450 acres in the heart of Snoqualmie Valley.* This preserved farm was the site of a Native American village and, later, the world's largest hop ranch.

MOUNT BAKER-SNOQUALMIE NATIONAL FOREST. *21905 64th Ave W, Mountlake Terrace (98043). E and S of Seattle, reached via I-90. Phone 425/775-9702; toll-free 800/627-0062. www.fs.fed/us/r6/mbs/.* The Snoqualmie section of the National Forest includes several ski areas, eight wilderness areas, picnic and campsites, fishing, and hunting in more than 1 million acres.

MONORAIL. *370 Thomas St, Seattle (98109). Phone 206/441-6038. www.seattlemonorail.com.* Seattle's monorail provides a scenic 90-second ride between Center House and Westlake Center, downtown. A legacy of the 1962 World's Fair, the Swedish-built train makes frequent runs throughout the day. Closed Jan 1, Thanksgiving, Dec 25. **$$**

MUSEUM OF FLIGHT. *9404 E Marginal Way S, Seattle (98108). Phone 206/764-5700. www.museumofflight.org.* As a major hub for plane-maker Boeing—even since the aviation giant's headquarters bolted for Chicago in 2001—Seattle is the ideal location for this impressive air and space museum. The facility is highlighted by the soaring Great Gallery, home of more than 50 vintage aircraft, many of which are suspended in formation six stories above the ground. On display here are the original presidential Air Force One and a replica of the Wright Brothers' biplane from Kitty Hawk, North Carolina, alongside mint-condition models of the first fighter jet (a 1914 Caproni Ca 20) and the first jumbo jet (a prototype Boeing 747); many planes are open for visitors to sit in the cockpit or explore the hold. Located near Seattle-Tacoma International Airport in southern Seattle, the museum is also home to the restored "Red Barn," where the Boeing Company was founded nearly a century ago, and several space-themed exhibits. Open daily; closed Thanksgiving, Dec 25. **$$$**

★ **PIKE PLACE MARKET.** *85 Pike St, Seattle (98101). Phone 206/587-0351. www.pikeplacemarket.org.* Area farmers established the Pike Place Market in 1907, because they were tired of middlemen taking more than their fair share. Today, the indoor/outdoor market is a Seattle landmark and a cornucopia for the

Washington

I-90 ❈ Mountains to Sound Greenway

senses, with burly guys tossing fresh fish back and forth at the fish market; bin after bin of fresh, colorful fruits, vegetables, and flowers; the sounds and sights of street performers; and the wares of hundreds of artists on display. But it doesn't stop there: the astoundingly comprehensive Pike Place Market has dozens of restaurants and food stands, a day spa, a barbershop, a tattoo parlor, and a dating service onsite. Just two blocks east of the waterfront, the market is a quick walk from the center of downtown and is surrounded by eateries and bars. Guided tours are available Wed-Sun year-round ($$). Open daily; closed some major holidays. **FREE**

PIONEER SQUARE DISTRICT. *Roughly bounded by Columbia St, Elliot Bay, Second Ave S, Fourth Ave S, and Fifth Ave N, Seattle (98104). www.pioneersquare.org.* Seattle's Pioneer Square district, the city's original downtown, was built in the 1890s (after a disastrous fire) as money from the Yukon Gold Rush started pouring in. The architecture is amazingly harmonious (one architect was responsible for nearly 60 major buildings in a ten-block radius) and graciously restored. The area also features the underground tour and many galleries, cafés, and antique shops. A collection of totem poles can be found in tree-lined Occidental Park and in Pioneer Square itself. Open during business hours. **FREE**

SAFECO FIELD. *1250 1st Ave S, Seattle (98134). Phone 306/346-4000. www.safeco.com/safeco/safecofield.* First opened in 2002, SAFECO Field replaced the much-maligned Kingdome as the home of Major League Baseball's Seattle Mariners. It's easy to see why the $517 million ballpark quickly won the hearts of the Emerald City's sports fans, based on nostalgic architecture, stunning views of the Seattle skyline and the Puget Sound sunset, and a one-of-a-kind umbrella for the city's infamous rainstorms: a retractable roof that weighs 22 million pounds and covers 9 acres. Hour-long tours of the facility are available on a near-daily basis (except Mon during baseball's off-season and day game days during the season), and cover a walking distance of about 1 mile. Aside from the roof and old-time ironwork, some of SAFECO's can't-miss features are the works of public art integrated into its design, a playground for kids, and the official Mariners team store.

SEATTLE ART MUSEUM. *100 University St, Seattle (98101). Phone 206/654-3255. www.seattleartmuseum.org.* Its entrance guarded by an animated, 48-foot-tall sculpture named Hammering Man, the Seattle Art Museum (known locally as SAM) is the premiere facility of its kind in the Pacific Northwest. There is something for everybody here, from ancient Greek sculpture to modern Russian decorative art. Held in particularly high regard are the collections of contemporary art (with pieces by Andy Warhol, Jackson Pollock, and Roy Lichtenstein) and Northwest Coast Native American art (comprised of nearly 200 masks, sculptures, and household items). SAM's temporary exhibitions are similarly diverse. A dynamic events calendar helps distinguish the museum, offering up a bevy of concerts, films, lectures, demonstrations, family programs, and classes. Admission is waived on the first Thursday of every month, and a restaurant and two gift shops are onsite. Open Tues-Wed, Fri-Sun 10 am-5 pm; Thurs 10 am-9 pm; closed holidays. **$$**

SEATTLE OPERA. *1020 John St, Seattle (98109). Phone 206/389-7676. www.seattleopera.org.* This renowned company presents five operas per season (Aug-May). After a year and a half of renovation of the historic Opera House, performances return to their old home, now called Marian Oliver McCaw Hall. **$$$$**

SPACE NEEDLE. *400 Broad St, Seattle (98109). Phone 800/937-9582. www.spaceneedle.com.* First a sketch on a placemat, then the centerpiece of the 1962 World's Fair, and now Seattle's face to the world, the Space Needle is one of the most distinctive structures in the US. Capping the 605-foot tower, the flying saucer-inspired dome is symbolic of both the

Seattle World's Fair's theme—"Century 21"—and the coinciding national push into space. The dome houses an observation deck (with stunning city views) and SkyCity, a revolving restaurant that goes full circle every 48 minutes. A banquet facility sits 100 feet above street level; a gift shop is located at the tower's base, where you board an elevator for the 43-second journey to the top. The Space Needle is the setting for one of the West Coast's premiere New Year's Eve celebrations every Dec 31. $$$

SNOQUALMIE FALLS. *North Bend (98068). www.snoqualmiefalls.com.* Perpetual snow in the Cascade Mountains feeds the 268-foot falls. Power plant; park area; trail to the bottom of the falls. Salish Lodge overlooks the falls.

SNOQUALMIE VALLEY HISTORICAL MUSEUM. *320 S North Bend Blvd, North Bend (98068). Phone 425/888-3200. www.snoqualmievalleymuseum.org.* Displays, room settings of early pioneer life from the 1890s; photos, Native American artifacts; logging exhibits; farm shed; reference material. Slide shows; changing exhibits. Open Apr-mid-Dec, Thurs-Sun; tours by appointment. **FREE**

SUMMIT AT SNOQUALMIE. *1001 State Rd 906, Snoqualmie Pass (98068). Phone 425/434-7669. www.summit-at-snoqualmie.com.* About an hour east of downtown Seattle, the Summit at Snoqualmie is a top winter sports destination for skiers and snowboarders. The mountain has four distinct base areas—Summit West, Central, and East, as well as the daunting Alpental—each with its own amenities and lifts. Between the four, the resort has varied terrain with ample acreage for every skill level. Of special note: the snowboarding paradise called the Nissan Terrain Park and Halfpipe at Summit West; the Nordic Center at Summit East, the starting point for more than 30 miles of groomed trails. Restaurant and ski rental services are at all four base areas; the repair shop is at Summit Central. Lodging is available in the area at hotels, motels, and vacation home rentals. $$$$

THORP GRIST MILL. *From I-90, take exit 101, turn N, and go 3 miles to Thorp to reach the mill at the far edge of town. Phone 509/964-9640. www.thorp.org.* This flour mill, built in 1883, is the only one in the country with its machinery completely intact. **FREE**

THE WATERFRONT. *The Waterfront, Alaskan Way, Seattle (98101).* The most tourist-trafficked spot in all of Seattle, the downtown waterfront bustles with activity year-round. Abutting Puget Sound on the western fringe of downtown, such landmarks as the Pike Place Market and the Seattle Aquarium reel in visitors by the thousands. Then there are the crowds drawn in by the boats—including the ferry to Bainbridge Island and Victoria Clipper Charters—that depart from the piers, encrusted with touristy shops, seafood restaurants, and oyster bars. One particularly kitschy retailer that's worth a peek is Ye Olde Curiosity Shop on Pier 54, with a circus-meets-harbor atmosphere accentuated by the mummies and jar-encased, two-headed calves on display. As for recreation, some people fish here; others engage in a pursuit that is distinctly Seattle: jigging for squid.

WENATCHEE NATIONAL FOREST. *Wenatchee (98801). Phone 509/662-4335. www.fs.fed.us/r6/wenatchee.* Approximately 2 million forested, mountainous acres lying west of the Columbia River. Trail system leads to jagged peaks, mountain meadows, and sparkling lakes. Fishing, hunting, picnicking, winter sports; many developed campsites (some fees).

PLACES TO STAY

If you choose to include an overnight stay in your trip along this Byway, Mobil Travel Guide recommends the following lodgings.

★★★★ **BELLEVUE CLUB HOTEL.** *11200 SE 6th St, Bellevue (98004). Phone 425/454-4424; toll-free 800/579-1110. www.bellevueclub.com.* You instantly feel the hush of the Bellevue Club Hotel when you walk through the vine-covered entrance to this exquisite hotel. Visitors are

Washington

I-90 ❋ Mountains to Sound Greenway

instantly welcomed to this temple of serenity and contemporary elegance set on 9 acres in the center of Bellevue. While the Bellevue Club feels private and exclusive, hotel guests are warmly greeted with thoughtful touches and deluxe amenities. Each room has an inviting atmosphere, complete with luxurious bedding and baths crafted of marble, limestone, or granite. Stone fireplaces, oversized baths, or private balconies set each room apart from another. An Olympic-size pool, state-of-the-art fitness equipment, racquet courts, and spa make the fitness facility a true sanctuary. Regional and international flavors define the menu at Polaris, where alfresco dining by the fountain makes for an unforgettable experience. Quick bites are provided at two other establishments for those on the go. 67 rooms, 2 with shower only, 4 story. Pet accepted. Complimentary continental breakfast. Check-out 1 pm, check-in 3 pm. TV; cable (premium), VCR available. In-room modem link. Restaurant, bar; entertainment Thurs-Sat. Room service 24 hours. Children's activity center. In-house fitness room, spa, massage, sauna, steam room. Indoor pool, outdoor pool, children's pool, whirlpool, poolside service. Lighted outdoor tennis, indoor tennis. Valet parking. Business center. Concierge. $$$

★★★ **THE WOODMARK HOTEL ON LAKE WASHINGTON.** *1200 Carillon Point, Kirkland (98033). Phone 425/822-3700; toll-free 800/822-3700. www.thewoodmark.com.* With the blinking lights of Seattle's skyline only 7 miles in the distance, the Woodmark Hotel gently rests on the shores of scenic Lake Washington. Convenient to Bellevue and Redmond, the Woodmark is an ideal stop for travelers to the pristine Pacific Northwest. Set within a complex of specialty shops, restaurants, and a marina, the hotel is a true getaway enhanced by a marvelous destination spa. Characterized by the serenity and casual elegance of the region, the Woodmark instills a sense of belonging in its guests. From the friendly staff to the cozy furnishings, a relaxed, residential style pervades the hotel. The 100 rooms are luxurious without being pretentious and feature lake, marina, or creek views. The region's fresh, delicious cuisine is the highlight at Waters Lakeside Bistro, and the Library Bar serves a wonderful afternoon tea, complete with a special menu and china service for children. 100 rooms, 4 story. Pet accepted. Check-out noon, check-in 4 pm. TV; VCR available. In-room modem link. Fireplace in suites. Restaurant, bar. Room service 24 hours. Babysitting services available. In-house fitness room, health club privileges, spa. Pool, poolside service. Marina; three lakeside parks. Valet parking. Concierge. $$

★ **BEST WESTERN PIONEER SQUARE HOTEL.** *77 Yesler Way, Seattle (98104). Phone 206/340-1234; toll-free 800/800-5514. www.bestwestern.com.* 75 rooms, 4 story. Complimentary continental breakfast. Check-out noon. TV; VCR available. Health club privileges. In a restored 1914 building. $

★★ **COURTYARD BY MARRIOTT LAKE UNION.** *925 Westlake Ave N, Seattle (98109). Phone 206/213-0100; toll-free 800/321-2211. www.courtyard.com.* This chain hotel is near many of Seattle's popular attractions, including the Space Needle, Woodland Park Zoo, and the Seattle waterfront. 250 rooms, 7 story. Check-out noon, check-in 3 pm. TV; cable (premium). In-room modem link. Laundry services. Restaurant, bar. In-house fitness room. Indoor pool. Business center. Concierge. $

★ **HAMPTON INN & SUITES.** *700 Fifth Ave N, Seattle (98109). Phone 206/282-7700; toll-free 800/426-7866. www.hamptoninn.com.* 198 rooms, 74 suites, 6 story. Complimentary continental breakfast. Check-out noon, check-in 3 pm. TV; VCR available. In-house fitness room. Business center. $

★★ **HILL HOUSE BED & BREAKFAST.** *1113 E John St, Seattle (98102). Phone 206/720-7161; toll-free 800/720-7161. www.seattlebnb.com.* 9 rooms, 3 story. No A/C. Some room phones. Weekends, holidays 2-4-day minimum. Children over 12 years only. Complimentary full breakfast. Check-out 11 am, check-in by appointment. TV in suites; cable (premium). In-room modem link. Restored 1903 Victorian inn. $

★★ **HOLIDAY INN SEATTLE-ISSAQUAH.** *1801 12th Ave NW, Issaquah (98027). Phone 425/392-6421; toll-free 800/465-4329. www.holiday-inn.com.* 100 rooms, 2 story. Check-out noon. TV; cable (premium). Outdoor pool; wading pool, poolside service. Restaurant, bar. Room service. Coin laundry. Meeting rooms. Business services available. $

★★★ **INN AT THE MARKET.** *86 Pine St, Seattle (98101). Phone 206/443-3600; toll-free 800/446-4484. www.innatthemarket.com.* One of the most romantic hotels in Seattle, this inn is known for its spectacular views of Puget Sound, Mount Rainier, and the Olympic Mountains. 70 rooms, 10 suites, 4-8 story. Check-out noon, check-in 4 pm. TV; cable (premium), VCR available. Restaurant, bar. Health club privileges. Parking $17; valet. $$

★★ **SIXTH AVENUE INN.** *2000 6th Ave, Seattle (98121). Phone 206/441-8300; toll-free 800/648-6440. www.sixthavenueinn.com.* 167 rooms, 5 story, no ground-floor rooms. Check-out noon, check-in 3 pm. TV; cable (premium). In-room modem link. Restaurant, bar. Room service. $

★ **SUMMERFIELD SUITES.** *1011 Pike St, Seattle (98101). Phone 206/682-8282; toll-free 800/996-3426. www.wyndham.com.* 363 rooms, 9 story. Complimentary continental breakfast.

Check-out noon, check-in 4 pm. TV; cable (premium), VCR available. In-house fitness room. Outdoor pool, whirlpool. Valet parking. $

★★★ **WARWICK HOTEL.** *4th and Lenora St, Seattle (98121). Phone 206/443-4300; toll-free 800/426-9280. www.warwickhotel.com.* Located downtown, this hotel offers many recreational facilities. 233 rooms, 17 story. Check-out noon. TV; fireplace in lobby. Restaurant, bar. Room service 24 hours. In-house fitness room, sauna. Indoor pool, whirlpool. $$

★★★ **THE WESTIN SEATTLE.** *1900 Fifth Ave, Seattle (98101). Phone 206/728-1000; toll-free 888/625-5144. www.westin.com.* 919 rooms, 40 story. Pet accepted. Check-out noon. TV; VCR available. Restaurant, bar; entertainment. Room service 24 hours. In-house fitness room. Indoor pool, whirlpool. Business center. Concierge. Tower rooms with panoramic view. $$

★★★ **SALISH LODGE AND SPA.** *6501 Railroad Ave, Snoqualmie (98065). Phone 425/888-2556; toll-free 800/2-SALISH. www.salishlodge.com.* This lodge is located near the 268-foot Snoqualmie Falls in the wilderness of the Pacific Northwest, and only 35 minutes from downtown Seattle. 91 rooms, 4 story. Check-out noon, check-in 4 pm. TV; cable (premium), VCR available. Fireplaces. Restaurant, bar. Room service. In-house fitness room, spa, sauna. Whirlpool. Concierge. $$$

PLACES TO EAT

A long day of driving is sure to make you hungry. At the end of your journey, take a table at one of the following restaurants.

★★★ **AL BOCCALINO.** *1 Yesler Way, Seattle (98104). Phone 206/622-7688.* This intimate Italian restaurant features muted antique light-

Washington

I-90 ✤ Mountains to Sound Greenway

ing and candlelit tables that set the stage for many marriage proposals. Italian menu. Closed major holidays. Lunch (weekdays only), dinner. No A/C. Casual attire. $$
[D]

★★★★ **BRASA.** *2107 3rd Ave, Seattle (98121). Phone 206/728-4220.* Seattle's trendy residents gather at Brasa on a regular basis to indulge in this hotspot's robust, Mediterranean-inspired fare. While the crowd at the bar tends to be young and hip, the folks filling the rustic but sleek dining room, decorated with terrazzo floors, black and tan accented wood, and wrought-iron railings, are a stylish set of 30- and 40-somethings. No matter what your age, however, the vibrant cuisine at Brasa is easy to love. Two of the signature dishes show off the kitchen's culinary brilliance: the roast suckling pig and the mussels and clams served oven-steamed in a cataplana, a double-domed copper pot that's used to cook stews in Portugal. From the open kitchen and a stunning wood-burning oven, you'll find exciting dishes layered with the bold flavors of Spain, Portugal, France, and Brazil. Brasa serves wonderful food that dazzles the palate and the eye and expertly balances the rustic and the sophisticated. Iberian, Mediterranean menu. Closed holidays. Dinner. Bar. Entertainment. Casual attire. $$
[D]

★★ **BROOKLYN SEAFOOD, STEAK & OYSTER HOUSE.** *1212 Second Ave, Seattle (98101). Phone 206/224-7000.* Seafood menu. Closed Jan 1, Dec 25. Lunch, dinner. Bar. Children's menu. In an 1890s building; artwork. Reservations accepted. Valet parking (dinner). Patio/courtyard dining. $$$
[D]

★★★ **CASCADIA.** *2328 1st Ave, Seattle (98121). Phone 206/448-8884.* Continental menu. Closed Sun; holidays. Dinner. Entertainment: pianist Wed-Sat. Children's menu. Casual attire. $$$
[D]

★★ **CHUTNEY'S.** *519 1st Ave N, Seattle (98109). Phone 206/284-6799.* Indian menu. Lunch, dinner. Bar. Reservations accepted. Indian prints and carved deities decorate the walls. Totally nonsmoking. $$
[D]

★★★ **FLYING FISH.** *2234 1st Ave, Seattle (98121). Phone 206/728-8595. www.flyingfishseattle.com.* Here, you will find artfully presented fish items with an Asian influence. Seafood menu. Closed most major holidays. Dinner, late night. Bar. Casual attire. Outdoor seating. Totally nonsmoking. $$
[D]

★★★★ **THE HERBFARM.** *14590 NE 145th St, Woodinville (98072). Phone 425/485-5300.* Set in an enchanted old farmhouse, The Herbfarm is a place where nature rules the dinner table. Each evening's gourmet nine-course menu is finalized only hours before the meal to best reflect the harvest of the season. (Dinner is served with five or six matched wines; nonalcoholic beverages and beers are available upon request.) But it's not just the last-minute nature of the menu that is impressive. The really wild and wonderful thing about The Herbfarm is that for most of the year, the harvest used for your dinner comes directly from The Herbfarm's own house-run gardens and farm, as well as from small, local growers and producers of wild mushrooms, heritage fruits, handmade cheeses, and rare ingredients like water-grown wasabi root and artisanal caviars. This is a gourmet's dream. In the summer, bocce ball is played on the restaurant's grass court and a pre-dinner outdoor hosted garden tour (weather permitting) begins 30 minutes before service each evening. This unique and spectacular dining experience will stay with you well after you have licked your plate clean. Seasonal Pacific Northwest menu. Closed Mon-Wed; holidays; one week in Feb or Mar. Dinner. Casual attire. Reservations required. Totally nonsmoking. $$$$
[D]

★ **IVAR'S ACRES OF CLAMS.** *Pier 54, Seattle (98104). Phone 206/624-6852. www.ivars.net.* Seafood menu. Closed Thanksgiving, Dec 25. Lunch, dinner. Bar. Casual attire. $$
D

★★ **MAXIMILIEN-IN-THE-MARKET.** *81A Pike Pl, Seattle (98101). Phone 206/682-7270.* French menu. Closed Jan 1, Thanksgiving, Dec 25. Breakfast, lunch, dinner, Sun brunch. Bar. Casual attire. Valet parking. $$
D

★★★★ **ROVER'S.** *2808 E Madison St, Seattle (98112). Phone 206/325-7442. www.rovers-seattle.com.* A small, white clapboard cottage houses Rover's, an intimate restaurant serving innovative and amazing contemporary cuisine. Thierry Rautureau, the chef and owner, stays true to the regional ingredients of the Northwest while paying homage to impeccable French technique, perhaps because he hails from France. The restaurant's modest but lovely décor does little to tip you off to the extraordinary culinary masterpieces that await you. Presented like precious little works of art, the portions are perfect in size, taste, and appearance. The miraculous part of Rautureau's menu is that as soon as you finish the course in front of you, you are ready and salivating for the next. (The restaurant offers five-course and eight-course tasting menus in addition to a five-course vegetarian menu.) Dishes are light but intense and wonderful, so you crave the next one immediately. Not only is Rautureau a gifted chef, but he is also a gregarious and witty host who makes a point of visiting and welcoming every guest personally. Northwest Contemporary menu. Closed Sun, Mon; holidays. Dinner. Entertainment. Casual attire. Totally nonsmoking. $$$$
D

★★★ **WILD GINGER.** *1401 Third Ave, Seattle (98101). Phone 206/623-4450.* One of Seattle's premier restaurants, Wild Ginger is a hotspot for celebrities who sometimes come for Monday night jazz sessions. Chinese menu. Closed Thanksgiving, Dec 25. Lunch, dinner. Bar. Satay bar. Near Pike Place Market. Casual attire. $$$
D

★★★ **SALISH LODGE AND SPA DINING ROOM.** *6501 Railroad Ave, Snoqualmie (98065). Phone 425/888-2556. www.salishlodge.com.* With views overlooking the magnificent Snoqualmie Falls, the word is casual elegance at this rustic lodge restaurant. New World menu. Breakfast, dinner. Bar. Entertainment Fri, Sat. Casual attire. Valet parking. $$$
D

Strait of Juan de Fuca Highway
SR 112 ❈ WASHINGTON

Quick Facts

LENGTH: 61 miles.

TIME TO ALLOW: 2 to 8 hours.

BEST TIME TO DRIVE: Spring, when rain keeps the country green and lush, and fall, when the maples turn color and the weather is its mildest. Summer is the high season.

BYWAY TRAVEL INFORMATION: Clallam Bay-Sekiu Chamber of Commerce: 360/963-2346.

SPECIAL CONSIDERATIONS: Gas is available on SR 112 at Joyce, Clallam Bay, and Neah Bay. Pets are not allowed on the trails at Lake Ozette. When on the Makah Reservation, follow their request to "take only pictures; leave only footprints." Posted speed limits change frequently depending on the nature of the road, population, and activities.

RESTRICTIONS: Flooding and/or landslides occasionally occur and can close the road for short periods. The only fee along the Byway is a nominal one at the Makah Cultural Museum.

BICYCLE/PEDESTRIAN FACILITIES: Bicyclists tend to stay at the east end of the corridor, between Port Angeles and the SR 113 junction, because it is well suited for bicycle travel. This segment has wider shoulders and good sight distances for much of its length. After the SR 113 junction, cyclist find either narrower shoulders or no shoulder areas at all, along with many curves and hills.

Reaching farther out into the cold waters of the North Pacific than any other point of mainland in the lower 48 states, this Byway, located in the northwest corner of Washington state, is a remote stretch of coastline with rugged cliffs and forests. The Strait of Juan de Fuca Highway follows the shoreline of a glacial fjord that connects Puget Sound to the Pacific Ocean. Natural wonders that are rare and exciting events in other places of the world are everyday occurrences here. For example, eagles search for food among intertidal rocks, and gray whales feed in the Strait of Juan de Fuca.

This Byway offers an uncommon adventure on an uncrowded stretch of Washington's coast. The highway provides access to Cape Flattery, the farthest northwest point in the continental United States. It also provides access to Olympic National Park beaches. Explore the wild shoreline, stroll windy beaches and fishing towns, fish for salmon and halibut, take a self-guided tour among timber forests, or just set off by foot, bike, boat, or kayak to actively explore the area.

The communities along the highway provide pleasant starting points for exploring the surrounding natural landscape. A boardwalk system provides access to remote shorelines, where Pacific Ocean waves crash against sea stacks and rocky cliffs. Along the route, you'll spy tree-covered hillsides, uncommon sea birds like puffins and auklets, bald eagles, and marine mammals (including sea otters, whales, and sea lions).

Whether you watch the waves break, take a ride on a salmon charter, learn about Native American cultures, or watch whale spouts, the Strait of Juan de Fuca Highway can be an adventure for a day or week.

Washington

SR 112 ✽ *Strait of Juan de Fuca Highway*

THE BYWAY STORY

The Strait of Juan de Fuca Highway tells archaeological, cultural, historical, natural, recreational, and scenic stories that make it a unique and treasured Byway.

Archaeological

Archaeology is quite prominent in this area because Native American artifacts are unearthed with relative frequency. The many Native American artifacts found here have been gathered into one of the nation's most significant displays of its kind, the Byway's own Makah Cultural and Research Center. This center chronicles the Native American people who have inhabited this region for millennia. Specifically, it features artifacts from two ancient Native American villages that have been unearthed here in recent years. An Ozette village was discovered in 1966; also, a Makah fishing village, estimated to be nearly 3,000 years old, was excavated in the 1980s. Some artifacts from this Makah fishing village include wooden fishhooks, harpoons, a gill net, and basket fragments.

Cultural

The longtime residency of Native American tribes gives distinctive seasoning to this area's already unique culture. The still-thriving Makah tribe contributes particular savor because it resides, continuing in its traditions, at the western end of the Byway. The Makah Cultural and Research Center, which sits on the Makah reservation, tells the story of the Makah. This center also tells the stories of other tribes that had great influence on the area, such as the Klallam and the Quileutes. The Klallam were especially influential; by the late 1700s, they had established 17 villages between Discovery and Clallam Bays and numbered about 2,000 people. The Makah and Ozette, headquartered near Neah Bay and Lake Ozette, also numbered about 2,000 people each. Evidence of the effect of these tribes is prevalent in the overwhelming amount of Native American artifacts that have been found here and are displayed at the center.

Historical

This Byway's communities treasure their history and have consequently taken care to renovate the buildings that tell the stories of its modern history. For instance, the restored train depot serves as the Joyce Museum, which recounts the area's logging history through logging artifacts displays. Another well-preserved building, the Joyce General Store (originally a hotel at the town of Crescent Beach) exudes the spirit of bygone days. The Byway's communities are also continually working to refurbish other structures, such as the West Clallam Schoolhouse. This finely crafted wooden building, built by one of the region's early timber companies, characterizes the region in that era. Efforts are also being made to restore the warning horn of the unique and well-preserved Slip Point Lighthouse Tender's Residence.

Natural

It's no surprise that the Strait of Juan de Fuca's many gorgeous variations—its rocky shorelines, snow-covered mountains, and nationally featured tide pools—support a wide range of remarkable and unique flora and fauna. You need only to walk on the beach or take a sea kayak out on the profound waters to see and feel a kinship with these plants and animals. For example, it wouldn't be atypical to slide past a gray whale, killer whale, or sea otter while on your sea kayak. Olympic National Park's Pacific Beach area offers wild and remote beaches that are yours to discover and are lined with nationally significant old-growth rain forests. Birds and sea mammals crowd around the sea stacks and rocky cliffs and in the waters off Cape Flattery, the most northwestern point in the mainland United States. You can feel close to these animals from your jutting vantage point from Cape Flattery's Cliffside boardwalk system and viewing decks.

These nearly mythic wonders continue as you travel farther inland. The glacier water and deep gorge of the Elwha River were once home to a legendary run of chinook salmon, fish that were large enough that Native American tribes used single skins as ceremonial robes. Unfortunately, these fish no longer exist in this river because populations have been in decline ever since the development of hydroelectric dams at the turn of the century. In fact, no type of salmon has been able to negotiate the dams, but funding has been allocated to begin removing the dams in what is likely to be the highest-profile fish habitat restoration project in the nation.

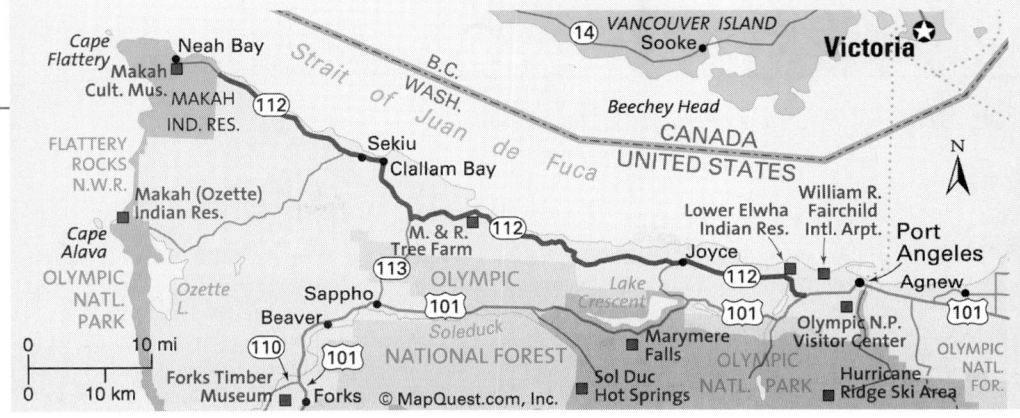

The Byway's rolling, tree-covered hillsides have been managed for timber production for more than 100 years, meaning that the length of time from harvest to "green-up" is minimal. These forests, consequently, are a dynamic mosaic of newly harvested areas and mature woodlands. Part of the mature woodlands is an area of dense bald eagle nesting, roosting, and feeding. It would be rare to drive through this particular area and not see an eagle hunting or perching. In fact, when the eagle population is at its peak in the spring and fall, it is common to see a dozen eagles in one day.

Recreational

When driving along the Strait of Juan de Fuca Highway, opportunities to stop and have a good time abound. Every stop affords a dazzling view and also offers a chance to make memories.

Salmon fishers have come here from throughout the country for decades, one of which was the nation's most famous sportsman, Eddie Bauer (of retail and catalog fame); he even had a fishing cabin along this route. Visitors love to fish for salmon, and the fishing is so good that a salmon season exists each summer. Boats of all sizes can be used to fish for mighty Pacific halibut, several kinds of rockfish, resident blackmouth salmon, beautiful coho salmon, and giant chinook salmon. In the area near Neah Bay, the state's record 288-pound flatfish was caught. While fishing is best in the summer, you can also enjoy great fishing in the winter: keep an eye on the wind forecasts, enjoy the solitude, and catch some good-sized fish.

Kayaking and scuba diving are a thrilling way to immerse yourself (quite literally) in the marine life of the area. The Strait of Juan de Fuca from Pillar Point to Cape Flattery offers several places where you can launch and kayak through kelp forests and offshore sea stacks to view the variety of marine life while paddling. There are both freshwater and saltwater kayaking opportunities in the area. For a different kind of adventure, consider scuba diving. The Strait of Juan de Fuca and the Olympic Coast National Marine Sanctuary offer world-class diving. Rocky reefs and kelp forests enable you to catch views of large and colorful invertebrates, including fish-eating anemones, giant mussels, and the world's largest octopus. Plenty of darting fish also keep you company.

The surrounding area is incredibly diverse. The shores of the Strait of Juan de Fuca and adjacent forests accommodate more than 200 species of birds. Located in the middle of the Pacific flyway, trumpeter swans, falcons, hawks, and sandhill cranes may easily be sighted during the spring and fall migration periods. In addition, expect the excitement of shores crowded with bald eagles in the winter months. Swimming in the waters below the winging

Washington

SR 112 ❋ Strait of Juan de Fuca Highway

birds are a variety of whales for the watching. During the summer, California gray whales and orcas travel the Strait of Juan de Fuca from Tatoosh Island to Clallam Bay. Pilot and humpback whales also frequent the waters south and east of Cape Flattery. Other marine life will catch your eye, including sea lions, porpoises, white-sided dolphins, and harbor seals. In fact, during the winter, you may be able to glimpse an occasional "raft" of up to 100 male sea otters off the shore along the beaches. Female otters with pups reside between Cape Alava and Cape Flattery all year.

Scenic

The Strait of Juan de Fuca Highway takes you through an incredibly diverse landscape. The Byway travels along the north edge of Washington state right next to the sandy beaches and shoreline of the Strait of Juan de Fuca. The greenery of the Olympic National Forest and Park borders much of the other side of the Byway. The sights and sounds of the culture of various communities in the area add to the rich scenic qualities of this Byway.

The beaches of the Strait of Juan de Fuca themselves are complex and diverse, ranging from rocky coastlines to sandy white beaches. Immense sea stacks—erosion-resistant rock separated from the land by a bit of sea—tower offshore, dwarfing people strolling near the surf. Sea stacks are frequently photographed for their massive yet elegant profiles. The burnished reds of the setting sun cast a delicate light on the sea stacks and the shore, making exquisite photographs. Tide pools abundant in brightly colored marine life dot the rocky shores of this Byway.

A look to the other side of the Byway hides the view of the shoreline and brings into focus the thickly forested mountain knolls and flowering alpine meadows. The world's only coniferous rain forest is near the highway, showcasing a stunning world of gigantic trees and overwhelming greenery. The world's largest specimens of western red cedar and Sitka spruce stalk the terrain, with moss hanging like drapery from their ancient branches. The glacier-capped peaks of Mount Olympus rise in the distance.

HIGHLIGHTS

This tour takes you through some of the highlights of this Byway. If you're starting on the western end, read this list from the bottom up.

- Start your drive in the early middle of the day at the eastern end of the Byway, which is just west of the city of **Port Angeles.** After 10 miles of enjoying the scenic drive, you'll come upon **Joyce General Store,** where you can get food (like a picnic lunch for later) and other traveling items. This charming establishment was built in the early 1900s and still maintains old-time charm.

- Adjacent to the store is the **Joyce Museum.** This former railroad station displays early area history; it has general store items from the 1920s through the 1940s, old photos, and more.

- Twenty miles west of the museum is **Pillar Point,** offering an imposing profile of Pillar Point and a view of the Pysht River estuary.

- About 15 miles west of the Point is **Clallam Bay County Park,** a gorgeous saltwater agate-strewn beach. You can wade and picnic here and see Seiku Point and Vancouver Island.

- A few miles west of the Park is Hoko-Ozette road. Take this road for about 10 miles to the southwest to get to **Lake Ozette,** a really large lake in and around which you can backpack for a couple of days or do a little light hiking, bird-watching, and picnicking by the water. Watch the sunset here and travel home in the gentle dusk.

THINGS TO SEE AND DO

Driving along the Strait of Juan de Fuca Highway will certainly keep your senses engaged, but if you yearn to get out of the car and stretch your legs, or if you'd like to make a mini-vacation out of your trip, check out these attractions along the route.

FERRY SERVICE TO VICTORIA, BC. *Port Angeles (98362). Phone 206/622-2222 or 604/386-2202 (in Victoria).* A 90-minute trip, the ferry departs from the Coho ferry terminal to Victoria's Inner Harbour. Open daily; four trips in summer; two trips in spring and fall; one trip the rest of the year. $$$$

HURRICANE RIDGE. *Olympic National Park (98362). www.huricaneridge.net.* Pomalift, intermediate, and beginner's runs; school, rentals; snack bar. Also snowshoeing and cross-country ski trails. Open late Dec-late Mar, Sat and Sun.

JOYCE GENERAL STORE. *50883 Hwy 112, Port Angeles (98363). Phone 360/928-3568. www.joycewa.com.* Built in the early 1900s, the Joyce General Store still has the same false front, beaded ceiling, oiled wood floors, and original fixtures. Much of the interior came from the Markham House Hotel, which stood in the now-extinct town of Port Crescent. Joyce's namesake, Joe Joyce, transported much of what was used to build the store from Port Crescent (now Crescent Bay) to its present location. The store has been in the same family for more than 48 years.

JOYCE DEPOT MUSEUM. *www.joycewa.com/museum.htm.* The museum is located in a former railroad station. Visitors can browse through general store items from the 1920s through the 1940s, logging equipment, and historical railroad equipment. Old photos of the area have been preserved, as well as articles from the former *City of Port Cresent* newspaper. Stop for a short trip back to the early days of this area.

MAKAH CULTURAL AND RESEARCH CENTER. *Hwy 112 and Bay View Ave, Neah Bay (98357). Phone 360/645-2711. www.makah.com/museum.htm.* Exhibits 500-year-old artifacts uncovered at the Ozette archaeological site, and a Makah village dating back 2,000 years. Craft shop, dioramas, canoes, and a complete longhouse. Open daily Memorial Day to mid-Sept; rest of year, Wed-Sun; closed Jan 1, Thanksgiving, Dec 25. $$

MERRILL AND RING TREE FARM INTERPRETIVE TOUR. *Hwy 112, Port Angeles (98363). Phone 800/998-2382. www.nps.gov/olym/.* Merrill and Ring Tree Farm and Forestry Trail offers self-guided tours of the Pysht Forestry Trail. Along the trail are interpretive resources explaining resource management and reforestation, providing an opportunity to educate visitors about the clear-cuts along the SR 112 corridor. The Merrill and Ring Tree farm also offers a bit of history, as the site still has the original cabins built by Merrill and Ring to house its loggers in the early 1900s.

OLYMPIC NATIONAL PARK. *3002 Mt Angeles Rd (98362). Phone 360/565-3130. www.nps.gov/olym/.* In these 1,442 square miles of rugged wilderness are such contrasts as the wettest climate in the contiguous United States

Washington

SR 112 ✽ *Strait of Juan de Fuca Highway*

(averaging 140 to 167 inches of precipitation a year) and one of the driest climates; seascapes and snow-cloaked peaks; glaciers and rain forests; elk and seals. The Spanish explorer Juan Perez was the first European explorer to spot the Olympic Mountains in 1774. However, the first major western land exploration did not take place until more than a century later. Since then, generations of adventurous tourists have rediscovered Mount Olympus, the highest peak (7,965 feet), along with several other 7,000-foot peaks and hundreds of ridges and crests between 5,000 and 6,000 feet high. The architects of these ruggedly contoured mountains were and are glaciers, which have etched these heights for thousands of years. About 60 glaciers are still actively eroding these mountains; the largest three are on Mount Olympus.

From November through March, the west side of the park is soaked with rain and mist, while the northeast side is the driest area on the West Coast except southern California. The yearly deluge creates a rain forest in the western valleys of the park. Here, Sitka spruce, western hemlock, Douglas fir, and western red cedar grow to heights of 250 feet with 8-foot diameters. Mosses carpet the forest floor and climb tree trunks. Club moss drips from the branches. Some 50 species of mammals inhabit this wilderness, including several thousand elk, Olympic marmots, black-tailed deer, and black bears. On the park's 60-mile strip of Pacific coastline wilderness, deer, bears, raccoons, and skunks can be seen; seals sun on the offshore rocks or plow through the water beyond the breakers. Mountain and lowland lakes sparkle everywhere; Lake Crescent is among the largest. Some roads are closed in winter.

Fishing is excellent in the park. Streams and lakes have game fish including salmon, rainbow, Dolly Varden, eastern brook trout, steelhead, and cutthroat. No license is required in the park; a permit or punch card is necessary for steelhead and salmon. Mountain climbing is another enticing recreational opportunity.

From the novice to the experienced climber, you'll find something for everyone. Climbing parties must register at a ranger station. The Olympic Raft and Guide Service (phone 360/452-1443) offers river rafting in the park. The excellent visitor center (open daily, $$) has information, natural history exhibits, displays of American Indian culture, and an orientation slideshow.

OLYMPIC VAN TOURS, INC. *731 W 4th St, Port Angeles (98362). Phone 360/457-3545.* Unique, interpretive sightseeing tours into Olympic National Park (eight hours). Reservations are required. Call for schedule and fees.

PORT ANGELES. *Phone 360/457-0411. ci.port-angeles.wa.us.* Sitting atop the Olympic Peninsula, Port Angeles has the Olympic Mountains at its back and the Strait of Juan de Fuca at its shoreline; just 17 miles across the Strait is Victoria, British Columbia. Ediz Hook, a sandspit, protects the harbor and helps make it the first American port of entry for ships coming to Puget Sound from all parts of the Pacific; there is a US Coast Guard Air Rescue Station here. A Spanish captain who entered the harbor in 1791 named the village he found here Port of Our Lady of the Angels, a name that has survived in abbreviated form. The fishing fleet, pulp, paper and lumber mills, and tourism are its economic mainstays today.

PLACES TO STAY

If you choose to include an overnight stay in your trip along this Byway, Mobil Travel Guide recommends the following lodgings.

★★★ **CHITO BEACH RESORT.** *7639 Hwy 112, Clallam Bay (98326). Phone 360/963-2581. www.chitobeach.com.* 4 cabins, 2 story. Long regarded as one of the state's best waterfront accommodations, Chito Beach is home to an amazingly beautiful stretch of Washington's rugged coastline. $

AMERICA'S BYWAYS - WEST COAST

★★ **KING FISHER INN.** 1562 Hwy 112, Neah Bay (98357). Phone toll-free 888/622-8216. www.kingfisherenterprises.com. 4 rooms, 3 story. Overlooking the Strait of Juan de Fuca and international shipping lanes, with views of Vancouver Island in the background, this inn is a perfect base for year-round hiking, surfing, and kayaking. $$

★★★ **DOMAINE MADELEINE.** 146 Wildflower Ln, Port Angeles (98362). Phone 360/457-4174; toll-free 888/811-8376. www.domainemadeleine.com. The guest rooms at this intimate bed-and-breakfast are individually decorated. The views of Victoria, British Columbia, and the San Juan Islands are magnificent. 5 rooms, 2 story. Children over 12 years only. Complimentary full breakfast; afternoon refreshments. Check-out 11 am, check-in 4-6 pm. TV; cable (premium). VCR (movies). In-room modem link. Massage. Lawn games. Airport, ferry transportation. Totally nonsmoking. $$

★★ **FIVE SEASUNS BED & BREAKFAST.** 1006 S Lincoln St, Port Angeles (98362). Phone 360/452-8248; toll-free 800/708-0777. www.seasuns.com. 5 rooms, 2 story. No A/C. No room phones. Children over 12 years only. Complimentary full breakfast. Check-out 11 am, check-in 4-6 pm. TV in common room; cable, VCR available (movies). Lawn games. Restored Dutch colonial inn built in the 1920s; pond, waterfall. Totally nonsmoking. $

★ **PORT ANGELES INN.** 111 E 2nd St, Port Angeles (98362). Phone 360/452-9285; toll-free 800/421-0706. www.portangelesinn.com. 23 rooms, 3 story. No A/C. Check-out 11 am. TV; cable (premium). Restaurant nearby. Business services available. Some balconies. $

★ **QUALITY INN UPTOWN.** 101 E 2nd St, Port Angeles (98362). Phone 360/457-9434; toll-free 800/858-3812. www.qualityinn.com. 35 rooms, 1-3 story. No A/C. Pet accepted, some restrictions. Complimentary continental breakfast. Check-out 11 am. TV; cable (premium). Scenic view. $

★★ **RED LION HOTEL.** 221 N Lincoln, Port Angeles (98362). Phone 360/452-9215; toll-free 800/733-5466. www.redlion.com. 186 rooms, 2 story. No A/C. Pet accepted. Check-out noon. TV. Outdoor pool, whirlpool. Restaurant. Sundries. Health club privileges. Private balconies. Overlooks the harbor. $

★ **SOL DUC HOT SPRINGS.** Sol Duc Rd and US 101, Port Angeles (98362). Phone 360/327-3583. www.northolympic.com/solduc/. 32 cottages (1-bedroom), 6 kitchen units. No A/C. Open mid-Mar-late Sept and Apr, Oct weekends; closed rest of year. Check-out 11 am, check-in 4 pm. Outdoor pool, wading pool, mineral pools. Dining room. Grocery. Massage. Picnic tables. Originally conceived as a European-style health spa (circa 1912); mineral pools range in temperature from 98 to 106 degrees. $

★★ **TUDOR INN BED & BREAKFAST.** 1108 S Oak St, Port Angeles (98362). Phone 360/452-3138; toll-free 866/286-2224. www.tudorinn.com. This European, Tudor-style bed-and-breakfast offers guests a historical location from which to enjoy the Pacific Northwest. Visitors can relax in the living room, the library, or the inn's natural surroundings while enjoying the view of the Strait of Juan de Fuca and the Olympic Mountains. 5 rooms, 2 story. No A/C. No room phones. Children over 12 years only. Complimentary breakfast. Check-out 11 am, check-in 4-6 pm. TV in sitting room; VCR available (free movies). Totally nonsmoking. $

Washington

SR 112 ❋ *Strait of Juan de Fuca Highway*

★★ **STRAITSIDE RESORT.** 241 Front St, Sekiu (98381). Phone 360/963-2100. www.straitsideresort.com. 7 rooms, 2 story. Located on the Strait of Juan de Fuca with waterfront views, full kitchens, and plenty of outdoor excursions available. $

PLACES TO EAT

A long day of driving is sure to make you hungry. At the end of your journey, take a table at one of the following restaurants.

★★ **BELLA ITALIA.** *118 E 1st St, Port Angeles (98362). Phone 360/457-5442. www.bellaitaliapa.com.* Italian menu. Closed Thanksgiving, Dec 25. Lunch, dinner. Bar. Children's menu. Totally nonsmoking. $$
D

★★ **BUSHWHACKER.** *1527 E 1st St, Port Angeles (98362). Phone 360/457-4113.* Northwest menu. Closed Thanksgiving, Dec 24-25. Dinner. Bar; Sat, Sun. Children's menu. $$
D

★★★ **C'EST SI BON.** *23 Cedar Park Dr, Port Angeles (98362). Phone 360/452-8888. www.cestsibon-frenchcuisine.com.* Elaborate paintings and floral wall coverings and fabrics give this restaurant its classic French feel. A gracious host and talented chef deliver a delightful dining experience. Closed Mon. Dinner. Bar. Children's menu. Outdoor seating on terrace with gazebo and rose garden. Romantic atmosphere. $$
D

★ **LANDINGS.** *115 E Railroad Ave US 101, Port Angeles (98362). Phone 360/457-6768.* American menu. Closed Jan 1, Dec 25. Breakfast, lunch, dinner. Bar. Outdoor seating. $$
D

★★★ **TOGA'S INTERNATIONAL CUISINE.** *122 W Lauridsen Blvd, Port Angeles (98362). Phone 360/452-1952.* The menu at this quaint, intimate restaurant shows influences from all over Europe and highlights Northwest ingredients. The dining room is located in a remodeled 1943 home and boasts beautiful Olympic Mountain Range views from its back window. Continental menu. Closed Sun, Mon; some major holidays; also Sept. Dinner. Children's menu. Reservations required. Outdoor seating. Totally nonsmoking. $$
D

NOTES

NOTES

NOTES

NOTES

NOTES

NOTES